CAPITALIST COLONIAL

CAPITALIST COLONIAL

*Thai Migrant Workers
in Israeli Agriculture*

MATAN KAMINER

STANFORD UNIVERSITY PRESS
Stanford, California

Stanford University Press
Stanford, California

Printed in the United States of America on acid-free, archival-quality paper

Library of Congress Cataloging-in-Publication Data

Names: Kaminer, Matan, author.
Title: Capitalist colonial : Thai migrant workers in Israeli agriculture /
    Matan Kaminer.
Description: Stanford, California : Stanford University Press, 2024. |
    Includes bibliographical references and index.
Identifiers: LCCN 2024027046 (print) | LCCN 2024027047 (ebook) |
    ISBN 9781503640511 (cloth) | ISBN 9781503641099 (paperback) |
    ISBN 9781503641105 (ebook)
Subjects: LCSH: Foreign workers, Thai—Israel. | Foreign workers,
    Thai—Arabah Valley (Israel and Jordan) | Agricultural laborers,
    Foreign—Israel. | Agricultural laborers, Foreign—Arabah Valley (Israel
    and Jordan) | Thais—Israel—Social conditions. | Thais—Arabah Valley
    (Israel and Jordan)—Social conditions. | Israel—Emigration and
    immigration. | Thailand, Northeastern—Emigration and immigration.
Classification: LCC HD8660 .K34 2024 (print) | LCC HD8660 (ebook) |
    DDC 331.6/2095694—dc23/eng/20240711
LC record available at https://lccn.loc.gov/2024027046
LC ebook record available at https://lccn.loc.gov/2024027047

Cover design: Michele Wetherbee
Cover art: Tomer Taledano
Typeset by Newgen in 10/15 Source Serif Pro

This book is dedicated to the memory of my grandfather, Reuven Kaminer (1929–2020), and my father, Noam Kaminer (1953–2014), whose belief in the dignity of working people never flagged.

CONTENTS

ILLUSTRATIONS

FIGURE 0.1

The Central Arabah. Map by the author.

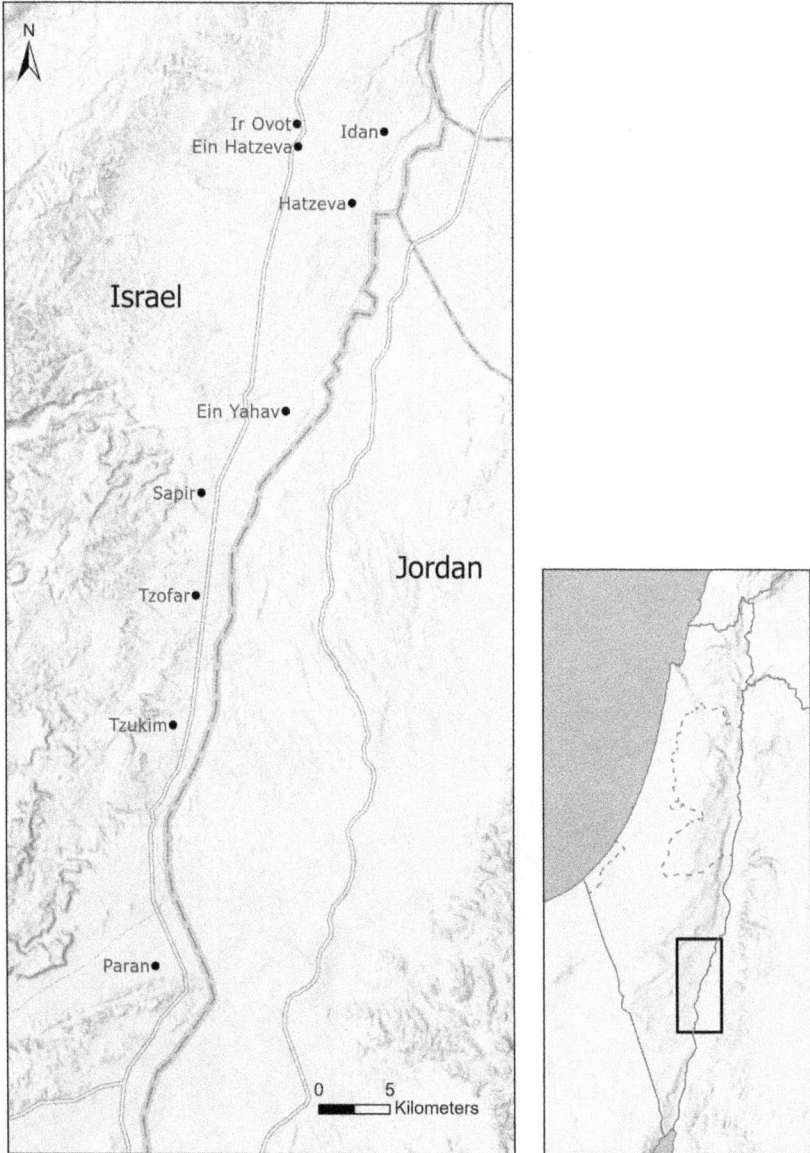

FIGURE 0.2

Isaan (Northeast Thailand). Map by the author.

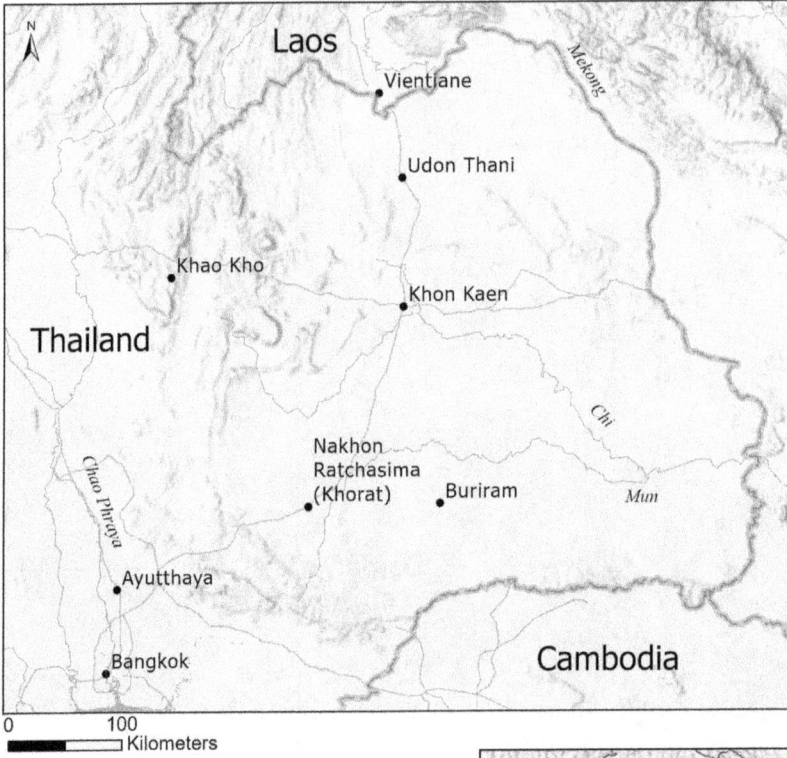

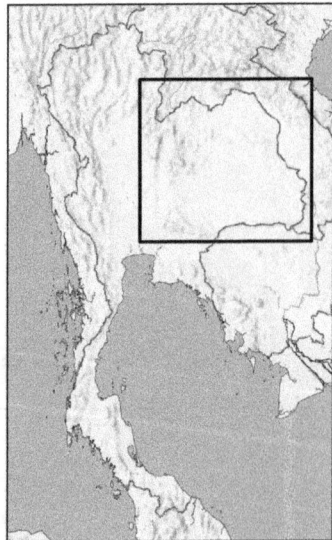

PREFACE

The "ethnographic present" is always a pretense: in the time that passes between participant observation and the publication of its findings, things change. Even if this book had been published before October 7, 2023, it would have been a history of the recent past rather than a snapshot of the current state of things, but that is all the truer now. Hamas's attack of that day on the Israeli region surrounding the Gaza Strip, and the horrific onslaught unleashed by Israel on Gaza in its wake, will certainly be a milestone in the country's history.

Thai migrant farmworkers found themselves at the miserable epicenter of this historic event: thirty-nine were murdered by Hamas and thirty-one abducted, of whom eight remain captive at the time of writing. For the first time, parts of the Israeli public, so far overwhelmingly indifferent to migrant farmworkers, have recognized the victims and their kin as members of the "family of bereavement." But the subsequent exodus of workers, encouraged by the Thai government, has been received more ambivalently. Some politicians have even gone so far as to accuse workers of "abandoning their posts," as if they were soldiers, and to threaten them with denial of legally owed payments.[1] Many returned workers, facing spiraling debt and unemployment at home, have already taken advantage of loosened migration controls and returned to Israel. Nevertheless, the manpower deficit, compounded by the blanket ban on entry of workers from the Occupied Palestinian Territories that has been in effect since the war began, has plunged the farm sector into deep crisis.[2] It is too early to know how this crisis will be resolved, but days into the war representatives of the sector were at pains to clarify that as far as they are concerned there is no replacement for migrant labor, whether from Thailand or elsewhere.[3]

If my argument in this book is valid, it will not be as easy as some suppose for Israeli farmers to sever their connection to Thailand and start over with a migrant workforce from Sri Lanka or Malawi (to name two countries that have already entered into negotiations on labor exportation with Israel). Over the last thirty-five years, Thai migrants—the vast majority of whom come from Isaan, Thailand's northeast—have made an indelible mark on Israeli agriculture. The rapid transformation that the neoliberal Emergency Stabilization Plan and the first Palestinian intifada imposed on the sector, from diverse cultivation for a protected national arena to specialized production for fiercely competitive global markets, may well have been impossible without them. As I try to show, Thai migrants have contributed not only a capacity to work diligently in the fields, but also a delicate sensitivity to the complicated but unstated ideological demands of their employers and a paternalistic "interaction ideology" that helps to govern hierarchical relations in the workplace. Other groups of migrants might possess equivalent skills and goodwill, but they might not. And despite the retreat to well-trodden ideological ground triggered reflexively by the war, the strategic (not to mention economic) significance of agriculture is still very much up for debate among Israeli decision makers. So nothing is preordained.

But despite the deep uncertainty they have introduced into all aspects of life in Palestine/Israel, the repercussions of the war also corroborate some of my main arguments, indicating strong continuities with the past. Unlike the "Gaza Envelope," the region under study in this book, the Central Arabah, lies near a border that has been officially peaceful for three decades, and practically so for much longer. Unlike Gaza's hinterland, which is naturally fertile and historically agrarian, the Arabah almost certainly would not be a center for agricultural production or for the employment of migrant workers if it were not first a strategic frontier region. The link between the cultivation of cash crops and the assertion of sovereignty, which has been so central to capitalist colonization on a world-historical scale, remains strong in Israel today. Heretofore, as the book argues, Thai migrants have been framed as neutral actors in this antagonistic process. Their political neutralization has made it easier for Israelis to think of them as "here to work, not to live," and thus undeserving of any claim to the land or right to political participation. Hamas' targeting of Thai migrants and the subsequent departure of so many suggest that this particular jig may be up. As time goes on, it will become more difficult for Israel to place migrants—of any origin—in the line of fire and then renounce responsibility for their fates.

That said, the project of picking hopeful strands out of the jumbled knot of ideologies I found in the field now seems more utopian than ever. While war takes its toll, the simple but terrible spiral of bad karma—do evil, get evil—proliferates beyond measure. At a time when dependence on people who are slightly different from us comes increasingly to be viewed as a dangerous trap, even the "binational" horizon of decolonization that I criticize as insufficient in the book's conclusion appears entirely foreclosed. Some readers may therefore find my suggestion that this horizon should be *broadened* to encompass equal rights and political membership for those residents of the country who are neither Palestinian nor Israeli a bit over-the-top. On the other hand, none of the principals is going anywhere. The mythic Zionist aspiration to a pure "Jewish settlement" will never come true, and neither will its mirror image of an "Algerian-style" decolonization. Arabs, Jews, *and others* will live in the country from here on, as indeed they have for millennia, and they will live better to the extent that they find ways to make their relations with one another (and their natural environment) democratic and equitable rather than exploitative and exclusionary. This book was written in the fervent hope of facilitating the work involved: that hope is not dead, and the work remains to be done.

Jaffa, February 2024

NOTE ON NON-ENGLISH TERMS

In transliterating both Hebrew and Thai, my main goal has been read-ability. For Hebrew, I use the official Hebrew Academy system, minus the duplication of consonants with a *dagesh* and the macron below the *h* representing the letter *het* (an unvoiced pharyngeal or velar frica-tive). I use an apostrophe to mark glottal and guttural stops (*alef* and *ayin*) where they separate a succession of vowels (as in the name Ya'ir), or an *s* and a consonantal *h*; particles such as the definite article *ha* are separated from the word they are affixed to with a dash. I transliterate Arabic using a simplified version of the IJMES system, using an apos-trophe to mark the letter *'ayn*. For Thai (Central and Isaan), I use the ISO 11940–2 standard of transliteration, omitting tone markers.[1] For both Israelis and Thais who prefer a different Romanization of their names, I respect their preference. I follow Thai usage in referring to Thai scholars and other Thais by their first name and alphabetizing in accordance. (In everyday life in Thailand, nicknames are normally used, and I refer to my Thai interlocutors by fictional nicknames.) I have attempted to retain the original morphology of non-English terms, using the Hebrew plural suffix for Hebrew terms (generally masculine *-im*, feminine *-ot*) and no suffix for terms in Thai, which does not have grammatical number. For ease of reading, I use an italic typeface for all such terms unless they are proper nouns.

Places in Palestine/Israel often have different names in Hebrew and Arabic and sometimes an additional one in English. For the most part, I acknowledge this by citing all relevant names upon first mentioning a place; in subsequent mentions, for simplicity, I choose one of these as seems fit and stick with it. Where there is a common English term, I use it. Because the term "Arabah" appears so frequently in the text, its selection may merit an explanation. This English spelling is first found in the sixteenth-century Geneva Bible and has been used in this form at least since then, a use that attests to its rootedness in the common imaginary that informs Jewish, Muslim, and Christian understandings of the Holy Land. Using the Arabic *al-'arabah* would be pretentious, given the lack of Arabic-speaking voices in the text. But to use the modern Hebrew *ha-arava*, except in names of institutions and publications, would be to privilege the voice of the Israeli state and its nomenclature, a nomenclature employed consciously in the service of colonization and state-building in the "wilds" (*'aravot*) of the South. Finally, *Arabah* has the fortuitous advantage of being the closest of the available options to how the region's name is pronounced in Thai.

NOTE ON ANONYMIZATION

Of the many debts I owe, one is to the members of the Sadot family, who trusted me enough to open their farm and their home to me for six months. While I hope that nothing I have written will offend the Sadots or make trouble for them, given the sensitivity of the subject matter I cannot be certain that this will be the case. Moreover, the Central Arabah is at once a small place where everybody knows everybody, and a very globally connected one where everyone has access to media, both old and new. While I have used a pseudonym for the community in which the Sadot family lives, anyone with even a cursory knowledge of the region will be able to guess easily enough which of its five *moshavim* has here been dubbed "Ein Amal."

Obviously, many people in the *moshav* were aware of my presence, and I have no way of keeping those people in the dark about my host family's identity. If I were to content myself with the ethnographic gold standard for anonymization, the use of pseudonyms, anyone else acquainted with the region could also surmise precisely which family it is that I worked for.[1] While I don't think the Sadots would necessarily wish to hide any of the information divulged here, they have a right to privacy according to both the institutionalized "ethics" of the University of Michigan's Institutional Review Board (Study ID #HUM00098440) and my own sense of decency. While the former might be content with pseudonyms, I have taken the further step of fictionalization.[2] The Sadots are, in essence, a real family with a real farm. However, several details about the family and the farm have been changed, in order to make it more difficult for them to be identified on the basis of the text only.[3] None of these details are in any way pertinent to the argument; moreover, wherever I have changed details I have done so with a view to remaining well within the range of what is common in the *moshav* and the region. The result is nothing like a composite or a "typical" farm, whatever that might mean from a qualitative perspective. The details that have been changed are of the kind that, while making identification difficult, do not change any of the essentials of the argument.

I have followed a different procedure to protect the privacy of interviewees who provided me with historical information, either as part of my dissertation research or in follow-up research done during my postdoctoral fellowship at the Hebrew University (Social Sciences Ethics Committee Approval #2023–01031). The field of actors involved in the migration stream on the Israeli side is quite small, and if I were to provide any information at all about the identity of these interviewees, they might be identified by others involved. Hence, when referring to facts they provided I specify only the date of the interview.

ACKNOWLEDGMENTS

The seeds of this book were planted at the University of Michigan in the fall of 2012. Four years into the Great Recession, and a year after the wave of uprisings that swept the world, there was a welcome sense of political urgency in the air in Ann Arbor. A top school made our chances better than most, but we could expect nothing like the clear path to tenure that our predecessors had enjoyed. We were particularly fortunate, even by elite university standards, to benefit from the struggles of previous generations of members of our union, GEO, and the strong contract they had achieved. Thanks to the union, everyone in my cohort enjoyed adequate funding, enabling an easy solidarity. Among my cohort-mates, special thanks go to Adrian Deoanca, John Doering-White, Georgia Ennis, Obed Garcia, Adrienne Lagman, Prash Naidu, Niku T'arhechu, and Warren Thompson. Valuable friends from other cohorts and departments included Seçil Binboğa, Maayan Eitan, Drew Haxby, Yanay Israeli, Maire Malone, James Meador, Sam Molnar, Regev Nathanson, Rachna Reddy, Sam Shuman, and Lauren Whitmer. Ben Schuman-Stoler was a precious possession—a friend outside academia, keeping me sane on visits to Chicago.

Ruth Behar, Krisztina Fehervary, Stuart Kirsch, and Bruce Mannheim were generous readers and advice-givers. Jason De León, Alaina Lemon, Dan Nemser, and Scott Stonington supplied the confidence I lacked and showed me arcane professional ropes. Andrew Shryock's confidence in my abilities has been a constant comfort. I am told that it is not unusual for friendship to blossom between adviser and advisee only after the formal relationship is discontinued, but I have nevertheless been surprised by the new profundities that our dialogue has reached in the last few years. I hope for many more ahead.

At Tel Aviv University, where I took my first steps in anthropology, I owe much to Ilana Arbel, Naama Friedman, Khaled Furani, Ofra Goldstein-Gidoni, Ran Hacohen, Adriana Kemp, Simha Menahem, Nissim Mizrachi, Dan Rabinowitz, Ronen Shamir, and Seffi Stieglitz. The bulk of the work that has gone into making the very unripe manuscript into a hopefully digestible book took place in my two postdoctoral homes, the Department of Sociology at the University of Haifa and the Martin Buber Society of Fellows at Hebrew University. At Haifa I am particularly grateful to my supportive supervisor, Tali Kristal. At Buber, special thanks are due to director Raz Chen-Morris, administrators Sofi Efremov, Hadeel Jafar, and Gabi Schneider, and peers Natalia Gutkowski, Amit Gvaryahu, Netta Green, Mirjam Lücking, Nora Derbal, and Ido Wachtel. The record for reader of most drafts of my writing over the last few years is split three ways between Geoff Hughes, Liron Mor, and Hadas Weiss—you're all champions in my eyes!

Work on this project spanned some of the most difficult times in my life. I dare say that some of my empathy for the plight of Thai migrants in Israel derives from the suffering I experienced myself as a (very privileged) transnational migrant. My father, Noam, was already ill when I left Israel, but made his support clear, as did my mother and my sister, who never once questioned whether I was right to leave home as his situation worsened, though I often did. I will always be grateful for the care they provided on his deathbed, as did my uncle Micah and aunt Tali; this is also a gift I cannot repay. Since then, we have also lost my grandfather Reuven, the family's undisputed head and a beloved mentor and adoptive father to many others. But the clan perdures— hence, eternal gratitude to my mother Smadar and sister Carmel, my grandmother Dafna, to Micah, Tali, Shalom, Sybil, and their children, and to Selma and the Midwestern branch of the family. Love also to the Nehabs in Kibbutz Hazorea and the diaspora, and to Dorit and Tsur Shezaf, their daughters and son-in-law and adorable grandchildren.

Besides my "real" family, I am deeply fortunate to have a strong network of intimate friends and comrades. Noam Bahat, Yoav Beirach, Michal Baror, Matan Boord, Dror Boymel, Basma Fahoum, Eyal "Giuseppe" Goldstein, Tamar Gomel, Edo Konrad, Eran Hakim, Alma Itzhaky (who drew the amazing illustrations in chapter 4), Noa Kaufman, Noa Levy, Adam Maor, Eilat Maoz, Haggai Matar, Hemi Paska, Tslil Regev, Assaf Tamari, Danya Vaknin, Or Yizhar—much love to all. Comradely salutations also to the dogged members of my Marx reading group, Uri Cagan, Tal Giladi, Michael Sappir, Tomer Shore, and Guy Tal. The bulk of my political energies in the last few years have been dedicated to activism in Academia for Equality—a network whose importance emerges at moments of crisis like the current one. Thanks to my many dear comrades there, including Yael Berda, Hilla Dayan, Karin Loevy, Anat Matar, Areej Sabbagh-Khoury, Guy Shalev, and the late Hayim Katsman and Eyal Shimoni, who are both greatly missed. Zvi Ben-Dor Benite, who started as a political comrade at A4E (and unofficial uncle), has since also become a close intellectual interlocutor and mentor. Outside of Israel, my peri-academic activism has taken place mostly at LeftEast, where particular love and gratitude go out to Rossen Djagalov, Sonja Dragovic, Mariya Ivancheva, Tibor Meszmann, and Mary Taylor.

Our commitment is to a world where education and research are activities open to all, not only a competitively selected few—an outcome that would contribute greatly to the pursuit of knowledge as well as to social justice, not to mention saving everyone a lot of boring desk work. I am nevertheless grateful to the University of Michigan for various forms of financial support and to the Social Science Research Council's International Dissertation Research Fellowship, the US Department of Education's Fulbright-Hays Doctoral Dissertation Research Abroad program, the University of Haifa, and the Hebrew University, for providing me with funding to complete my research, as well as to Atalya Ben-Abba for her research assistance. Elsewhere in the academic world, I am thankful for the advice, encouragement, and camaraderie of Joel Beinin, Naor Ben-Yehoyada, Anthony Dest, Paul Durrenberger, Sai Englert, Sue Ferguson, Gökçe Günel, Michael Herzfeld, Raja Khalidi, Andreas Malm, Oded Nir, Alejandro Paz, Josh Stacher, Hebatalla Taha, and Rafeef Ziadah. At Queen Mary University London, where I am taking my first steps, I already have cause to be grateful to Elena Baglioni, Liam Campling, Neve Gordon, Giuliano Maielli, Sharri Plonski, Keren Weitzberg, and Shreya Sinha.

Doing research on a Buddhist society while setting out on my own dharma practice has provided me with insights that are difficult to verbalize, especially in academically acceptable terms. I am deeply thankful to the unbroken chain of dharma that links the Tathāgata with Galia Tanay, my first teacher, and my subsequent *ajaan*, all of whom are in some way associated with the noble refuge at the Tovana Meditation Center, among them Keren Arbel, Nathan Glyde, Zohar Lavie, Simi Levi, Shahar Matan, and Keren Sheffi. *Sabbe sattā sukhī attānam pariharantu dukkhā muccantu.*

Care for their privacy prevents me from naming most of the people who made my fieldwork possible (see also the Note on Anonymization). I would like to thank everyone who spoke to me, but especially my Israeli coworkers and the "Sadot" family. If I have been critical of their community, I have done so in what I hope is a fair and honest way: I am of their flesh and any critique applies to me as well. Special thanks are due to Arabah native anthropologist Liron Shani, who assisted me in countless ways; to Manh Nguyen, who made me laugh and watched my cat; to Rivka Ofir and Boaz Horowitz at the Dead Sea and Arava Research Centre; and to Shosh Shirin at the Ein Yahav archive.

I owe an enormous debt to all Thai migrant workers in Israel and their kin, whose sweat and suffering I have turned into my bread and butter. I have rarely encountered anything but generosity from Thai interlocutors, and the kindness of my coworkers on the Sadot farm and their kin in Isaan was sometimes almost too much to bear. No demands were ever made on me, but I believe many of my interlocutors expected me to try to do something to alleviate their plight, and I have tried to make good on this expectation. Happily, I am not alone in this endeavor. In addition to Yahel Kurlander and Shahar Shoham, who have been scholarly and activist cartel-mates for years, I am grateful to the other leaders of the new group Aid for Farm Workers—Naama Ben-Shimol, Yannai Kranzler, Yonatan Omer Mizrahi, Danit Rosner, and Zohar Shvarzberg. AFW joins the veteran NGO Kav La-oved/Worker's Hotline in advocating for Thai migrants. Over the years, I have had cause to thank many of the Hotline's dedicated workers, including Miriam Anati, Adi Behar, Mijal Grinberg, Angie Hsu, Adi Maoz, Orit Ronen, Noa Shauer, and Sophie Shannir. Thanks also to Nelly Kfir at CIMI and to Petra Neumann at IOM for believing in my work and assisting it.

In Thailand, I was welcomed at CIEE Khon Kaen, and I am thankful to then-director David Streckfuss, to my teachers there, Jeab, Joong, and Nitnoy, and to *ajaan* Kannikar of blessed memory at the Southeast Asian Studies Summer Institute (SEASSI) in Madison, Wisconsin, who made the connection. Thailand was a strange land to me and I could not have made much progress without their help and that of a great number of other wise people, including Felicity Aulino, Ian Baird, Buapun Promphakping, Erik Cohen, Dusadee Ayuwat, Fabian Drahmoune, Junya Lek Yimprasert, the late Charles Keyes, Yukti Mukdawijitra, Patcharawalai Wongboonsin, Pitch Pongsawat, Piya Pangsapa, Premjai Vungsiriphisal, Katie Rainwater, Samarn Laodumrongchai, Shayaniss Kono, Soimart Rungmanee, Somchai Phatharathananunth, Sudarat Musikawong, Ara Wilson, Supang Chantaravanich, Thanapauge Chamaratana, Tony Zola, and especially Claudio Sopranzetti. Nothing at all would have been possible without my research coordinator, interpreter, driver, teacher, drinking buddy, and intellectual collaborator, "P. Mee," Vorachai Piata. For translation, language training, and many other things besides, I am grateful to Meedee Srilert, Nathaporn Peach Suwannathada, and Supang Lamputha. None of these generous people bears any responsibility for my misrepresentations of "Thai culture."

For their help with various other aspects of making this book happen, I would like to thank Iair G. Or, Adi Elmaliah, Zohar Shvarzberg, and Alma Itzhaky for permission to use their work; Ido Wachtel for his help with the maps; Amir Elizur for legal advice; Shiraz

Grinbaum for aesthetic inspiration; and Tomer Toledano for the colorful, chaotic cover art. At Stanford University Press, Dylan Kyunglim White and Austin Araujo were a joy to work with, a feeling I hope they reciprocate. Many thanks to the two anonymous reviewers of the manuscript, and especially to Reviewer 1, who went beyond the call of duty to provide references and rescued me from several terrible blunders. Of course, any remaining errors of fact and judgment are entirely my fault.

Hagar Shezaf is not only my life partner but also my model for hard work, modesty, and unblinking commitment to truth and justice. My work on this project has not always made our life together easy, but her faith in me and the example of her own cool steadfastness in her work have always encouraged me to push forward. Much is changing in the world around us, mostly—it often seems—for the worse, but our love is the anchor that keeps the storms at bay.

CAPITALIST COLONIAL

INTRODUCTION
DOMINATION ACROSS DIFFERENCE

THIS IS A BOOK ABOUT domination—the power people exercise over others—and its relationship with the forms of difference that are often called "cultural." It examines a relationship of domination across such difference, that between the residents of an agricultural settlement in Israel's desert Arabah region and the migrants from northeast Thailand who work their farms. Each of these two sets of people has a long and very different history of dealing with domination, and the grossly unequal encounter between them is at once rather new—no more than a generation old—as well as dependent on the sediments left in each group's accustomed approach to such hierarchical relationships by much deeper histories. Despite this gap—in part thanks to it—the relationship seemed to be working out when I was in the field, in 2015–16. Bell peppers were grown; profits were made from their sale; the Israeli settler community retained its cohesion; and transnational migrant families survived. Instead of eroding the difference between the two groups, moreover, these successes reinforced it. How do domination and difference become interdependent in this way?

Though the question seems local, the answer is not. The vegetable farms of the Arabah are integrated into a structure that is at once planetary and intimate: capitalist coloniality. The encounter between Israeli employers and laborers from northeast Thailand, or Isaan, is historically contingent, but also determined by the workings of a *world-system* in which the production of commodities for profit depends on a dynamically racialized division of labor.[1] Reactions to the encounter, which range from the embodied and visceral to the deliberate and codified, are marked by particular trajectories of integration into that system.[2] Following previous scholars who have sought to combine the critiques of capitalism and colonialism, I show how cultural heterogeneity—at once real and reified—fits into this system's "combined and uneven" development, as well as how it points toward possible avenues of escape from that system's destructive tendencies.

My investigation of domination across difference joins historical methods, which trace these trajectories of integration into the system, with those of the ethnography, which explores interactions through "close-up, on-the-ground observation of people and institutions in real time and space."[3] This research began in the autumn of 2015 with fieldwork on the Sadot family farm, in a *moshav*, or cooperative settlement, in the Central Arabah. After spending a full growing season working for the Sadots, I traveled to Isaan to meet former co-workers and family members of one who was still in Israel.[4] I also conducted research in local and national archives in Israel and interviewed Thai and Israeli actors who had been involved in the development of the migration regime.

Why did Israeli farmers decide to recruit an agrarian workforce to replace their rebellious Palestinian employees in Thailand, of all places? I trace the roots of this linkage to the period immediately following World War II, when integration into the world-system through commodity agriculture spread together with the projection of colonial state power in both countries. In the Israeli case this was a matter of replacing the indigenous agrarian and pastoral economy of Palestinian Arabs with a collectivist settler agriculture. In Isaan, a hotbed of regionalist and left-wing opposition to the Bangkok-centered monarchic order, the spread of commodity agriculture into previously wooded areas was explicitly conceived as a counterinsurgency measure. A common understanding of commodity-producing "frontier settle-ment" as a useful strategy for the pacification of border zones thus enabled the elites of the two countries—connected by their shared par-ticipation in the Cold War on the "Western" side—to lay the groundwork for a migration circuit in the late 1980s. Though the developmentalist strategy of agrarian "frontier settlement" was fast becoming obsolete as the Cold War wound down and countrysides the world over emptied out, this discourse remained comprehensible to both state elites, form-ing a crucial ideological bridge into a new era.

The resonances and the differences between previous histories of capitalist coloniality in the two countries became evident in the encounter that began as large groups of migrants arrived in Israel in in the early 1990s. The settlers of the Arabah were second- and third-generation children of the erstwhile vanguard of Zionism, the "labor settlement movement" (LSM). Focused on extending control over territory through the establishment of exclusionary but egalitar-ian agrarian settlements (*kibbutzim* and *moshavim*), the LSM inculcated members with a deep anxiety about the exploitation of non-Jewish wage labor, as well as a suspicious attitude toward circumspection and politesse in interpersonal interaction. In Isaan, the peasantry's experience of steeply inegalitarian and repressive integration into the Thai polity brought home the importance of sensitivity to one's place in the hierarchically constituted "social body." In the initially anomic encounter between the settlers and their new employees, it was the latter who provided the paternalistic ground rules for relationships within the "private" yet economically productive unit of the family farm, and a public culture acknowledging, even celebrating, the Thai presence briefly sprang up around them.

These paternalistic norms of behavior were still in effect on the Sadot farm when I arrived. An intimate but hierarchical reciprocity continued to define the relationship between workers on one hand, and the boss and his family on the other, both at work and off. But though Thai workers were as crucial to the settlement's economic survival as ever before, by the time I started my fieldwork, there was no room for them in its public sphere. The migrants—ever conscious of subtle social cues—had carefully removed themselves from the *moshav*'s "face"; meanwhile, changes in the migration regime, intended to cut out middlemen, took away much of the incentive to sustain paternalistic relations on both sides. Nevertheless, emotionally laden ties of moral responsibility continued to connect migrants' female kin back in Isaan not only to their breadwinning emissaries in Ein Amal, but to the boss as well.

ISRAEL'S THAI FARMWORKERS IN THE CAPITALIST-COLONIAL WORLD-SYSTEM

Today agriculture accounts for less than 3 percent of Israel's GDP, and employs an even smaller proportion of the citizen workforce. Occasional official genuflections to food security notwithstanding, in an economy whose prime motor is a capital-intensive, military-adjacent information technology sector, food production appears as an afterthought. As countryside in the heavily populated center and north is swallowed up by suburbanization and as neoliberal economic policy exposes producers to global competition, farming has receded to enclaves in peripheral regions such as the "Envelope" surrounding the Gaza Strip and the Arabah, the desert valley that forms the southern segment of Israel's border with Jordan.[5] Over the past few decades, the latter has shifted from cultivation of a variety of fruits and vegetables for domestic sale to monocultural specialization in products slated for export to much larger markets in Europe.

However, agriculture's role in Israeli society cannot be understood simply through the lens of its contemporary economic marginality. The Zionist colonial project has historically been invested in agricultural settlement for strategic and ideological reasons, developing the ideology of "Hebrew labor" during the push for land purchase before 1948. In practice, the windfall of confiscated farmland it received following the Nakba and Israeli independence led the farm sector to abandon this ideology and recruit large numbers of wage laborers—Palestinians as well as Mizrahi Jews—but its activities remained closely connected to national developmentalist policy. Beginning in the 1970s, shifts in military strategy, ideological hegemony, and economic policy rendered farming increasingly marginal, and after the breakout of the First Intifada in 1987 the sector's Palestinian workforce became marked as a security liability and a political danger. Nevertheless, the sector's survival was regarded as a national priority.

The solution to Israeli agriculture's compounding problems was found in the form of migrant "guestworkers" from Thailand, whose numbers reached 20,000 by the mid-1990s. As integration into global markets brought lower unit prices and pressure to step up production, farmers' hunger for land and water and the pressure they put on fragile ecosystems increased greatly. Competition with European producers, who employ the cheap labor of migrants from North Africa and Eastern Europe, also fueled Israeli employers' drive to keep down labor costs. Thus, while in theory migrants are protected by the same labor laws as Israeli workers, in reality their earnings amount to about 70 percent of the Israeli minimum wage, and regulations meant to guarantee health, safety, and decent housing are flouted. These workers, today almost all male, are only allowed to stay in the country for five years and three months, and their freedoms of movement and association are curtailed in an effort to prevent their permanent settlement. Thais are prohibited from working in any sector other than agriculture, and their right to change employers within that sector, though enshrined on paper, is heavily restricted in practice. Their hyper-exploitation—extreme not only in comparison to Israeli workers, but to other non-Jewish migrants in the Israeli labor market—is directly tied to their geographic, social, and linguistic isolation. This isolation also serves the interest of the farm sector in protecting its image as a pillar of the Zionist project by keeping migrant labor out of the public eye and rendering it politically innocuous. Employers and their representatives have a vested interest in maintaining that isolation, although the rigidity of the labor supply also has negative consequences for their bottom line.

Employees, for their part, hail overwhelmingly from Isaan, Thailand's poorest region, exposed for several generations to ecological despoliation, racial discrimination, and methods of political repression ranging from coercive indoctrination, through assassination, to all-out counterinsurgency and economic underdevelopment. Consequently, Isaan has become an exporter of migrant labor, sending millions of sons and daughters to the Bangkok metropolis and hundreds of thousands abroad to work in construction, consumer services, industry, and (less often) agriculture. In a rural economy already heavily dependent on remittances, migration is often the only way to keep a family's head above the rising waters of debt and poverty. Work in Israel is not particularly coveted, no one gets rich off it, and for many migrants, Israel is only one station in the chain of peregrinations making up a "laborious life."[6] And though it has become normative, long-term separation continues to extract a heavy emotional price from migrants and their families and to apply severe pressure to their family bonds.

Random as it may seem at first glance, the newly forged link between Isaan and the Arabah continues a deep history of connections between residents of the Middle East and Southeast Asia, who have made use of the monsoon winds to sail around the "Indian Ocean world" for thousands of years.[7] Though peripheral to this world, both the Arabah and Isaan have long been scenes of mobility, the former connecting the Mediterranean and Red Sea basins and the latter linking the valleys of the Chao Phraya and Mekong Rivers, at the western and eastern ends of this world.[8] Beginning in the late fifteenth century, the Indian Ocean littoral was gradually subsumed under a new, European-dominated world-system.[9] By the nineteenth century, when imperialism condemned millions of Asians to death by starvation and disease and millions of others to indentured labor on plantations within the region and far abroad,[10] a tripartite global racial schema had begun to emerge, opposing the figure of the European not only to the African or American savage, who "embodied untamed liberty that vitiated the orderliness necessary for material advancement," but also to the Oriental, who "emblematized customary submission to despotic authority. . . . The savage was free but uncivilized, whereas the Oriental was civilized but unfree."[11] This image of the servile Asian, juxtaposed to both the free Westerner and the savage native, is one of the deepest templates for the racialization of Thais in Israel today.

At the end of World War I, the British Empire exercised hegemony over most of the Indian Ocean littoral, including both Palestine (taken from the Ottoman Empire) and the Kingdom of Siam (which retained formal independence). But fast on the heels of the next world war came the collapse of the old empires, and ruling elites throughout the non-European world faced the need to accumulate the capital needed for development while extending control over peripheral zones and populations. The result was a rapid extension of commodity relations over huge territories where subsistence had previously held sway, accompanied by enormous and often forced population movements.[12] In many cases, the polities enforcing the new "rule of difference" had themselves recently emerged from under the boot of European imperialism, a formal shift that did not prevent critical observers from analyzing their strategies—usually supported if not instigated by the old imperial actors—as "neo-colonialism," "internal colonialism," or "colonialism without a metropolitan home-base."[13]

As the strength of communism and the Non-Aligned Movement grew across Asia, the Western bloc—now headed by the United States—lent support to trustworthy allies, including the Kingdom of Thailand and the new settler State of Israel. In the 1950s and '60s, both states dedicated resources originating in the capitalist core—German reparations and American philanthropic funds in Israel, US military aid in Thailand—to extending commodity production into frontier zones that had become strategic theaters of the Cold War, as a method for both territorial control and economic development. The history of the Arabah and Isaan in this period was strongly marked by their role as Cold War agricultural frontiers. In 1949, in one of the last acts of the Nakba, the indigenous Bedouin of the Arabah were chased over the Jordanian border. A decade and a half later, agricultural settlements were established in the valley, with the goal of fortifying control of the frontier against Palestinian "infiltration" through the production of vegetables for a national market. In Isaan, consolidation of the conservative militarist regime, a Bangkok-centric development policy, and growing involvement in the Vietnam War all accelerated the region's "opening" to the extraction of forest resources and pulled its natives into labor migration to the booming capital as well as farther abroad, while social movements based in the region were methodically put down.

As the global economy entered secular stagnation in the 1970s, underdeveloped countries were increasingly burdened with "surplus populations" that could not be profitably integrated into capitalist production.[14] The export of parts of these populations to countries of the capitalist core, whose own working classes had come to resist hard labor at low wages, became an alternative avenue to wealth for southern elites. Actors ranging from the village middleman to the state itself emerged to facilitate migration and siphon off remittances through fees, interest on loans, and taxation. In many parts of the world, the new migration circuits reversed the paths of former imperial dominion: from North Africa to France, Latin America to the US, and the Caribbean to the UK, for example.[15] In the Indian Ocean, however, migration revived trajectories that had been suppressed by Western imperialism, as masses began to move from South Asia, East Africa, and Southeast Asia to oil-wealthy Arab countries, to the region's financial center in Lebanon, and later to Israel.[16]

Coloniality—the "rule of difference" between populations, often divided into "native" and "foreign" along racial lines—has been a fundamental characteristic of the capitalist world-system from its emergence.[17] For Marx, the imbrication of capitalist exploitation with colonial rule and violent racialization was clear: he considered the "chief moments" of capital's "primitive accumulation," besides the enclosure movements in the British Isles, to be the "extirpation, enslavement and entombment in mines of the indigenous population of [the Americas], the beginnings of the conquest and plunder of India, and the conversion of Africa into a preserve for the commercial hunting of blackskins."[18] Every subsequent stage of the spread of capitalism has been marked by the extension of political control from cores into peripheries, almost always accompanied by a racialization of the inhabitants of these newly incorporated zones, and often by their relocation, more or less forced, to zones of intensive commodity production. Writers working within Marxism and adjacent traditions such as black radicalism, social-reproduction feminism, and radical political ecology have advanced the theorization of this link in various ways.[19]

"Extra-economic" categories such as race and gender, then, have been essential to the construction of a globally integrated, capitalist world-system.[20] In many cases, colonial rule has deprived the colonized of the resources necessary to produce for their own subsistence while also denying them the juridical status and employment opportunities necessary to undertake wage labor "freely."[21] What Marx called the "general law of capitalist accumulation," the generation of an unemployable "surplus population" due to technological advances and a lack of adequate effective demand, has always hit racialized populations, those hired last and fired first, with the cruelest effect.[22] While in theory capitalism may be possible without a colonial rule of difference, in historical reality this has never been the case.

The reality of capitalist coloniality powerfully structures relationships between in the Arabah, and not only at work, where Thai migrants are obliged to do backbreaking labor for long hours and little pay, but also outside it, through their brutal exclusion from the public sphere and all political claims. It is possible to separate out these forms of domination—economic (class) and political (citizenship, race)—and then examine how they "intersect." Such analyses present the situation's contradictory features—such as how state regulation intended to prevent migrants' permanent settlement in Israel makes it harder to lay them off—as resulting from a clash between employers' economic interests and the state's political priorities.[23] Useful as such analyses are in some respects—as for lobbying the state to curb employers' excesses—they make little sense from the perspective that encompasses these actors as participants in a unitary, capitalist-colonial system of domination. More to the point, the state of affairs in Ein Amal itself militates against such a separation. Here domination, though not homogeneous, is certainly continuous, and exercised in closely interdependent ways on and off the clock.

INTERACTION IDEOLOGIES AND THE REPRODUCTION OF DOMINATION

In order to perpetuate itself, any social phenomenon—including domination—must create the conditions for its continued existence: in other words, it must be *reproduced*. Marx posited the reproduction of capitalism as a question of finding profitable avenues for the reinvestment of revenues, while Louis Althusser expanded the problematic to include the ideological processes that legitimize and stabilize the system.[24] Socialist feminists have developed a theory of social reproduction that analyzes the unpaid labor, mostly performed by women, without which the proletariat could not live to serve the accumulation of capital.[25] Finally, the ecological conditions for production and human life must also be reproduced if a "metabolic rift" is not to appear between human inputs and outputs on one hand, and the carrying capacity of the natural environment on the other.[26]

Reproduction is relevant to the case at hand in all these senses. Thai migrants reproduce the settlements of the Arabah by working hard for low wages, thus securing the profits that provide livelihoods to farmers, their families, and the other Israeli inhabitants of the region. The unpaid reproductive labor performed by migrants in Ein Amal and by their wives, mothers, and other kin back in Isaan plays an indispensable role in keeping the migrant workforce available for the hard labor of producing vegetables. Natural systems such as the hydrological cycle are exploited without recompense through the unsustainable withdrawal of water from ancient aquifers and the destruction of desert ecosystems, endangering the settlements' reproduction in the long term.[27] Finally, Thais' deferential behavior and willingness to erase their own presence from the settlement's public "face" are necessary to the community's ideological reproduction.

However, the relationship between reproduction and ideology is much more intimate than this list of topics might suggest. Building on use of the term in linguistic anthropology as well as in Marxism, I use "ideology" to refer not only to ideas consciously upheld by individuals and the institutions that inculcate them, but more generally to patterns of meaningful behavior structured by social context, which generally serve the interests and needs of one social actor or another.[28] In this broader sense, ideology is everywhere, in texts read and rituals performed, but also in everyday conversations and even in mute gestures. It is as active at the greenhouse, the factory floor, or the office as it is in the classroom, the temple, or the parade ground.

Treating capitalist coloniality as a unitary mode of domination makes it possible to understand the role of ideology in the exercise of domination across difference in Ein Amal. The capitalist wage-labor relation posits employer and employee as equal, autonomous, self-ruling juridical subjects—quintessential "Western" individuals on a secularized Protestant model—and, at the same time, as parties to a self-evidently legitimate (because voluntary) relationship of domination. The various forms of coercion that force workers to accept this bargain are obscured by an ideological "violence of abstraction," as Derek Sayer terms it, whose effects arise from the very form of the exchange, even in the absence of any deliberate propagandization by interested parties.[29] However, insofar as workers are deemed to belong to racialized groups separated from employers by a colonial rule of difference, their domination also depends on modes of justification that treat the hierarchical distinction between the two parties as prior to their economic encounter—even if the distinction is partly a product of the encounter itself.[30] Beyond the violence of abstraction, then, capitalist coloniality also creates and depends on what one might call, following Alfred Whitehead, a "violence of (misplaced) concretion."[31] This is, at least in part, how race becomes the modality through which class is lived, in Stuart Hall's famous formulation.[32]

The two forms of ideological violence work in this insidious way throughout the world-system: it is not that fully enfranchised citizen-workers are *only* subjected to the dialectical violence of abstraction, while the racialized masses are pure victims of the violence of concretion. Anyone who participates in wage-labor relations and possesses some conception of a fair wage or a good boss, as migrants certainly do, is in practice endorsing the possibility of an equitable relationship of domination. Conversely, "fear of falling" into the depths of the abject surplus population haunts even the most privileged members of the global working class.[33] Without taking account of these forms of ideology, both of which are *internal* to capitalist coloniality, it would be difficult to explain either why Thai migrants expect to be included under the minimum wage protections of Israeli law, or why Israelis are so indifferent and even hostile to this demand.

The reproduction of domination depends heavily on the action of such everyday ideological orientations, especially insofar as they prescribe manners of dealing with hierarchical relationships. What I propose to call "interaction ideologies" are norms, morally charged but not always formally articulated, that apply to verbal and nonverbal interactions between persons, especially where relations of domination apply. Because such ideologies do not subsist solely in the mind or habits of any individual, but also in the interactions between them, they are never entirely arbitrary, but take part in what Webb Keane calls a "material semiotic," in which nonlinguistic signals clump together in "bundles" of meaning.[34] Keane's conceptualization is ripe with potential for an anthropological theorization of the links between domination and the modes of its legitimation, since such links are neither naturally given nor arbitrary, but echo previous histories of domination and resistance.[35] As long as they are shared by the parties to the relationship, such ideologies are often taken for granted. But in places like Ein Amal, divergent ideologies of interaction are thrown into relief—not on equal terms, but across the gradient of domination.

For this reason, the interaction ideologies that distinguish settlers and migrants from one another and draw them together play a central part in this book. The *dugri* attitude and karmic reciprocity, in particular, contrast with one another, while paternalism serves as a sort of rickety bridge between them. The *dugri* attitude, first analyzed by Tamar Katriel, is an ideology upheld by many Israelis, valorizing forthright and even blunt conduct over tact, subtlety, and deference.[36] Within the settler community, such forthrightness is valued as producing cohesion and trust, while overly deferential behavior is read as duplicitous, marking the interlocutor as a suspicious outsider. My analysis relates this ideology to the LSM's historical ethos of exclusionary egalitarianism, in which the substantive equality of all community members depends on the strict policing of its boundaries. During the LSM's struggle for hegemony within Zionism, these virtues were inculcated quite deliberately in the movement's membership. Forged in the fires of successive rounds of violence against indigenous Palestinians, valorization of the *dugri* attitude is closely related to the LSM's ideological anxiety vis-à-vis the direct economic domination of those who do not belong to the collective, especially if they are Arab.

Conversely, "karmic reciprocity" is my term for the interaction ideology pithily summated in the Thai adage *tham dii day dii*, or "do good, get good." As discussed throughout the book, beginning in chapter 2, this approach is closely related to the vernacular Buddhist concept of karma.[37] Karmic reciprocity enjoins participants in social interaction to respect the hierarchical constitution of the "social body" and to refrain from making direct demands, instead expecting interlocutors to recognize one's respectful attitude and to reciprocate of their own accord.[38] But though this ideology relies in part on ancient religious notions—as the labor settlement ethos also does—it owes at least as much to recent projects of ideological indoctrination like the one revealed in Katherine Bowie's study of the social-engineering Village Scouts movement in 1970s Thailand.[39] Like *dugriyut*, karmic reciprocity is a palimpsest of a long history of domination, resistance, and accommodation.

The ideological reproduction of domination is always a risky business of gathering together preexisting orientations, a process of the kind sometimes called "bricolage" or "assemblage."[40] But even people as different as Isaanite peasants and Israeli settlers do not emerge from entirely incommensurable histories; they share not only the contemporary predicament of capitalist coloniality but much older forms of domination that subtend it—most prominently patriarchy, the rule of fathers over women and the young. The interaction ideology that stipulates that superordinates and subalterns should treat one another like members of one patriarchal family, with unequal but undeniable responsibilities toward one another—that is, like fathers and children—is called paternalism. Affirmed, even assumed, by interaction ideologies prevalent in Thailand, paternalism is frowned upon in the LSM's foundational ideology, which makes ample room for fraternity but not so much for parentage. Here as elsewhere, though, settler disavowal only goes so far, and especially in the sphere defined as domestic—which includes the scene of agricultural production—paternalism provides the glue that sticks Israelis and Thais together.

The ideological success of domination across difference is far from guaranteed. True, the encounter between settlers and migrants in the Arabah has produced a structural misunderstanding that, in the immediate term, is very conducive to the farmers' goal of making profits while protecting their community's face (see chapter 5). But the plastic nature of interaction ideologies like *dugriyut* and karmic reciprocity makes them potentially unreliable parts of the assemblage that reproduces capitalist-colonial relations. After all, neither the idea that people should be approached honestly as equals nor the notion that kind and respectful behavior brings its own reward is itself conservative. In fact, both contain kernels of a liberating understanding of social life—and thus may have a part to play in its transformation. If a political project that aims to disrupt and dismantle domination is to have any hope of success, it must take these ideas into serious consideration and attempt to cast its critiques immanently, in their terms. This is a task that I begin to take up in the book's conclusion, in which I briefly discuss several sparks of utopian possibility embedded in these ideologies.

HOW I LOST MY JOB: DOING THE ETHNOGRAPHY OF DOMINATION

Even abstracting from difference, domination is not an easy object to investigate: in situations of relative equilibrium, when the subaltern party is not in open revolt, it seems consensual nearly by definition. As I discovered during previous research among Israeli workers in a warehouse in the port city of Ashdod, in such situations the ethnographer's ostensibly impartial interest in ascertaining the reality of unrest might pose a risk to the fragile balance of social peace.[41] In other words, the ethnographic study of domination can never be a simple reflection of the surface reality of the social field: its very insistence that something oppressive might be going on constitutes an active intervention in that field. As I learned when attempting to speak to my warehouse coworkers about our inchoate collective response to the removal of our forewoman Oksana, it is far from certain that subalterns will always embrace such moves toward escalation, not only for tactical reasons but because material domination has real effects on consciousness. The very fact that their labor was considered "unskilled" and remunerated at the minimum wage made it difficult for the workers in my unit to verbalize pride in their work and solidarity with one another.[42] As scholars like Timothy Mitchell and Susan Gal have argued in responses to James Scott's celebrated thesis about "hidden transcripts" of resistance, part of what makes domination effective is precisely its capacity to invade the supposed sanctum of individual subjectivity; this is a key aspect of what I have been calling its ideological side.[43]

At the Ashdod warehouse I quickly became aware of the effect of ethnic and gender differences, which stranded middle-aged immigrant women from the former Soviet Union permanently in "temporary" positions, while young men of more diverse origins cycled in and out of the workplace rapidly. Such complex effects are everywhere, but as I was to learn when comparing the situation of the Ashdod workers to that of Thai migrants in the Arabah, the state's reifications of difference have a strongly reinforcing effect. By being de facto denied the very minimum wage that caused my coworkers in Ashdod to devalue their own labor, migrants are effectively cast as "below the minimum" of legitimate concern to state authorities, and thus definitively removed from the political community.[44]

Influential as state policy is in determining consciousness, then, the relevance of difference cannot be reduced to administrative fiat. As I have mentioned, the conception of the human subject as a partible individual capable of withholding consent and of expressing choice sincerely is closely related to the "violence of abstraction" inherent in capitalist relations. The "largely Protestant cultures of Western capitalism," as Rosalind Morris writes, "have assumed and demanded a relationship of transparency between inner truth and outward appearance, between value and its sign."[45] One might suggest that this is precisely because the capitalist-colonial world-system has racialized the working men of these societies as white, and thus fully capable of consenting to domination. Concomitantly, other ways of understanding subjectivity—as collective, ambivalent, or guileful, for instance—are devalued and associated with the racialized Oriental other. This is especially true of the people of Thailand, who have long been associated in anthropological discourse with a "regime of images" in which appearance trumps essence and acquiescence can never be judged sincere.[46] In contexts wherein cultural difference is not only reified but instrumentalized to facilitate domination, as when the quasi-nongovernmental organization CIMI advises employers on "effective work in a multicultural environment" with Thai migrants, trying to hold both domination and difference in focus becomes a serious epistemological challenge for the ethnographer—especially one belonging to the superordinate category and embodying its ideologies of interaction, like me.

I did not approach the encounter between Israeli settler employers and Thai migrant workers from a neutral position, by any means. Like many middle-class Ashkenazi Israelis, I have kinship and social ties to the erstwhile service elite of the labor settlement movement.[47] Both my parents were born on *kibbutzim,* and though both sides of the family broke with LSM orthodoxy—my father's parents were expelled from their *kibbutz* for communist sympathies when he was an infant, and my mother left hers in her twenties to join the urban student left—this project has brought home the extent to which its exclusionary egalitarian ideology survives in me. Family social capital (including that of my in-laws, who also have strong LSM connections) was indispensable in opening doors for me in the Arabah. My inherited radical background also played a role in determining my approach to the Arabah, as well as the tone of my public interventions on the topic, which have since caused some of those doors to shut.[48] Finally, I was interested in Buddhist meditation, and though at first I saw little connection between my practice and vernacular Thai Buddhism,[49] and did not speak much about the latter with my coworkers, I doubt that I could have reached an understanding of their interaction ideologies without having studied and practiced dharma myself.

Innocent at first of many of these complexities, I approached field-work in the Arabah in keeping with my previous experience in Ashdod, looking to get a paid job on a farm. This might have been possible, but while Israelis of my background and age (thirty-two at the time) do work on farms in the region, the positions they hold are usually of a kind from which Thai migrants are excluded, in management and marketing. I was not naïve enough to try to simulate the migrants' experience, but I wanted to do the same work as them, both so I could build rapport and in order to learn firsthand about their experience of the job. It was important to me to be paid for my work, not so much because I needed the money (although this was a consideration, as I had no funding for the first year of fieldwork), but because this was the only way to gain intimate experience of the employer-employee relationship: when someone is paying you, they try to get their money's worth back.

I thus went about looking to work "as a *taylandi*"—not my phrasing but that of potential employers when they realized what I was asking for. I started about a year in advance, and quickly got an affirmative response from Gadi, one of the last of the first generation of Ein Amal to still be running a farm. "You'll work like a *taylandi* and get paid like one," he promised gruffly, to my satisfaction. But as the beginning of my fieldwork came near, Gadi began to hesitate and eventually decided against hiring me. I can only speculate as to the reasons, but it may have been the second part of the promise that eventually gave him cold feet: paying me "like a *taylandi*" would have been illegal, after all, and while migrants are helpless to defend themselves against violations of labor law, I could have made a stink. The legal alternative—to pay more than the prevailing wage for undoubtedly subpar labor—would not have been worth his trouble.

I did not have long to ponder Gadi's reasons, because within a week I had found another job. My new boss, Udi, was managing a farm belonging to another *moshav* member while working a second job and strapped for time. He agreed to let me do the same work as the Thais most of the time, and the additional tasks he gave me, like monitoring irrigation systems and filling fertilizer tanks, were not supervisory ones. But it became apparent that Udi wanted me to perform a disciplinary function after all when, a few days into my employment, he asked me to spend the morning in a greenhouse with the farm's Thai workers, but without working, explaining that he preferred me not to do the farm's *avoda shhora*—literally "black work." So I did nothing that morning, fiddling with my phone while the Thais worked. But Udi didn't like me to be loafing in this manner either; it "sets a bad example," he said afterward. If I was not supposed to work or to zone out, it seemed that the only option was to supervise the workers, but this was exactly what I had told Udi I didn't want to do. "This will continue to be a front line," I wrote in my field notes. "I have to make sure I handle it carefully."

Apparently I failed, since about two months into my employment Udi found a pretext to fire me. To fulfil my tasks, I had been provided with a small all-terrain vehicle. I was allowed to park it near the apartment I was renting, but only when I was home. When away from the *moshav*, I was supposed to leave it in the farm's parking lot. Running late to catch a bus one day, I left the ATV in the public lot at the entrance to the *moshav*. When Udi called to confront me, I confessed and apologized, but he was adamant that I had violated his trust and would not take me back. I don't know why Udi reacted so harshly to this minor infraction; whatever the reason, I found myself without a job or an alternative plan in the middle of the growing season, with no openings on any farm in the *moshav*. After a few weeks, through family connections, I was able to secure a spot on the Sadot farm, where I ended up staying on for six months. However, I had to give up my aspiration to a paid position: now I was a volunteer.

On the Sadot farm I made my own schedule: five days a week, eight hours a day, usually beginning together with Ya'ir and the Thais at the break of dawn and taking off in the early afternoon, but sometimes beginning later and working until the end of the day, which usually lasted ten or eleven hours. At first the boss insisted on asking me what I preferred to do, though eventually he agreed to allocate me to whatever jobs needed to be done. Some of the time this meant that I was assigned tasks the Thais could not do, like taking orders from clients, but most of the time I did what they did alongside them, took breaks with them, shared their meals, and occasionally spent evenings with them as well. The six months I spent on the Sadot farm in 2015 and 2016 in this manner are the heart of this book. It was there that I was able to gain a close understanding of the labor process as well as to find a vantage point from which to make observations about communal life on the *moshav*.

As the season drew to a close and the temperatures outside crept up to insufferable levels, I was glad to get out of the fields and to start doing interview and archival work. Interviews with coworkers took place in an unusual setting: on one hand, my interlocutors had already known me for six months or so, and some degree of mutual affection obtained. However, the interviews were short (between an hour and two), rather formal in tone, and held on the farm, where the boss's authority loomed large despite his physical absence and my assurances of privacy. Interpreter Supang Lamphutha navigated this difficult territory with aplomb, and we nevertheless managed to learn quite a bit. In the archive of the region's oldest *moshav*, Ein Yahav, I found a wealth of documentation that I was later able to supplement with papers from the Israel State Archives, interviews with Israeli players in the migration regime, and secondary sources. The relationships I forged on the Sadot farm also laid the foundation for my 2017 fieldwork in Thailand. With the crucial support of my charming and indefatigable research coordinator, Vorachai Piata (aka P. Mee), I was able to establish some real rapport with Daeng, whom I had met in Ein Amal, as well as with Moon, whose husband, Boy, was still on the farm at the time, and with Song, who had worked for the Sadots years before I met them.

Like most novice ethnographers, I longed to become close friends with my interlocutors and fantasized about spending hours in deep conversation with them. This didn't happen, probably primarily because I never became fluent in Isaan or Central Thai. Though I studied both languages and was certified advanced in the latter, I never became confident in my abilities, and my limited conversations with coworkers were held in farm pidgin, with its simplified grammar and mix of English, Hebrew, Isaan, and Central Thai vocabulary. However, language was not the only issue; as I was to learn, interaction ideologies prevalent in Isaan discourage the expression of negative emotions in front of strangers, in contrast to Israel, where griping (*kitur*) is a common way to forge intimacy with new acquaintances.[50] Moreover, despite the politically inflected sympathy I tried to communicate, my coworkers surely saw me as an Israeli first, a coworker second, and a comrade probably not at all. Despite my protestations (and the ethical duties formalized in the University of Michigan's IRB stipulations), I imagine they suspected that any criticism of their working and living conditions might eventually reach the employer. Thus, even though I solicited criticism in what I hoped were gentle ways, interviewees supplied it in very small doses. It was only after I left the farm, during the production of the informational web series *Cheewit Nay Israel*, that I became exposed to a more critical discourse on their part.

———

This book attempts a risky gambit, trying to speak to both anthropologists and activists. At a time when many radicals trained in anthropology are asking what the discipline is even for, and some even flirt with calls for its immolation,[51] *Capitalist Colonial* hopes to make the case that much of the seemingly apolitical theory that anthropologists produce can become an instrument in the struggle against domination. This is not only a matter of employing the ethnographic method, which forces the activist/researcher to test her ideas and concepts against those thrown up by the everyday life of the people she wishes to work with; militant researchers of various kinds have already appropriated this method, either under the influence of anthropology or independently.[52] The move I am trying to make is a trickier one, having to do with anthropology's traditional interest—what some might call its unhealthy obsession—with cultural difference. Since focusing on such difference all too often leads anthropologists to bracket out domination, radicals' impatience toward too much harping on about culture is certainly understandable. But capitalist-colonial domination has not culturally homogenized the globe; for good and for ill—and there are plenty of both—different groups of people still see the world in very different ways, ones directly relevant to struggles against domination.

Let me then assure the radical reader that I leave the field as I entered it, convinced that migrant workers in Israel suffer unconscionable exploitation. However, my ethnographic experience and my theoretical formation in anthropology have forced me to rethink the role I had automatically assigned them. In many important senses, I learned, Thai migrants in the Arabah—and even their kin back in Isaan—participate in setting the terms of their exploitation. This is not because they desire such exploitation, but because under current circumstances, in which it is unavoidable, there are ways to make it more bearable. The interaction ideologies that enable them to do so, just like those that Israelis employ to ignore their suffering, are malleable, and I suspect that they can be used not only to ameliorate this exploitation, but to challenge it, and perhaps even to abolish it altogether.

1 THE SETTLEMENT OF THE CENTRAL ARABAH

THEY SAY YOU NEED TO get your passport stamped at the Arabah Junction, after winding down the descent at Sodom. They say it facetiously, in the Israeli style of aggrandizement; after all, it is only a two-hour drive from the country's urban heartland to the junction, and another two hours to the Red Sea port of Eilat, at the other end of this narrow rift valley. But the drop from the mountainous scrub of the Negev into this nether country, more than two hundred meters below sea level, does feel something like crossing a boundary, especially if the sun is setting behind you and the ruddy mountains opposite are burning bright as the lights come on at the gas station far below. It is thirty kilometers south from here to Idan and Hatzeva, the most northerly *moshavim* of Israel's vastest regional council, the Central Arabah, and another fifty to Paran, the southernmost *moshav* of the council. South of Paran lies the Eilot Regional Council, whose *kibbutzim* are in the hinterland of Eilat, at the northeastern tip of the Red Sea (see Figure 0.1).

Despite Israel's tiny size, the Central Arabah is an economically peripheral and phenomenologically remote part of the country.[1] Though it has been inhabited for many thousands of years, hyper-aridity and extreme heat place it at the tip of the global climate spectrum. This chapter explores the history of the Arabah from the earliest sources to the period of its integration into the Israeli state and the capitalist market through agricultural settlement, which began in the 1960s. After describing the modes of subsistence and far-flung geographic connections that have characterized human habitation of the valley since ancient times, I narrate its colonial takeover by Israel in the 1948–49 war and the subsequent expulsion of the indigenous Bedouin population. To place the settlement drive of the 1960s in context, I then move away from the region and back in time to theorize the "labor settlement movement" (LSM), to which the region's *moshavim* belong, as a capitalist and colonial project. I draw connections between the political goals of this movement, which once dominated the Zionist project and the Israeli state, and the ideological orientations that continue to play a crucial role in social life in the Arabah. I then return to the historical narrative with the debates over colonization of the region in the first decades of statehood. This debate was won by Israel's founding father, David Ben-Gurion, and his voluntarist allies among the young guard of the LSM. Once established, the settlements of the region carved out an ecological and economic niche protected by state developmentalist policies. These policies were dropped in the neoliberal rollback of the late 1980s, which together with the Palestinian rebellion of the First Intifada threw the entire Israeli agricultural sector into crisis. The chapter ends as this crisis deepens in the Central Arabah.[2]

THE ARABAH BEFORE ISRAEL

The narrow sliver of land known as Palestine or Israel[3] encompasses diverse ecological zones, enabling a variety of modes of subsistence and long-standing commercial and cultural links to the Mediterranean world and, for long periods, also far to the east.[4] The hills of the country's central spine and the Galilee have long sustained peasants and herders, while lowlands and seasonal marshes historically supported smaller populations reliant in part on foraging.[5] The south of the country is "desert"—a very broad term encompassing zones where agriculture has been regularly practiced, areas in which the Bedouin inhabitants combined farming with pasture, and arid stretches where

Bedouin herders' camels and goats rubbed shoulders with a diverse wildlife. While always lightly populated relative to the better-watered areas to its north, the south is the country's historical gateway to the Red Sea, the Arabian Peninsula, and the monsoon world of the Indian Ocean.

Palestine's shift from subsistence economy toward enclosure, privatization of natural resources, and profit-oriented commodity production began slowly, over the centuries of Ottoman rule. The country's integration into the growing world-system accelerated in the nineteenth century as coastal towns like Jaffa, Haifa, and Gaza forged commercial links to Europe. Population and economic activity shifted to the west, and the crown sold large tracts of lowland to urban commercial families, some of whom began to grow citrus fruit for export using water pumped from coastal aquifers with animal power and employing commuting peasants as well as a new peri-urban proletariat.[6] South of the line connecting Gaza and Hebron, arability, population density, and wealth all fell away as tribal territories grew larger and the Ottoman military's coercive power faded. Over the nineteenth century, the empire began encouraging its nomadic subjects to settle down and cultivate, a shift exemplified by the establishment of the garrison town of Beersheba.[7] But the roughly 80,000 Bedouin residents of the southland retained ownership of their tribal territories (Ar. *dirāt*) and connections with kin in the Sinai and Transjordan throughout the Mandate period.[8]

One of the remotest parts of the Palestinian desert, from the Ottoman perspective, was the Arabah Valley. Geologically, this valley forms the southern half of a tectonic gap known as the Dead Sea Transform (DST), separating the Arabian Plate, which includes Jordan, from the African Plate, which includes Palestine/Israel. The plates are sliding past each other while also pulling slowly apart, creating the world's lowest terrestrial elevation on the gaping shores of the Dead Sea, 435 meters below sea level and dropping. The northern half of the DST, which receives precipitation from the Mediterranean and runoff from mountains in Lebanon and Syria, is traversed by the Jordan River, which drops from the foothills of Mount Hermon to the shores of the Dead Sea. But the southern half of the valley is hyper-arid and very hot for much of the year. A few times per winter, rainstorms arrive from the Red Sea, which touches its southernmost point; more often, Mediterranean storms break over the Negev massif in Israel and the neighboring mountains in Jordan. Their rushing waters flood the creek beds that flow into the valley, seeping into the ground and feeding a string of springs and minor oases.[9] At such times the Wadi Arabah itself becomes an evanescent river, dragging branches ripped from the acacia trees that dot its banks.[10] The acacia is the keystone species of the local ecosystem, a food source for herbivores, including the Nubian ibex and the endemic Palestine gazelle, who were once hunted by leopards, wolves, and other predators.[11]

The word "Arabah" is an ancient Semitic one meaning "desert" or "wilderness."[12] In a region where heat and lack of precipitation are the limiting climactic factors, the term was used to refer to places too hot and arid for cultivation, and may be cognate with the word "Arab," once used to refer to residents of such areas.[13] In the Hebrew Bible, it is a toponym understood to refer to the entire DST, or at least to the part of it south of the Sea of Galilee.[14] But the part of this zone in which fresh water was regularly obtainable from rain, springs, and the Jordan is quite different from the southern part, which begins at the Dead Sea. In the valley's fertile northern half, known in Arabic as the *ghor*, the combination of year-round heat and easily available water has enabled winter agriculture and engendered a pattern of seasonal but stable settlement.[15] The most salient ecological difference between the *ghor* and the Arabah is in water availability. While both areas are extremely hot,[16] the latter lacks the easily accessible water of the former, and before the arrival of modern pumping technology the most reliable watering places on its western side were a chain of springs where wadis bringing floodwaters from the Negev would enter the rift, at (from south to north, in Arabic and Hebrew respectively) 'Ayn a-Dafiyeh/Avrona, 'Ayn Ghadyan/Yotvata, el-'Amar, 'Ayn Weiba/Ein Yahav, and 'Ayn Hosb/Ein Hatzeva.[17]

Remarkably, human occupation of the Arabah dates to the Paleolithic Era and remains have been found from every period since.

The world's first systematic copper mine was probably located in Wadi Feinan, today on the Jordanian side of the valley. Hundreds of years later, the first great power to evince an interest in the region was the Egyptian empire, which ran its own copper mines in Timna, near Eilat.[18] Beginning in the eighth century BC, important trade routes crossed the wadi, among them the Incense Route, leading from Yemen to the Mediterranean. This caravan route was controlled by the Hellenized Semitic kingdom of the Nabateans, whose capital was at Petra, just off the Arabah.[19] After the rise, in the second century CE, of the Roman-sponsored sea route to Yemen that passed through the Gulf of Suez, bypassing Petra, the importance of the Incense Route declined.[20]

Nevertheless, comfortable winter temperatures made the area attractive for seasonal grazing of camels, sheep, and goats, and in the early Islamic period, the city of Ayla (now 'Aqaba) was established at the tip of the Red Sea and the Arabah became a hinterland and passage point for caravans undertaking the hajj pilgrimage from Egypt to Mecca.[21] Throughout this period the valley provided winter pasture and opportunities for agriculture. Researchers building on the firsthand knowledge of Bedouin native 'Ali al-Misk have uncovered a unique system channeling rainwater to fields through stone terracing, practiced in the region from ancient times until the Israeli conquest. In wet years the Bedouin planted barley and wheat for human consumption, and in dry years animal feed was grown. Together with the threshing floors, livestock enclosures, and storage sheds discovered by the researchers, these constructed fields provide evidence of intervention in the environment to support a "smallholder, mixed crop-livestock" mode of production, with imported artifacts testifying to connections outside the region.[22]

From the seventeenth century on, the Arabah was under the de facto control of Bedouin tribal federations. The valley often served as a rough border between these federations, which sometimes clashed over water, pasturage, and political dominance. State power was very weak, and European travelers were wary of approaching the region for fear of being caught up in intra-Bedouin rivalries.[23] In his *History of Beersheba and Its Tribes*, Palestinian historian 'Aref al-'Aref wrote that the Arabah, nicknamed "the wadi of fire" after the many victims of tribal warfare who had fallen there, belonged to the Sa'idiyyin tribal federation.[24] In 1942, a Zionist exploratory expedition provided a more detailed account, describing the valley as divided from south to north between the territories of the Ahaywat, Sa'idiyyin, and 'Azazma federations, and estimating that at the yearly peak of occupation it was home to 15,500 goats, 7,800 camels, and 2,040 Bedouin tents, perhaps housing about 10,000 people.[25]

The opening of the Suez Canal in 1869, which greatly facilitated the shipment of goods from Asia to Europe, fueled renewed imperial interest in neighboring areas, including the Arabah.[26] Following the British conquest of the Negev at the end of World War I and the imposition of Mandatory rule by the League of Nations, the territories of Palestine and Transjordan were administratively separated, with their border—at this point entirely unmarked—running down the center of the wadi. The British, who had depended on Bedouin allies to win the war in the Middle East, attempted to cement the alliance locally through the establishment of a Bedouin desert police corps. This corps staffed a series of police stations along an ancient Roman route, descending from Kurnub in the eastern Negev through the winding path of 'Aqareb (Heb. Ma'aleh Aqrabim), reaching the Arabah at 'Ayn Hosb (today's Ein Hatzeva) then cutting south along the DST to Umm Rashrash on the Red Sea coast, near 'Aqaba in Transjordan. This policy had mixed results, with some Bedouin policemen participating in the Arab Revolt of 1936–39, but the posts established throughout the Arabah were staffed until the end of Mandatory rule.[27]

Until the mid-1940s the southland played a minor role in Zionist colonization. The strategic interest of the British in retaining control over this zone led them to ban Jewish settlement; the ban, combined with Bedouin landowners' organized refusal to sell land to settlers, was left mostly unchallenged.[28] Only in 1946 did the Zionist movement move to expand into the arable northern reaches of the Negev, when eleven Jewish settlements were rapidly established in order to pressure the United Nations to include the area in the planned Jewish state.

The desert nevertheless played an important role in competing visions of the country's future. Mandate officials and Palestinian nationalists interested in reducing Jewish immigration pointed to the limits of water and land resources, prompting the Zionist leadership to turn its interest to the possibility of "improving" arid lands through grand ecological transformations such as the diversion of water from the Jordan basin to the northern Negev.[29]

The 1937 Peel Commission's partition plan, which assigned the entire country south of Jerusalem to a future Arab state, split British officialdom, with influential officers arguing that only the Jews could make proper use of the desert.[30] This view won over the UN Special Committee on Palestine, which justified its assignment of the whole Negev to the Jewish state in its 1947 partition plan by a logic of improvement, arguing that the region's "sparsely populated" parts could be developed through "heavy investment of capital and labour and without impairing the future . . . of the existing Bedouin population."[31] However, after the breakout of war in late 1947, Zionist military strategy did not prioritize making good on this allocation. While the northwestern Negev saw intense fighting between Israeli and Egyptian armies beginning immediately after the British withdrawal and Israeli declaration of independence in May 1948, its wedge-shaped south was not conquered until March 1949, when the Israel Defense Forces (IDF) swept to Umm Rashrash with little resistance, expelling the Bedouin population over the Egyptian and Jordanian borders as they passed through.[32]

THE RISE OF THE LABOR SETTLEMENT MOVEMENT

Zionism is not the only settler-colonial movement to possess a "labor wing." In the late nineteenth and early twentieth centuries, several movements representing European populations who had settled in colonies or planned to do so moved in what they considered a socialist direction, arguing that the best way to achieve colonial goals was through the creation of a settler working class protected by legal privileges from the competition of indigenous labor. In South Africa,

Australia, and the United States, "white labor" movements argued that a stable settler polity could not be constructed in a colonial economy dominated entirely by the free market and the profit motive.[33]

In the Zionist case, the tenacity with which the indigenous Palestinians managed to hold on to their land made the need for a class compromise between proletarian and bourgeois colonizers particularly pronounced. Residing at the very center of the Afro-Eurasian landmass, Palestinians were not vulnerable to the communicable diseases carried by settlers, as the indigenous peoples of Australia and America had been.[34] Moreover, on the eve of colonization, Palestinian agricultural and pastoral producers were already integrated into regional trade networks and showed substantial initiative in responding to the pressures and opportunities which came along with this integration.[35] Finally, under Ottoman rule, and to an eroding but still significant extent under the British Mandate, the complex communal arrangements by which Palestinian peasants regulated land tenure continued to carry the force of law, making the alienation of their property difficult.[36]

The Zionist aspiration to the "redemption of land" (ge'ulat ha-karka) was in some ways equivalent to the imperial doctrine of terra nullius, "no one's land," which played a central role in the colonization of the non-European world from the sixteenth century on. For seventeenth-century English philosopher John Locke, "in the beginning all the world was America," a primeval, unowned wilderness, which could only become private property once man's "improvement" molded it to his needs.[37] This primal appropriation, however, need only be undertaken once; henceforth the land would belong to the heirs of the initial cultivator, whether they invested any additional work in it or not. Onur Ulaş Ince makes sense of this rather arbitrary-seeming notion by arguing that for Locke, the goal of enclosure of property is nothing other than the establishment of "social interdependence mediated by the commodity form"—that is, of capitalist relations.[38]

There was an obvious problem with applying a Lockean justification to the appropriation of land in Palestine—namely, that the indigenous population had already established its claim under the Ottoman legal system. The first Zionist settlers, arriving from Eastern Europe in the late nineteenth century, worked within the framework of capitalist property relations that was already emerging in the Ottoman Empire. They bought land from local or absentee landowners and availed themselves of the skilled labor of Palestinian peasants, who often owned their own subsistence plots but struggled to pay onerous cash taxes and were hence available for seasonal wage labor at attractively low wages. However, the next wave of settlers, who came in the early twentieth century, were mostly destitute Jews of working age, and many of them had imbibed socialist as well as Zionist ideas. Influenced as much by German romantic nationalism and Russian agrarian populism as by Marxism, the ideologues of the new immigration believed, with Locke, that sweat mixed into the soil established a property right. However, they conceived of this right as pertaining to the nation rather than the individual, and demanding perpetual reaffirmation through repeated investment of labor.[39] By withholding work from the young settlers, the employment of Arab peasants constituted a threat to this reaffirmation; moreover, the supplement to their incomes provided by wage labor on the Zionist colonies could end up *strengthening* peasants' hold on the land—a clearly counterproductive effect from the standpoint of colonization.[40]

The wing of the Zionist movement in which the new generation of settlers was organized gradually developed a solution to this problem of "low frontierity," as Baruch Kimmerling would term it.[41] The terms "socialist Zionism" and "labor movement," by which this wing is often known, can be misleading. I prefer to follow Michael Shalev in translating a synonymous and widely used term, *tnu'at ha-hityashvut ha-ovedet*, as "labor settlement movement," or LSM.[42] This term has the advantage of highlighting the movement's commitments to labor and rural colonization without the misleading imputation that it sought to represent a working class in conflict with capital. An orientation toward class struggle was not lacking at the outset, but it was snuffed out during the movement's climb to hegemony.[43] This turn toward class peace was greatly facilitated by the massive injections of capital that Zionism was able to enlist and redistribute according to nonmarket criteria by mobilizing a network of wealthy private benefactors abroad (as well as, later, with the help of West German reparations and US aid).[44]

Organized in political parties and a trade union federation, the Histadrut, the new immigrants initially embarked on a "battle for labor," demanding that Jewish farmers employ them rather than Palestinians, and at higher wages.[45] The battle ended in the late 1920s with a class compromise that cemented the character of the LSM and the larger Zionist movement. Though the wealthy industrialists and financiers who bankrolled the World Zionist Organization were naturally disinclined to socialism, they came to realize that large-scale Jewish immigration could not be sustained by private employment alone, especially when immigrants could also go elsewhere, to the US for example. Moreover, most employment opportunities were in the coastal cities, leading the settler population to concentrate in a small part of the country. Thus, in addition to funding public works projects, the WZO also undertook to buy land from Arab landowners and turn it over to groups of immigrants supplied with the most advanced agrarian technology available, so as to enable a high standard of living.[46]

Two organizational models were made available to these groups. The first was the *kibbutz*, or communal settlement, in which all means of production were shared, and reproductive labor such as child-raising socialized. The alternative was the *moshav*, or cooperative settlement, in which nuclear families settled on private plots attended independently to both production and reproduction, but shared machinery and marketing arrangements. Settlers could choose whether to join or set up a *kibbutz* or *moshav* based on personal predilections as well as the judgment of movement experts with regard to the exigencies of location. While enjoying a variety of subsidies and protective economic measures, both *kibbutzim* and *moshavim* were always committed to producing commodities and measured their own success according to market criteria of earnings and losses, while never losing sight of their "national" objectives as organs of colonization.[47] Thus, the economization of reproductive labor produced by collective life on *kibbutzim* was perceived as conducive to its military tasks, and the mixed-crop farming adopted in the *moshavim* was planned not to enable farmers to provide for their own needs, but to distribute the labor-time required for commodity production throughout the year in order to avoid the need for hired day labor.[48] Throughout the Mandate period, and especially following the Great Arab Revolt of 1936–39, the Jewish consumer market was carefully and consciously placed out of bounds for Palestinian producers through aggressive boycott campaigns.[49]

The proportion of the country's population living in *moshavim* and *kibbutzim* would always be small, and the center of political gravity remained closely moored to the growing urban centers of Jewish population around Tel Aviv, Haifa, and Jerusalem. Nevertheless, the parties of the labor settlement movement—including the rising hegemon, Ben-Gurion's Land of Israel Workers' Party (MAPAI), as well as the smaller Union of Labor (*Ahdut Ha-avoda*) and Unified Workers' Party (MAPAM), each of which possessed its own press, school system, and youth wing—quickly went about constructing an ideology that promoted "pioneering" in rural settlements as the epitome of Zionist practice. The practice of what Gershon Shafir calls "pure settlement" was codified in the twin ideological pillars of *avoda atzmit* and *avoda ivrit*: "self-labor" and "Hebrew labor" respectively.[50]

Precisely because it was not an obviously self-interested choice for urban youth, "pioneering" could be construed by the parties of the LSM and their powerful youth movements as a regulative ideal, something to aspire to in defiance of narrow economic interest rather than a calculated, egotistical move. Sociologist Jonathan Shapira offers a Bourdieusian analysis of the "voluntarism" of the labor settlement movement, suggesting that what pioneers gave up in immediate economic opportunities they made up for in symbolic capital, which could later be reconverted into economic capital through various public subsidies or through placement in the proliferating state and para-state apparatuses.[51] By defining itself on the basis of this self-denial, the labor settlement elite could distinguish itself both from bourgeois city dwellers—who had the opportunity to renounce consumption and did not do so—and from those Middle Eastern Jews who could not make an "ideological" sacrifice by definition, because to be workers was their "natural" fate.

Middle Eastern, or Mizrahi, Jewish workers only began to play a quantitatively significant role in the Israeli labor market following the mass immigration of the 1950s. However, Zvi Ben-Dor Benite argues that a disastrous earlier experiment in importing cheap but Jewish labor-power from Yemen made a crucial contribution to the later racialization of the Mizrahi proletariat through its impact on the LSM leadership, which was closely involved in the project. Yemeni immigrants were hyperexploited by the veteran Zionist planters, then summarily rejected as fellow pioneers by the LSM, leading to horrific casualties in the community.[52] Arabs as well as Jews, the Yemenis were considered workers "by nature," whereas to be a pioneer and a *subject* of the colonization process, one had to adopt proletarianization voluntarily, out of "idealism"—something only a European could do.[53] It was precisely the supposed ease with which they could take up agricultural labor that disqualified them from full belonging to the pioneer collective.

Before we move on, one important aspect of the LSM's "socialism" remains to be examined: its commitment to internal equality. Whatever its attitude to Palestinians, Mizrahim, or even Ashkenazi Jews living in the cities, it may be argued, the movement was socialist insofar as it insisted on the distribution of resources according to need and used its powerful ideological apparatuses to reject individualism and inculcate a strong tendency to symbolic as well as material "levelling." Even in the LSM's classic era, the applicability of this ethos varied widely between *kibbutzim* and *moshavim* and within each of the submovements; nevertheless, its essential contribution to the cultural life of the LSM and to the *dugri* ideology of interaction that will be discussed in Chapter 5 cannot be denied. However, the flip side of this egalitarianism was always exclusion: as Domenico Losurdo argues in his counterhistory of liberalism, here too the equal distribution of resources within the community of equals could not be sustained except through denial of entry to those who must remain unequal.[54] In the case of the LSM, this exclusionary egalitarianism was distilled into a horror of entry into wage-labor relations with those essential others— indigenous proletarians.

THE ROOTS OF EXPLOITATION ANXIETY

In *Land and Desire in Early Zionism*, historian Boaz Neumann provides an "existential" account of LSM pioneers' desire for the land that is explicitly opposed to materialist analysis of the kind offered by sociologists like Kimmerling and Shafir. But despite his contention that this desire is "a primal, irreducible condition, a state of being that precedes need or purpose,"[55] it can be demonstrated from his own materials, culled from the private and public writings of early pioneers, that the movement's ideological apparatuses deliberately inculcated it. This desire served concrete, material purposes: to facilitate the takeover of land and to justify the hegemonic role of the LSM. *Land and Desire* can thus be read against the author's intent, as a phenomenology of the strongly embodied effects of ideology, which include an erotic dimension (which he recognizes) as well as an aggressive one (which he does not).

For LSM pioneers, as Neumann shows, agricultural labor played an essential role in overcoming the estrangement between recent immigrants and the land they had come to inherit, as well as in articulating the difference between the land that would become theirs and that which would remain in the hands of the Arab enemy.[56] The long-neglected but intense link between the People of Israel and its land was conceived as taking root through the pioneers' offering up of their own bodily fluids. Shedding their blood to slake the thirst of the land was the most dramatic of these exchanges, but far more important, in many pioneers' eyes, was the offering of sweat and tears.[57] The pioneers read the biblical injunctions "by the sweat of your brow shall you eat your bread" (Genesis 3:19) and "they who sow in tears shall reap in joy" (Psalm 126:5) in this light—not as the wages of primordial sin or as grim universal truths, but as a formula of exchange: agricultural labor and its bodily indexes in return for livelihood and a permanent stake in the country.

If for the pioneers such intercourse was crucial to forming a direct bond with the land, it followed that the employment of Arabs in agricultural work would be not only counterproductive but downright dangerous. The pioneers viewed the plantation-colonies (*moshavot*) of the First Aliyah, where Palestinian workers were a common sight, as landscapes "abandoned, derelict . . . open to incursions by strangers who uprooted saplings and trees and stole property."[58] While Arab peasants' own attachment to the land they lived on was strongly disavowed, the possibility that they, too, might sanctify a bond with the soil thanks to the carelessness and greed of Jewish planters had to be carefully foreclosed: "Only where the soil is manured with the sweat of the [Jewish] peasant will the land become nationalized," wrote political economist Franz Oppenheimer, "[a]nd only where the cooperative association owns the land which it cultivates is there a guarantee that it is not Arab sweat that manures and wins the land."[59]

In the pioneers' disgusted reaction to "Arab labor" and in their strong ambivalence toward Yemeni workers we can begin to trace the contours of an affectively imbued ideological orientation I propose to call "exploitation anxiety." For socialists, exploitation is wrong primarily due to its immiseration and degradation of the exploited, whatever their nationality; but for the labor settlement movement, exploitation was immoral primarily due to its effects on the *exploiters*, as it would deny them the opportunity to form an immediate, intimate, and permanent link with the land. Such exploitation would thrust them back into the condition of exilic *luftmenshen* ("air people" in Yiddish) who make their living from "nonproductive" pursuits. Overcoming this condition through labor was a supremely difficult task and so long as "strangers" were available for exploitation, the possibility of a backslide into reliance on their labor would continue to loom.[60] The severe anxiety surrounding this possibility found expression in a fervor for "purity" that was at once strategic and moral. This was a slow process, and by the end of the Mandate, Zionist organizations and Jewish individuals only controlled about 7 percent of Palestine's arable territory.[61] However, following the establishment of the state and the Nakba, the conditions under which the LSM labored changed drastically. On one hand, the vast majority of Palestinians were expelled, and their fertile lands confiscated and leased to LSM communities.[62] On the other, a substantial stock of new proletarians was quickly made available for wage labor. One part of this new proletariat was composed of the remaining Palestinians, now subjected to military administration and dispossessed of large swaths of their land through the invention of Orwellian categories like "present absentees" and other bureaucratic maneuvers.[63] Its counterpart was the growing mass of Jewish immigrants from the Middle East who would come to be known as Mizrahim.[64]

Palestine had had an urban Sephardi Jewish community for centuries, but until World War II, most Zionist immigrants to Palestine came from Eastern Europe, and—with the significant exception of the Yemeni venture—the movement's leaders mostly ignored the smaller Jewish communities in Asia and Africa. Only after the greatest reserve of potential settlers was annihilated in the Nazi Holocaust did Zionists step up their recruitment efforts in the Middle East, and in the decade following Israel's establishment, which also saw a steep rise in exclusionary Arab nationalism, the vast majority of Middle Eastern Jews immigrated to Israel.[65] Many were subjected to policies of compulsory proletarianization and settlement in peripheral areas, whether in new, ethnically segregated *moshavim* or in "development towns," where they served as a landless reservoir of industrial and agricultural labor as well as a human barrier against Palestinian incursions.[66] Following Ben-Dor Benite, Liron Mor argues that the construction of the Mizrahi immigrants as expendable pawns rather than heroic volunteers in both labor and defense has been crucial to their stigmatizing racialization in Israel.[67]

Upon the heels of the rapid primitive accumulation of the Nakba and the assembling of a Palestinian and Mizrahi proletariat almost ex nihilo, the late 1950s and early 1960s were a period of rapid expansion for the LSM. Agricultural production was stepped up, with government support, to meet the demands of a growing population, and living standards rose as profits flowed into settlement coffers.[68] Yet as Tal Elmaliach has shown for the National Kibbutz Federation, the most ideologically orthodox component of the LSM, economic success triggered ideological crisis: the shift to manufacturing, the rise in living standards, and the newfound dependence on wage labor all ran directly counter to the ideological tenets upon which the movement had staked its claim to hegemony within the Zionist movement writ large.[69] The movement's economic reproduction was now in conflict with its ideological reproduction—a contradiction that would eventually destroy its political hegemony, if not its members' privileged class position.

Responses to the heightened exploitation anxiety incurred by this new situation were varied. Some members of the LSM came to terms with the gap between ideals and reality; others, especially the young, abandoned its settlements, embracing New Left politics or individualistic upward mobility in the cities.[70] Among those who continued to work in agriculture, a defensive attitude prevailed; many felt they had to defend themselves from the charge of being *frayerim*, or "suckers."[71] But one group reasoned differently: if in the agricultural heartlands it had become too difficult to resist the temptation to exploit, the movement's original principles could be put into practice in a new *terra nullius* unpolluted by "foreign labor."

THE ISRAELI SETTLEMENT OF THE CENTRAL ARABAH

Though the Arabah was ethnically cleansed in 1949, it was not permanently settled until the 1960s. The region's hyper-aridity made agricultural colonization of the kind in which the Zionist movement had gained expertise difficult, and parts of the state bureaucracy, including the military, were skeptical about the viability of farming in the region. However, it was precisely this challenge that attracted second- and third-generation pioneers, repelled by what they saw as the degeneration of their home settlements, to lobby the state for aid in settling the area. They found a powerful ally in the state's first premier, David Ben-Gurion, who envisioned the southland as both a strategic reserve and a field for ideological regeneration. Due to their remoteness, the settlements of the Arabah that Ben-Gurion helped to establish were able to extend the life span of the classic model of "Hebrew labor" far beyond what was possible in Israel's core. Only in the 1980s, when the shift to a neoliberal model of accumulation transformed Israel's preferred modes of colonization, were Arabah settlers forced to scramble for new modes of livelihood and self-justification.

Initially, Israeli interest in the deep south focused on its outlet to the Red Sea, which the new state's leaders saw as crucial for future trade links with Asia. Generous funding and attention were devoted to developing the port of Eilat, which opened in 1955; the *kibbutzim* established in its hinterland, in the southern Arabah, would later come to make up the Eilot Regional Council. As traffic between the port and the country's center grew, strategic importance devolved onto the Jordanian border. Fearing "infiltration" by Palestinian guerrillas and the displaced Bedouin inhabitants, the IDF placed the Central Arabah under military administration, establishing bases at the former British police posts at 'Ayn Hosb and 'Ayn Ghadyan (renamed Ein Hatzeva and Yotvata) as well as at Be'er Menuha and Paran.[72] In 1953, the Bedouin al-Misk and 'Amrani families of the Sa'idiyyin federation were allowed to return from Jordan and settle near 'Ayn Hosb in return for military services, which included patrolling the border.[73]

Zoologist Giora Ilani, who served as a military wireless operator at 'Ayn Hosb in 1956 and later settled in the Arabah, provides an account of the post in which wonder at the area's natural splendor clashes with disgust at the army's destructive actions:

> [T]he limestone mountainside sloped wildly towards Wadi Fuqra . . . dotted with tamarisks and acacias. . . . To the north, the gray eminence of mesquite, seepweed and nitre-bush dominated the landscape . . . ample trees—twisted acacia, umbrella thorn acacia, and even Christ's thorn jujube—grew and cast their gladdening shade across the land, but the jewel in the crown was the hundreds of desert gazelles. . . . Abu Ghanim and his friends estimated the distance to the camp at 'Ayn Hosb, and after ascertaining that no one would hear the shots, tried to kill as many gazelles as they could. The gazelles had learned from experience to run out of the rifles' range, so I could only see them from afar. . . . [The soldiers] smiled apologetically after missing their shots; they promised me that at night they would kill as many gazelles as they wished using spotlights.[74]

These Druze soldiers also served as hunting guides for high-ranking Jewish officers, who had "learned to enjoy free hunting" while serving "in the British Army in the Western Desert and North Africa." Ten gazelles were turned over to the camp's cook every week, but others were killed in such a reckless way as to render their carcasses unfit for consumption.[75]

As far as the army and much of the government bureaucracy were concerned, military administration of the region was adequate to the need of retaining security control; but others warned that if the Arabah were not permanently settled, it would never be stably integrated into the national territory. Wearying of the hypocrisy of the veteran settler leaders, who they perceived as enriching themselves while shirking their duty to the nation, these young traditionalists found an ally in Ben-Gurion, who felt an urgent need to furnish fresh ideological content to the hegemony of his MAPAI over other parties within and without the LSM, as well as to ensure the ascendancy of the state over all parties, including MAPAI itself.[76]

Since the end of the war Ben-Gurion had been concerned about two problems, for which he envisioned interconnected solutions. First was what he saw as the waning of the pioneer spirit among the younger generation in general and within the labor settlement elite in particular. Second was the need to settle the Negev in order to fortify and perpetuate Israel's control over its newly acquired expanses. The dissolution of the LSM's armed forces, the PALMAH and Haganah, and their integration into the Israel Defense Forces (IDF) was the first manifestation of Ben-Gurion's strategy of *mamlakhtiut,* or statism.[77] In time, state organs were also to take over many of the functions hitherto performed by the LSM's parties, its youth movements, and its trade union federation, the Histadrut. Rather than throw themselves into the challenges of state-building, in Ben-Gurion's eyes both the movement and the government bureaucracy (which drew its cadres from the LSM's ranks) were dragging their feet and obstructing necessary work. Worse, these cynical actors were exerting a pernicious influence on the youth, steering them away from the idealistic path of the pioneer and toward the multiplying comforts of life in the prosperous settlements of the center and north.

In Ben-Gurion's eyes, the necessary work included the settlement of the deep south, including the Arabah. Until the war the Negev housed less than 5 percent of Palestine's population, almost none of it Jewish.[78] After the Nakba, the remaining Bedouin inhabitants were concentrated in a reservation area east of Beersheba known in Hebrew as the Seyag, or "enclosure."[79] The half of the country that lies beyond Beersheba remained sparsely populated. As we have seen, before Israel's independence rural colonization was aimed at establishing control over thinly inhabited but strategically important wetland and lowland zones by converting them into commercially productive agricultural territories. While purchasing this land was expensive, the investment in productive capacity made long-term economic sense, with new settlements expected to provide foodstuffs and textile fibers for rapidly growing cities as part of a newly segregated Jewish economy.

The expanses of desert conquered in the war were a different matter. Ben-Gurion's running battle with cabinet "pragmatists" led by Finance Minister Pinhas Sapir was not over the need to anchor settlement in agricultural commodity production, which both took for granted, but over the expenses that the developmentalist state could afford to incur to establish such production. Over the pragmatists' objections, Ben-Gurion devised several schemes for the creation of new bodies—either entirely under state direction, or state-LSM hybrids—that were to undertake the task of settling the deep south.[80] But for the duration of his first term as prime minister, from 1948 to 1953, he was spectacularly unsuccessful in getting any of these projects off the ground. Some, like the fishermen's village in Eilat or the spiny rush farms at 'Ayn Ghadyan, proved economically untenable; others, like the first attempt at settling Ein Yahav, experienced social collapse and even internal violence.[81] These failed experiments convinced experts that precipitation in the region was not enough to sustain commercial agriculture; it was, however, known since the IDF's Corps of Engineers undertook a survey in 1949 that a vast but nonreplenishing aquifer of ancient water lay underneath the Wadi Arabah.[82] To draw up this alkaline water and make it usable for irrigation would require massive investment in drilling, pumping, and treatment, and government experts in charge of settlement infrastructure were skeptical about the possibility of recouping this investment.[83]

After being pushed out of the premiership in 1953, Ben-Gurion "retired" to Sdeh Boker, a new settlement in the central Negev that refused to affiliate with any of the LSM's constituent organs. His little house in the desert quickly became a hub of political intrigue, attracting figures hostile to the new government of Moshe Sharett. By 1955, Ben-Gurion had returned to the premiership and the Defense Ministry. When a group of youth intensely committed to initiating agricultural settlement in the Arabah received no support for its project from subordinates, it was an obvious move to turn to him.[84] With his help, the Arabah's first permanent Jewish settlement, Ein Yahav, was organized as an outpost (*he'ahzut*) of the NAHAL, or "Pioneer Fighting Youth." The most successful of Ben-Gurion's state-pioneering projects, perhaps because it also served the interests of the LSM, the NAHAL was a unit of the Israel Defense Forces composed of conscripts from the movement, who spent part of their service establishing and running paramilitary agricultural settlements, or "outposts," in frontier zones, with a view to their eventual "civilianization." Though quite controversial at times, and openly attacked by figures as eminent as IDF chief of staff, later minister of defense, Moshe Dayan, throughout the 1950s and beyond the NAHAL held an attraction for pioneering-minded LSM youth.[85]

The idea of establishing a NAHAL outpost in the Arabah was hatched by Shai Ben-Eliyahu and Hagi Porat, two young men of urban origins who had spent their teenage years together in Kfar Yehoshua, one of the oldest and wealthiest *moshavim* of Israel's north.[86] The two toured the country in search of a worthy spot to settle, and eventually homed in on the failed experimental station and military base in Ein Yahav—"spring of hope" in Hebrew, a euphemistic inversion of the original Arabic *'ayn weiba*, or "spring of disaster."[87] Near the point where a wadi draining much of the Negev entered the Wadi Arabah, the site had relatively good access to water but was difficult to get to.

One hundred twenty-five kilometers from both Eilat and Jerusalem as the crow flies, this was one of the remotest spots in the country, distant not only from Jewish metropolitan centers and transport infrastructure, but also from concentrations of Palestinian labor in the country's north and center.[88]

For Ben-Eliyahu and Porat's vision to become reality, administrative and financial support was needed, and as we have seen, the military and civilian bureaucracy could not see any strategic need for settling the Arabah.[89] Using personal connections, the two managed to reach Ben-Gurion and secure his active support for the creation of their NAHAL outpost, overcoming the objections of these officials.[90] In 1960, final permissions were received, and the first group formally settled at Ein Yahav. Within two years, the outpost was "civilianized" and temporarily became a *moshbutz*, a transitional form that served as a compromise between the settlers, most of whom hailed from veteran *moshavim* and desired to remain affiliated with that branch of the LSM, and the institutional actors who saw the *kibbutz* as the most appropriate format for settlement in such hostile conditions.[91] The settlers soon had their way: in 1962, Ein Yahav became a *moshav* and was accepted into the national Moshavim Movement. It was quickly followed by Hatzeva in 1965.

The 1967 Israeli occupation of the remnant of historic Palestine, together with the Egyptian Sinai Peninsula and the Syrian Golan Heights, gave additional impetus to the settlement of the Arabah. Under a semi-official plan authored by statesman Yigal Allon, the newly occupied southern part of the Jordan Valley was marked as crucial for preventing territorial continuity between the dense Arab populations of the West Bank and the Jordanian massif.[92] The new eastern frontier was quickly dotted with agricultural settlements manned by the younger generation of the LSM, from Neve Ativ on the slopes of Mount Hermon (Ar. Jabal esh-Sheikh) in the Golan to Mitzpe Shalem on the shores of the Dead Sea in the West Bank. The Central Arabah was thus linked to a chain of socially and economically similar settlements stretching along Israel's eastern flank.[93] Following a national pattern in which settlements of the same type were grouped together regionally and institutionally in order to maintain political homogeneity,[94] the settlements established in the Central Arabah following Ein Yahav and Hatzeva were also organized as *moshavim*: Paran in 1971, Tzofar in 1976, and Idan in 1980.[95] Unlike the border zones in which Mizrahim were more or less forcibly settled in the 1950s,[96] but like the occupied Golan Heights and Jordan Valley, the "isolated and climatically difficult" Central Arabah was deemed appropriate only for the pioneering spirit of "sons and daughters of the [LSM] and graduates of agricultural schools," who were assumed to "have a greater chance of managing the complex spatial challenge."[97] Here again idealism is construed as a limited and differentially distributed resource. "Rising to the challenge" of colonial settlement, as opposed to merely carrying out agricultural drudgery, appears once more as a form of racialized class privilege to which not just anyone can aspire.

The youth who set up the *moshavim* of the Arabah were not motivated primarily by a desire to escape the temptations of a readily exploitable labor force. Rather, they were attracted by the romance of the frontier. They were enthralled by proximity to the "majesty of nature" in a region that contrasted sharply with the rain-fed valleys to the north and seemed to belong on "another planet," as Ben-Eliyahu wrote. Inspired by the Spartan spirit required to live in this "uncompromising, hard and cruel land,"[98] they were eager to raise children who would work beside them in the fields and eventually take over as natural-born peasants. Unlike many of their peers, however, they were committed to the realization of the ideology on which they had been raised, and this did mean—first and foremost—refraining from employing "strangers." This is how Yossi, one of the first settlers of Ein Amal, put it to me:

> For many years we didn't let Arabs in here. Today it sounds a little racist, but in those years, there were grounds for it, ideological grounds, because in fact we had conquered them. . . . We had expelled them from their lands, and here we are employing them as . . . our workers on their own lands. There's something immoral about it. . . . Many places in the country, *moshavim* and *kibbutzim*, were on Arab lands. And for many years the position was held that it's immoral to

employ the people you have conquered and expelled from their lands, to employ them as workers. . . . The motto was: whoever works the land will in the end be its owner. That was the ideology. Not on racist grounds but rather on moral ones.[99]

Whether or not the young settlers realized it consciously, striking out far from concentrations of Palestinian laborers hungry for work would make the temptation to "let them in here" that much easier to resist. And while the Bedouin of the Negev were somewhat closer, their concentration in the Seyag also kept most of them well out of reach.[100]

Despite the authorities' initial reticence, once they had become a "fact on the ground," the settlements of the Arabah received enormous amounts of material support from the Israeli state and a panoply of para-state "national institutions" unbound by the legal strictures that prevent the state from openly discriminating between Jewish and non-Jewish citizens. While I cannot give a quantitative estimate of the magnitude of this support over the years, it is possible to assess these investments and the immense changes in the environment that they made possible qualitatively.[101] The most crucial intervention financed by these state and para-state institutions was in irrigation infrastructure. The springs and artesian wells used in the region before Israeli settlement could not provide anything like the amounts of water needed for commercial agriculture; for this it was necessary to locate deep, ancient, and nonrenewing aquifers, drill deep into them, and bring their contents to the surface. As water is sucked out of these aquifers, it becomes saline and silty, necessitating expensive repairs and eventually the drilling of new boreholes.[102] Irrigation water, making its way through the highly alkaline ground into the aquifers, pollutes them with alkaloids and fertilizer, and as the reserves degrade, lower-quality water must be extracted and subjected to expensive, energy-intensive treatment in order to be fit for farming, not to mention drinking.[103] Since the settlement of the Arabah, all investment in irrigation infrastructure has been underwritten by state and para-state actors; today, the region is covered by a grid of wells, pipes, dikes, and reservoirs capable, for now, of providing for its needs through periods of peak and slack demand.[104] Given the extreme salinity and compactness of the local soil (reg, also known as "desert pavement"), this investment had to be complemented by the importation of sandy soil appropriate for growing vegetables. Finally, like the rest of the labor settlement movement, the settlements of the Arabah also enjoyed cheap, state-sponsored credit for farming and industrial activities as well as production quotas and other subsidies.[105]

Without water and soil, it would be impossible to produce vegetables, but without roads it would be impossible to deliver them to markets. Until 1967, when Route 90 was completed, the only way out of the Arabah and to the center of the country was the unpaved Roman route of Ma'aleh 'Aqrabim. Using the new section of Route 90, known as the "Arabah Road," trucks could quickly bring the region's produce to the country's population centers as well as to its ports, from which they are now exported. The road—fully financed by the state—does not only serve the *moshavim*: as the fastest route to Eilat, it has played an important part in the city's development as a port and tourist destination. Nevertheless, without it, globally oriented agriculture in the region would be unimaginable.

A NICHE FOR SELF-LABOR

By the mid-1970s, an economic and ecological model that would enable the settlers of the Arabah to make an adequate living without violating the principle of self-labor was in place. Once supplied with water, suitable soils, and the appropriate infrastructure, the Arabah manifested a competitive advantage: high temperatures enabled the cultivation of summer vegetables such as tomatoes, cucumbers, and peppers in the wintertime. Out of season, in the protected national market, these vegetables initially drew prodigious prices: working hard in the cool months, local farmers made enough money to rest and recuperate during the hot, long summers when cultivation was impossible. Later to be emulated by farmers working in the western Negev, the settlers of the Arabah played a part in forming the culinary expectations of Israeli consumers, who are no longer satisfied with cabbage and carrots in the winter but expect year-round access to the summery ingredients of the ubiquitous "Arab salad": tomatoes, cucumbers, and peppers.

Even in the Arabah, outside labor, including Arab labor, was occasionally used. Both Bedouin from the Negev and Palestinians from the Occupied Territories worked in the *moshavim* sporadically. While the opprobrium they met with was not enough to prevent their entry altogether, it was—together with the geographical hurdles—sufficiently harsh to make complete reliance on their labor impossible for local farmers.[106] Combined with the strongly seasonal nature of farmwork, the practical unavailability of wage laborers meant that at peak times a considerable effort was required of all members of the community. Women worked in the fields besides men, gaining status and influence that they were later to lose.[107] Children, too, spent time in the fields with their parents, lending a hand as soon as they were able.

Another source of "outside" labor did play an important role in the moral and political economy of the Arabah's *moshavim*: foreign volunteers. Young people from around the Western world, drawn by Israel's global glory in the wake of the 1967 Six-Day War, developed an intense interest in the LSM's experiments in egalitarianism. As we have seen, in the two decades following 1948 the reality of the labor settlement movement tended to diverge even more from this ideal than it had before independence. Nevertheless, for a long time the image remained impressive—especially at a distance—and until the well-publicized atrocities of the First Lebanon War and First Intifada, tens of thousands of Western youth, both Jewish and gentile, volunteered their labor in order to learn firsthand about life and work on the *kibbutz* and *moshav*.[108] Unsurprisingly, many were particularly attracted to the Arabah.

Community institutions regulated the work of volunteers in a mostly successful attempt to prevent it from turning into wage labor pure and simple. In the most orthodox of the *moshavim*, Ein Yahav, only one volunteer was allowed per family until the early 1980s, when a second volunteer was permitted. Foreshadowing things to come, this arrangement was a strongly paternalistic one. In addition to an allowance, volunteers received room and board within the family home, intended to make sure each was treated as a *"ben bayit"*—a member, or literally "son" of the household—"and not a laborer [*po'el*]."[109] Usually single youth living for a few months with somewhat older couples and their young children, volunteers could comfortably be slotted into the role of impressionable youngsters in need of direction. Though neither side experienced the exchange as uniformly positive,[110] settlers could convince themselves that they were doing the volunteers and the nation a favor by taking them on, even as the relationship edged closer to that of hired day labor, as when *moshav* members drove to Red Sea resorts to recruit European tourists. "The assembly's decision to allow the employment of one volunteer per household farm," writes sociologist Avi Shnider, "was interpreted by the members to mean that one could hire anyone who had blond hair and spoke an Anglo-Saxon [*sic*] language." When, in 1983, settlers of the *moshav* he studied were permitted to lodge volunteers outside their homes, this opened the way to the employment of Israeli Jews, on the basis of the argument that "replacement of a Gentile volunteer with an Israeli represents a strengthening" of LSM values.[111] As with the distinction between Ashkenazi pioneers and Mizrahi grunts, here again we see racialization and the wage-labor relation lumped together in a semiotic bundle: while employment of Palestinians (Israeli citizens or not) remained illegitimate "exploitation," the labor of blond Europeans, even under similar conditions, was "voluntary" and thus legitimate.

The blurring of the distinction between volunteer and wage laborers throughout the 1980s can be understood, especially in retrospect, as an expression of a general tendency among capitalist employers to seek out cheap and flexible labor. However, so long as they served a protected national market and retained key elements of state support, the Arabah's farmers were able to prosper economically without capitulating entirely to the dictates of cost reduction, all the while respecting ideological strictures that had already been consigned to historic memory in the rest of the country. This here was a practical application of what Michael Herzfeld calls "structural nostalgia"—a "static image of an unspoiled and irrecoverable past" that "legitimizes deeds of the moment by investing them with the moral authority of eternal truth" in the service of an ongoing project of colonization.[112]

CRISIS

As we have seen, the initial approach toward colonization of the territories conquered by Israel in 1967 was governed by the familiar logic of labor settlement. But the debacle of the war of 1973, in which Syrian and Egyptian forces reconquered parts of these territories, spelled the end for this mode of colonization. Breaking free of the disgraced political establishment, the military turned away from the conception of territorial defense that prioritized agricultural settlement.[113] In the "turnaround" (*mahapakh*) of 1977, LSM hegemony over Israeli politics was broken by the rise of the right-wing Likud, whose leader, Menachem Begin, agreed two years later to return the Sinai to Egypt. The main thrust of colonization now shifted into the mountainous heart of the West Bank. A new generation of settlers called by a different name (*mitnahalim* rather than *mityashvim*), holding to a religious-messianic ideology, assumed the vanguard role.[114] New settlements were established with a view to preventing contiguity between urban areas within the Occupied Palestinian Territories (OPT), rather than between these territories and neighboring Arab countries. Though fresh legal strategies were dreamed up to nullify the tenure of the Palestinian *fellahin*, the new settlements were by and large suburban, with road connections to Jerusalem and Tel Aviv serving as means of cutting Palestinian villages and towns off from one another.[115] Since then, the commuter-oriented, non-agrarian "community settlement," which retains the right to exclude residents on arbitrary grounds of "incompatibility," has become the most common type for new settlements in the West Bank as well as Palestinian-majority areas within Israel proper.[116]

Neoliberalism emerged onto the Israeli political scene in response to an inflation crisis triggered by the first Likud government's policy of cutting taxes without trimming public expenditures or imposing monetary discipline. The Emergency Stabilization Plan of 1985 was

enacted by a "national unity" government in which MAPAI's successor, the Labor Party, led by Finance Minister Shimon Peres, embraced
the free market in keeping with the shifting interests of its upwardly
mobile constituency.[117] This turn spelled trouble for the whole of the
labor settlement movement, but most vulnerable were those communities that had managed to uphold orthodoxy thanks to the support
of the public purse. As barriers to international trade were lowered,
bringing competition and lower prices, expensive state investments
in agricultural infrastructure were called into question. At the same
time, the atrocities of Israel's war in Lebanon were driving world opinion against Israel and cutting off the flow of volunteers.

Perhaps the greatest shock was the withdrawal of agricultural
credit. Given its seasonal character and dependence on meteorological
vagaries, commodity agriculture is unavoidably a risky investment,
and private financial institutions are usually wary of providing loans
to small producers. As part of the Emergency Stabilization Plan, the
state raised interest rates on outstanding loans to the national and regional cooperatives in which agricultural producers were organized,
causing their debts to mushroom and many to go bankrupt. In the
drought year of 1985, water supplies to settlements that had not paid
for their quotas were cut off for the first time.[118] Left to negotiate with
banks for loans on their own, farmers were faced with a swift deterioration in the terms of credit.[119] But while many *kibbutz* and *moshav*
members near the country's center could look forward to converting their holdings into lucrative suburban residential properties, the
settlers of remote regions such as the Arabah had no such option. As
collective marketing and credit arrangements broke down, neighbors
were forced into competition with one another. In 1998, the antagonism between the defenders of the remaining cooperative institutions
in Ein Yahav and those who wanted to be released from their control
deteriorated into intra-community mayhem, ironically dubbed "the
intifada" after the Palestinian uprising that had broken out the previous year.[120] A cartoon in a local newsletter (Figure 1.1) expresses settlers' deep ambivalence about the new situation they found themselves
in. The caricature depicts a *moshav* farmer in conventional enough

FIGURE 1.1

"Capitalist." *Be'enenu*, 9 December 1988, p. 18.

פּסימיסט

terms: *tembel* hat, bushy mustache, and Histadrut membership card. The subtle but powerful satirical punch is provided by the caption, which reads, simply, "Capitalist."

If the Arabah's settlements were to survive in a global market, the comparative advantages of climate, capital investment, and high technical competence were not going to be enough. To this day no amount of research and development—in Israel or elsewhere—has made it possible for machines to efficiently replace humans in the delicate tasks of planting, pruning, and picking table vegetables and fruit. Fresh-produce cultivation remains one of the most labor-intensive of all economic sectors, hence any vegetable farm exposed to the global market has one sine qua non: cheap labor.[121] Since 1948 such labor had been available to the swiftly growing Israeli economy, first in the shape of Palestinian and Mizrahi citizens, and since 1967 in the form of the disenfranchised Palestinians of the Occupied Territories. But the former were no longer cheaply available, and the latter had just risen furiously, struggling for national liberation through workplace actions that ranged from rallies and strikes to the assassination of employers.[122] As farmers dependent on Arab labor scrambled to survive, the settlers of the Arabah must have felt vindicated in their insistence on cleaving to the colonial traditions of the LSM and remaining independent of such degradations. But now they felt the need for cheap labor as acutely as anyone else. Where would it come from?

2 TRANSNATIONAL CAPITALIST COLONIALITY

WHY DID ISRAELI AGRICULTURE END up recruiting a migrant labor force to replace its Palestinian workers, European volunteers, and Israeli "self-laborers" in northeast Thailand, of all places? In one sense, the process was entirely contingent, hinging on the imponderable decisions of individual actors, like Thai general Pichit Kullavanijaya and Israeli businessman Uzi Vered. Things could certainly have gone otherwise, and today Israel might have an agrarian workforce of a different nationality, or perhaps no agricultural sector to speak of at all. In another sense, however, this development was deeply structured by the workings of the capitalist-colonial world system, which was undergoing an important phase shift at the time. As we have already seen for the Israeli case, during the system's developmentalist phase, the post–World War II *trente glorieuses*, the extension of commodity-producing agricultural settlement into frontier zones was a primary tool for the projection of state power. The same was true of Thailand, though the differences are as important as the similarities. In Israel, capitalist colonization involved the dispossession and expulsion of the indigenous Palestinians and their replacement by an internally egalitarian but ruthlessly exclusionary "pure settlement" model of agrarian commodity production. In Thailand's Isaan periphery, by contrast, the process was marked by a deeply unequal and repressive integration of the Lao-speaking peasantry into both the national economy and the nationalist project.

Hence, at the dawn of the neoliberal era, the two regions posed diametrically opposed problems to their national ruling elites: while Israeli agricultural regions like the Arabah were facing depopulation due to the obsolescence of the region's state-protected agrarian business model, the closure of the land frontier and the lack of industrial employment opportunities rendered Isaan's agrarian population a political pressure cooker in need of a relief valve. But this new era was also one of "globalization"—that is, of tighter and tighter transnational integration within the world-system, comprising growing movements of capital, commodities, and labor. Against this background, one ruling class's problem could become part of another's solution: Israel's agricultural enclaves could reorient their production to global markets while at the same time absorbing some of Isaan's "surplus" labor-power and providing elite Thai actors with opportunities to draw arbitrage rents off the wage differential between the two countries.

Such transitions are often abrupt, however, and possibilities of failure abound. The remarkable success of the shift, especially in the Arabah, where "foreign labor" had previously been entirely anathema, owes much to the particular trajectory whereby Isaanite migrants were mobilized for work in Israel. This trajectory, determined by the two states' shared background as key US allies in their respective Cold War theaters, also leaned heavily on their experience with agrarian settlement as a strategic and ideological instrument. Though the "Frontier Settlement Project" initiated by Pichit and entertained by his Israeli interlocutors never really got off the ground, the links created thereby primed the pump of the migrant flow, not only in organizational terms but also in ideological ones. And though "frontier settlement" as military strategy was rapidly becoming irrelevant in both countries, its propagation abroad still provided a legitimate ideological vocabulary that made it possible for Arabah settlers, as well as the state officials whose approval they required, to accept the changes at hand and adjust to them. Whether the actors involved knew what they were doing or not—and there is good reason to suspect that they did—the discourse they employed was an instance of structural hypocrisy, a term I suggest by analogy with Herzfeld's "structural nostalgia."

But another ideological factor was no less important in the transition to total reliance on the exploitation of wage labor among Israeli settlers, especially in the Arabah. Exclusionary egalitarianism, by definition, provided farmers with few tools for the legitimation of hierarchical relations. But Isaan migrants, with their long history of hierarchical integration, knew how to relate to "superiors" at work as well as outside it. As I show in the next chapter, the paternalistic interaction ideology in large part dictated to them by the Thai state, a moral framework that bound those at both ends of domination into mutual responsibilities modeled on the patriarchal family, would step into the anomic breach to structure relations between workers and employers in the Arabah—at first publicly, before retreating into the "domestic" sphere of the farm.

This chapter thus begins by recounting the history of the Kingdom of Siam's colonization of Isaan, which was only belatedly accompanied by the imposition of capitalist relations. Lightly settled by Lao-speaking peasants in the nineteenth century, the region was densely forested and largely economically self-sufficient until after World War II. It was only in the second half of the twentieth century that Isaanites were hierarchically integrated into a Bangkok-centered capitalist economy and many pushed to migrate. Following this sketch of Isaan's colonization, I describe the paternalistic ideology whereby the Thai state interpellated its rural subaltern subjects as lesser organs of a unified "social body," part and parcel of its counterinsurgency strategy against the Communist Party of Thailand, which drew much of its support from the countryside. General Pichit's Frontier Settlement Project, the topic of the chapter's next section, was a cursory and possibly unserious attempt to seal Isaan off from the aftereffects of revolution and war through the establishment of agrarian commodity production on an Israeli model. To emplace the link between the two countries in its Cold War context, I go into some detail about previous such attempts and their questionable legacy, which made Israeli diplomats hesitant to go along with Pichit's plan. As I relate, while some settlements were established on the margins of Isaan in this period, the idea that these would bear an "Israeli stamp" never really came to fruition, though elite actors immediately seized upon the rent-seeking possibilities of dispatching Thai workers off for "training" in Israel, opening the door for the regularized labor migration that would be instituted once Israel decided to break free of its dependence on Palestinian labor-power in the early 1990s.

The very particularity of the narrative set out in this chapter, then, discloses its pertinence to a far larger story. In transitional situations like this one, by definition, something changes while something else persists. From the post–World War II period to the present, in both Israel and Thailand, the drive to deepen capitalist-colonial domination over peripheries and their populations abides. It is this basic homology, which is in no way limited to these two countries, that allowed their ruling classes to have mutually intelligible conversations about "frontier settlement." What changes is the role played by agriculture in this drive, as technological advance and global integration cause the sector to shed most of its workforce and, in wealthy and crowded countries like Israel, to recede into specialized enclaves. In this period, agricultural populations throughout the former Third World, today the Global South, tend to become "surplus," threatening to turn from bulwarks of stability into political liabilities if not funneled to places where their labor-power can still be exploited profitably. All the same, the central contradiction that the capitalist-colonial world-system is constructed to contain—the contradiction between capital's dependence on domination of a workforce for the production of profits and its vulnerability to that workforce's potential refusal—remains. By collaborating to institute a flow of migrant labor from Thailand to Israel, and from Isaan to the Arabah in particular, the ruling classes of both countries have contrived to deepen the pacification of their peripheries, while also producing commodities for a profit which is shared out between immediate employers and a ramifying network of rent-seeking intermediaries in both countries. The transnational capitalist coloniality that emerges has been latent in the system's dynamic from the start.

PUSHING BACK THE FOREST: CAPITALIST COLONIZATION IN ISAAN

Thailand, famously, has never been formally colonized. While the other vaguely demarcated and partially overlapping polities that had ruled mainland Southeast Asia succumbed to European imperialism in the nineteenth century, the Kingdom of Siam consolidated its sovereignty by forcibly incorporating peripheries, including the territory lying between its heartland in the Chao Phraya valley and French Indochina. However, the Kingdom was only able to maintain its formal independence by integrating into the colonial world order, both in the sense of subordinating itself to global imperial powers—first Great Britain and then the US—and in the sense of exerting its own colonial power over peripheries.[1] Accession to membership in the international community was facilitated by the Kingdom's adoption of the trappings of a nation-state, peaking in its 1939 renaming after the Thai ethnolinguistic group that predominates in the lower Chao Phraya basin, including the Bangkok area. The survival of the monarchy through the shift from a traditional, ethnically heterogeneous *mandala* empire to a modern nation-state granted the Thai elite a powerful claim to legitimate rule not only over this heartland, but over peripheral areas like the primarily Lao-speaking northeast, which was renamed Isaan, for "northeast"—a Sanskritizing, Bangkok-centric nomenclature.[2] The imposition of Siamese/Thai rule—at once interpellating the Lao-speaking peasantry as quintessentially Thai and racializing it as backward and rustic—paved the way for the unequal and uneven economic integration of Isaanites as a semiproletarian "reserve army of labor." After World War II, and especially during the Vietnam War, the capitalist transformation of the interior would kick into overdrive, catalyzing the massive conversion of forest into cropland and Isaan's integration into the global economy as an exporter of materials and labor-power.

This exploitative and hierarchical method of incorporation into the national body has met with explosion after explosion of resistance. The people of Isaan have lent their active support to a succession of insurrections and protest movements stretching from the *phuu mii bun* revolts of the early twentieth century to parliamentary activism in the

1950s, communist guerrilla war in the 1970s, the Red Shirt movement in protest of the military coup of 2006, and continuing support for the electoral opposition.[3] Exploitation, repression, and racism have led to the emergence of a strong collective consciousness among those who now understand themselves as *khon Isaan*. The Thai state, in its turn, has met this resistance with a distinctive mix of repression and piece-meal concessions, couched in a paternalistic idiom that Isaanites have learned to use for their own purposes in situations that preclude the chances of successful rebellion—including, as I shall suggest in the following chapters, as migrant laborers in Israel.

The Khorat Plateau, which covers most of Isaan, is bordered on the south and west by low mountain ranges, and undulates toward the Mekong River in the northeast at an average altitude of about two hundred meters above sea level. Until the twentieth century, it was heavily forested and lightly populated relative to neighboring lowland zones.[4] But as in the case of the similarly peripheral Arabah, marginality does not equal either desolation or isolation: Isaan has been peopled for millennia and connected to larger world of trade and cultural interchange for many centuries. Evidence of "some of Southeast Asia's earliest pottery, metallurgy and . . . rice cultivation [dating from] roughly 2,000 years ago" has been discovered in the region, and at sites such as Phimai and Prasat Phanom Rung there is plentiful evidence for the later influence of the Khmer-speaking Angkor Empire, which was participating in the Indian Ocean world-system by the tenth century.[5] Following the thirteenth-century collapse of the Angkor polity, the plateau was slowly resettled by speakers of the Tai language family (which includes Thai and Lao), who entered from the valleys of the Mekong and the Chao Phraya, its neighbors on the northeast and west respectively. Khmer, Mon, and other non-Tai languages continued to be spoken in the hills.[6] By the eighteenth century, local aristocrats (*chao*) ruling over small polities made up of villages combining wet-rice, dry-rice, and forest cultivation paid tribute to competing centers in today's Thailand and Laos, often to more than one simultaneously.[7] Buddhism was the religion of urban civilization, and the many monasteries supported by villagers throughout the region served, to a degree, as its emissaries, though Buddhist identification allowed for a great diversity of local interpretations.[8] But the forest, upon which villagers depended for a variety of products, held spirits who made their own demands and would punish incursions with outbreaks of disease and madness.[9]

Isaan's colonial subjugation began in the 1830s, when the Siamese empire sought to consolidate its victory over the Lao kingdom of Vientiane by deporting Lao-speaking subjects from the left bank of the Mekong (in today's Laos) into the plateau.[10] By the 1850s this Lao-speaking population formed one-third of the subject population of Siam—the same proportion it represents in Thailand today.[11] However, as Porphant Ouyyanont writes, the impact of Siamese administration in this period was "limited and indirect. Local rulers held sway, and as far as villages were concerned, local customs and traditions prevailed as they had done for several centuries."[12]

Following the Siamese-French War of 1893, the modernizing monarchy moved to replace its tributary relations with the local lords with the bureaucratized, colonial-style rule of appointed governors. Under powerful interior minister Prince Damrong, a project of deliberate historical revision was carried out, purposely striking the word "Lao" from official documentation, redefining the region as the Thai northeast, or Isaan, and its inhabitants as simply Thai.[13] Shortly after these reforms, the region erupted in millenarian convulsions centered around *phuu mii bun*, or "men of merit," who proclaimed the advent of the Buddha Maitreya. Charles Keyes analyzes these revolts, which kept recurring as late as 1939, as a cross-class anticolonial movement uniting peasants and the lower gentry against increased exploitation at the hands of Bangkok.[14] All the while, Isaan's peasant population was growing, and there are some indications that around the turn of the century it was already outpacing the region's capacity for subsistence cultivation at the given technological level, as witnessed by the first waves of seasonal labor migration into the Chao Phraya valley.[15]

Economically speaking, Isaan remained disconnected from Central Thailand due to the difficulties of transportation. Nakhon Ratchasima (Khorat), the Isaan town most closely linked to Bangkok, was up to nine weeks' travel distance from the capital until the railway opened in 1900, and it was twenty-five more years until the iron road reached Buriram, only a hundred kilometers or so farther east.[16] The railways expanded rapidly during the 1930s, with a French consular official remarking that "[e]ach kilometer of the railway cleared up what was once a dense forest. . . . Train cars filled to the brim with goods made their way to Bangkok," where "rice, leather, silk, spice, salt and valuable wood" were exchanged for imported goods.[17] But the region was still self-sufficient enough to be largely insulated from the effects of the global Great Depression, which began in 1929.[18]

The Japanese occupation of Thailand during World War II was followed by a brief political opening, presided over by social democrat Pridi Phanomyong. But in 1947 the right-wing Plaek Phibunsongkhram (Phibun), who had collaborated with the Japanese, returned to power with US support. During the reigns of Phibun and his successor Sarit Thanarat, Isaan was integrated into a national rice market dominated by the far more fertile central plain. The peasantry retained legal rights to its land, but new taxes on rice exports and lower prices drove millions of Isaanites to seek seasonal employment in the booming Bangkok metropolis.[19] By pushing the onus of reproducing labor-power onto families and farms, Bangkok-based industrial capital was able to enjoy a long period of economic growth, cited as a "miracle" by many outside observers.[20] This process of agrarian semiproletarianization was accompanied by racialization: the figure of the water buffalo (khwaai), a beast of burden essential to agrarian production, came to signify the Isaanite migrant, stigmatized as ignorant, brutish, and close to nature.[21] But this stigmatization also formed the basis for a regional cultural cohesion, which found expression in the popular musical genre luuk thung, "children of the fields."[22]

The polarization of the Cold War, the advances of revolutionary movements in nearby Vietnam and Laos, and an appetite for American aid encouraged the Thai elite to smear any opposition to its rule as "communist" long before there was any real support for communism in the country outside the Chinese minority in the cities.[23] In 1958, the reformist regional politician Khrong Chandawong was convicted of communist conspiracy and executed, exacerbating the anger and frustration of Isaanites just as migration was introducing many firsthand to the country's yawning class disparities. Agrarian transformation and political polarization were both boosted when Thailand joined the Vietnam War and Isaan was turned into a strategic base for the US war effort. American funds were poured into constructing transport infrastructure, primarily roads, as the US military made the region its staging post for sorties into Vietnam, Laos, and Cambodia.[24] While US military procurement ramped up demand for foodstuffs and lumber, the construction of military all-weather roads opened up forest frontiers for logging and agribusiness far more quickly than the railroad had before the war.[25] Forest cover, estimated at about 40 percent of Isaan's land surface in the late 1950s, was reduced to 15 percent by the early '80s.[26]

The invasion of the forest was not only a matter of arrogating space and natural resources for the elite's enrichment, but also of making forms of life outside the reach of the capitalist-colonial system impossible. Beginning in the mid-1960s, the insurgency of the Communist Party of Thailand (CPT) made progress in Thailand's most peripheral regions, including Isaan's hilly and still-wooded margins. The CPT's "forest soldiers" (tahaan paa) shared the woods with wandering forest monks (phra thudong) whose peripatetic living, as well as their democratic approach to the dharma and commitment to poverty, had brought them under suspicion of communist sympathies.[27] Both fell victim to US Air Force pilots' practice of emptying excess ordnance over the mountains upon their return from assaults on Laos.[28] Retreating from the forests, some forest monks began to assist the state-led incursion, offering to quell villagers' fears of their guardian spirits through meditation teachings. Others have become environmental activists, maintaining wooded reserves around their forest monasteries (wat paa) and working together with popular movements and environmental NGOs.[29]

In 1973, as the war in Vietnam was winding down, the Thai state indulged in another democratic opening, which came to a sudden and bloody end when growing collaboration between the student-led urban left and rural social movements such as the Farmers Federation of Thailand appeared to the military to be taking things too far.[30] The massacre at Thammasat University in Bangkok in October 1976, paralleled by a terror campaign in the countryside, pushed many student and peasant activists into the arms of the CPT. However, the party's adherence to Maoist orthodoxy rendered its political strategy unpalatable to New Left–inspired student activists and rendered it vulnerable to shifts in the geopolitical strategy of its patron, the People's Republic of China. The breakout of the "Third Indochina War," which pitted the Chinese against their former comrades in Vietnam and Laos and quickly degenerated into a horrific civil war in Cambodia, left the CPT isolated from supply routes running through Vietnamese-aligned Laos. Finally, in the early 1980s, in return for the Thai regime's tacit agreement to use its territory to funnel weapons to China's genocidal ally, the Khmer Rouge, the latter cut off support for the CPT, whereupon the insurgency quickly began to disintegrate.[31]

The defeat of the insurgent and civilian wings of the left cleared the way for the continued commercialization of agriculture in Isaan, where the farming frontier quickly closed, with all arable land put under cultivation by the mid-1980s.[32] As possibilities for independent subsistence continued to shrink and an industrial base in the region failed to materialize, Isaanites pushed farther afield in their search for livelihood. Masses of young women began to travel for work in Bangkok, while men increasingly undertook long-term migration to other parts of Southeast Asia and elsewhere, particularly the Persian Gulf.[33] The remittances that flowed back to their home villages garnered foreign exchange for the government while blunting the edge of rural poverty, amplifying inequality and fostering individualistic consumption of such goods as motorcycles, private education, and the iconic *baan sa'u*, the modern-style "Saudi house."[34]

Notwithstanding the hiccup of the 1997–98 financial crisis, Thailand has widely been considered a capitalist success story, one of Southeast Asia's "miracle" economies. But as Jim Glassman writes, the swift growth of the Thai economy (which has continued, in relative terms, into the current millennium) "occurred precisely because a highly internationalized state" dependent on the US military-industrial complex "positioned itself to achieve such growth through the very activities that lead to inegalitarianism and maldevelopment."[35] I now turn to the ideological mechanisms that enabled this inegalitarian maldevelopment to proceed in the face of the discontent it bred in the dispossessed and exploited.

PATERNALISM: AN IDEOLOGY OF HIERARCHICAL INTEGRATION

As scholars such as Thak Chaloemtiarana and Katherine Bowie have argued, elites seeking an alternative to communism deliberately inculcated rural Thai subalterns with a paternalistic ideology that likens the Thai collectivity to a family ruled by a benevolent father.[36] However, if paternalism were simply an elite imposition it would be difficult to explain why Isaanite migrants have brought it with them to Israel and interpellated their employers in its terms. It is more useful to approach subalterns' use of paternalist ideologies of interaction as an adaptation to conditions of domination in which the possibility of rebellion appears foreclosed. As E. P. Thompson points out in his study of eighteenth-century England, paternalism can be mobilized by those it casts in the role of dependent children to defend their customary rights.[37] Under the circumstances in which Isaanite proletarians find themselves, following the repeated defeat of collective action, "paternalism from below" makes sense both as a cognitive model of relations with "good" superiors and as a tactic for getting the most out of such relations. Paternalist ideology, like other forms of social control, is not a simple matter of hoodwinking subalterns into false consciousness but a much more difficult balance between the achievement of consent through integration into a hierarchically constituted collective and the use of violence to coerce those who threaten to reject the terms offered.

As a justificatory ideology, paternalism may be as old as the form of domination that invests male heads of families with power over women and the young—that is, patriarchy. For millennia, the patriarchal family has served as a template for the structuration and justification of hierarchical relations all over the world. Contrasting starkly with the amoral relations characteristic of the liberal "violence of abstraction," and in a more complex tension with the ideal of fraternity typical of modern nationalist projects,[38] paternalistic ideologies are heavily personalized and supported (in reality and imagination) by affects such as love, generosity, gratitude, and loyalty.[39] Because the presentation of domination as ancient and immutable can help to justify and naturalize it, those interested in introducing new forms of domination have every reason to dress them up in the vintage fashions of paternalism. This is especially true in the "Orient," where elites partake in a discourse of immutable cultural specificity as a smoke screen for the violence that they have proven willing to inflict in order to prevent social transformation.[40]

In Thai political ideology, Thak Chaloemtiarana has traced paternalism back to the Sukhothai Kingdom of the thirteenth to fifteenth centuries, with its ideal of the king as *phaukhun* (literally "father-lord"). After being eclipsed by the Hindu-influenced *devaraja* model of kingship, this ideal was revived as an elite discourse during the "Chakkri Reformation" of the late nineteenth century, but Thak argues that as a pervasive mode of social control, "despotic paternalism" is an innovation of Sarit Thanarat, who came to power in 1957. Unlike his predecessor Phibun, Sarit consolidated his power by promoting veneration of the monarchy while simultaneously promoting his own image as a stern but loving father.[41] Despite his virulent anticommunism, Sarit kicked off his rule with a spate of heavy-handed interventions in the economy, including not only cuts in electricity rates and provision of free drinking water but also controls on the price of iced coffee (to which sellers responded by watering down the drink) and "a directive to the navy to search for cheap coconuts to sell to the public."[42] The frivolous counterproductiveness of some of these gestures can be seen as part of the point of Thai paternalism in its "from above" variant: by catering to subalterns' supposed proclivity for "fun" (*sanuk*) through one-off acts of generosity, the superordinate is able both to forestall change and to represent them as whimsical, irresponsible children who cannot be trusted to defend their own interests. This charge is also reflected in the frequent appearance of accusations of vote-buying in the Thai elite's antidemocratic discourse.[43]

The "Thai way of counterinsurgency" that began to develop under Sarit was heavily influenced by this sort of paternalism. Both the government's budgetary priorities and its efforts at propaganda among rural populations were marked by a combination of authoritarian ruthlessness and theatrical generosity. While members of the royal family were parachuted into remote villages to hand out medicines and food, American aid was funneled into a panoply of state and para-state forces entrusted with counterinsurgency tasks, from the regular police to death squads like Nawaphon and the Red Gaurs.[44] Beginning in 1965, the "Communist Suppression Operations Command" (CSOC) took on a coordinating role in this murky sphere of competing state, para-state, and "deep-state" organs, which it continues to play as the "Internal Security Operations Command" (ISOC).[45] Under CSOC/ISOC, "winning hearts and minds" became a central tenet of Thai counterinsurgency. This encompassed a lenient amnesty policy for surrendering insurgents and rural investments directed at areas where they had made the most headway—though such investments, primarily in road infrastructure, often improved military capabilities while exacerbating rural inequality by encouraging extractive corporate agriculture and logging.[46] Quite as important was the reorganization of rural society along paternalistic lines through "voluntary" activities such as the infantilizing rituals of the state-sponsored Village Scouts Movement. As Katherine Bowie's ethnography of the movement shows, its creation was a deliberate attempt at instilling an interaction ideology that would bind rural subalterns to the national power structure via the mediation of local dignitaries such as police officers and wealthy merchants.[47]

As we have seen, both the CPT's insurgency and the land frontier in Isaan were exhausted by the mid-1980s. Hereafter the resistance of the rural population, as well as the state's modes of countering it, would have to take new forms. However, paternalism was as entrenched in the ideological matrix of the regime's rural policy as ISOC was in its organizational structure. Elite actors like Pichit felt a responsibility toward clients, including military subordinates, which they hoped could be fulfilled through their settlement on former battlegrounds, cementing patronal relations and pacifying border zones at the same time. As we shall see, this would turn out to be a dubious proposition; nevertheless, paternalism could survive as farmers turned into migrants. The latter needed patrons as much as the former, and here too there was a surplus to be extracted in return.

THE FRONTIER SETTLEMENT PROJECT AND THE BEGINNINGS OF THE MIGRANT FLOW

Following the Vietnamese occupation of Cambodia in 1978 and the initial defeat of the Khmer Rouge, Pol Pot's junta and allied groups retreated into bases inside Thailand, where they were supplied with Chinese arms.[48] By the mid-1980s, hundreds of thousands of desperate Cambodian refugees were mingling with these guerrilla forces in border camps that slipped out of the Thai government's control.[49] Like the Laotian frontier, which also threatened briefly to heat up in the mid-1980s, this hilly border belt—in parts still forested and largely populated by non-Tai minorities—was not only economically peripheral, but also a former center of CPT insurgency.[50] Like the nineteenth-century Siamese empire, the Thai military regime was interested in the possibility of using the colonial "mobilization and immobilization" of populations[51]—including formerly insurgent ones— to pacify the frontier. But unlike that predecessor, it took for granted that pacification would entail integration into capitalist relations of agrarian commodity production.

Emblematic of these attempts was the Khao Kho area of Phetchabun Province, in Thailand's north but bordering Isaan. Here the Thai Army's First Division had successfully subdued one of the CPT's most important bases, and the settlement of both surrendered CPT guerrillas and Hmong "hill-tribe war volunteers" was underway. At the same time, the hills, denuded by fire throughout the war years, were quickly taken over by what an FAO report later called "overexploitation for unsustainable agriculture."[52] In February and March 1982, division commander and West Point graduate Pichit Kullavanijaya hosted Israeli ambassador

Abraham Cohen on a tour of settlement activity in the area. According to Cohen, who noted King Bhumibol Adulyadej's "personal interest" in the project, it "epitomize[d] the development of a sensitive, strategic zone." In response to the Thais' request for "our advice and help" in this endeavor, Cohen referred Pichit to "Thais who have trained in Israel and who have already proven capacity for organization and action," as well as to an Israeli water expert serving nearby. As a training course "with an Israeli stamp" was planned for the near future, Cohen requested that his correspondents in the Ministry of Foreign Affairs look into the "possibility of organizing a training tour [in Israel] for a small group of Thais which will concern itself with organizing courses for youth."[53]

This visit, and the project that Pichit was later to propose to the embassy, did not come out of the blue. Cohen's references to the king's personal interest, to Thai graduates of Israeli training courses, and to Israeli experts in the area point to a continuous history of assistance in the field of agrarian development, part and parcel of a long-standing Israeli effort to extend soft power throughout the Third World on behalf of the West and in furtherance of its own interests. Israeli bodies like the Foreign Office's Center for International Cooperation (MASHAV) and the Histadrut's Afro-Asian Institute offered agricultural extension and settlement planning services to states in the Third World from the early 1950s onward.[54] Several paramilitary settlement units modeled on the NAHAL were established in sub-Saharan Africa, and when many of these failed, Israeli experts blamed the outcome on the top-down, authoritarian leadership prevalent in the Third World, which they opposed to the voluntarist context of Zionist pioneering. As we have seen, though, Israeli voluntarism was itself a mechanism for the justification of unevenly distributed privilege. As Eitan Bar-Yosef argues, the failure of the "African NAHAL" presented Israelis with a chastening mirror image of their own settlement project:

> The Israelis claimed that the Africans refused to stay in the countryside and preferred to move to the city, but the same could be said of Israel. The melting pot did not function correctly in the African NAHAL, but the NAHAL had also become an elitist framework which highlighted the mutual alienation between [Jewish] ethnic groups in

Israel. African rulers made cynical political use of youth projects, but the Israeli NAHAL too had been established to reproduce a limited group with a well-defined ideological outlook.[55]

In the early 1960s, a similar dynamic doomed the effort to establish dozens of *moshav*-like settlements in Burma, intended to "control the country's borders and minorities" through settlement in what Israeli experts called "huge empty areas" in the peripheral Shan States.[56] Israeli tutors expected the educated officials they had trained, who belonged to the Burman ethnic majority, to live in the new settlements. But much like the veteran settlers of the LSM whose indolence angered Ben-Gurion, "Burmans saw no reason to leave their privileged nucleus zone ('Burma proper') and go to what were the traditionally despised dependent peripheries."[57] The already faltering project was canceled following a military coup in Burma in 1962. Elsewhere, Israel's agricultural outreach dwindled until the 1973 Arab-Israeli War, when many Third World nations cut off their diplomatic relations and many of the remaining programs were shut down.[58]

Thailand, one of the West's staunchest Third World allies, was an exception to the trend. With the support of King Bhumibol, who was intensely interested in both agriculture and counterinsurgency, Israeli-inspired projects straddling this period of international isolation included a *kibbutz*-like cooperative established in 1967 at Hupkaphong in Phetchaburi Province and an ISOC-sponsored paramilitary group, the "Military Reservists for National Security," loosely modeled on the IDF's reserve corps.[59] Altogether, according to an internal MASHAV report, between 1976 and 1982 about 800 Thais participated in Israeli training courses, of whom about 300 traveled to Israel.[60] By the seventies, however, a new actor had entered the stage: private enterprise. Aiming to combine "capitalism and cooperatives," in 1977 the king enlisted Israeli magnate Shaul Eisenberg—himself a product of Israel's state-led developmentalism—

> to implement the farm cooperative concept on a more corporate basis, like the Israeli kibbutzes that melded farming with food processing. The idea was that the Eisenberg Group would introduce Israel's

innovative drip-irrigation systems and agriculture management skills in core demonstration farms. It would also set up and run processing plants for the crops produced by the demonstration farms and by independent Thai farmers using the new farm technology. With an airfield and well-equipped military patrols, the farms doubled as a buttress against the CPT in the area.[61]

"Eisenberg wasn't elsewhere involved in manufacturing or farming," remarks the king's biographer, "so presumably he had his eye on other deals in Thailand, possibly arms related."[62]

As this mysterious episode indicates, by the early 1980s the linkage between transnational infrastructure projects and capitalist profit-making—hitherto passing through the enabling policies of the developmentalist state—was becoming more and more direct. Between 1979 and 1982, three thousand Thais—most of them Isaanites with previous experience working for the Americans—were employed by the US military in the construction of an airport at Ovda, in the Negev, following the Israeli military's redeployment from the Sinai peninsula in the wake of the 1979 peace accords with Egypt.[63] These numbers paled in comparison to the hundreds of thousands of Thai migrants who were remitting hard currency from wealthy Arab states, and when in 1985 the Israeli ambassador complained to Thailand's deputy foreign minister about the latter's support for Arab resolutions in the UN Security Council, his colleague countered that Israel might consider employing more Thai workers in "development projects." Doing so, he suggested, "would make some flexibility in this area possible."[64]

In the same year General Pichit turned to the Israeli embassy in Bangkok with a detailed request for training and on-the-ground assistance for the creation of mixed military-civilian settlements modeled on NAHAL outposts near the Cambodian and Laotian borders. Now commander of the First Army Region, covering both the capital and parts of the border with Cambodia, and a rising star in military politics,[65] Pichit had not forgotten his admiration for Israeli frontier know-how. The diplomats were reticent; "wherever we've gotten into NAHAL [projects] we've had trouble," as one participant in a Foreign Office discussion remarked, and the Cambodian conflict in particular was not one they wished to get embroiled in.[66] Yet the Israelis could not afford to alienate Pichit, who they supposed might soon be in a position to improve relations, not only on the military and commercial levels, but in the arena of high diplomacy where Israel most needed help.[67] Finally, embassy staff decided to say yes to the first stage of the program—a crash course in "frontier settlement" for civilian and military Thai officials, to take place entirely in Israel, with Thai funding—but also to make certain that Israeli advisers would at no point be involved in the actual planning and construction of settlements in Thailand. The diplomats were willing to take a risk, gambling that Thai budgets would run out and that, without on-the-ground Israeli assistance, the "Thai NAHAL" would never materialize. Thus they could cultivate Pichit's goodwill without risk of embroilment in the Cambodian conflict.

On March 28, 1987, a delegation of twenty-five military and civilian officials arrived in Israel as guests of the IDF's Foreign Relations Department. Over two weeks, they were taken to visit *moshavim* and *kibbutzim* in Israel proper as well as settlements in the OPT, and received instruction from Israeli experts on the economic and strategic aspects of paramilitary settlement.[68] After the delegation's return, the Bangkok embassy's files fall silent on the project, but the silence of the archive only appears to fulfill the diplomats' wishes that the story end there; interviews with several Thai and Israeli actors, together with some sporadic documentation, confirm subsequent links between Pichit's Khao Kho settlement project and the beginnings of labor migration between the two countries.

Thus the next group to arrive in Israel from Thailand was composed of nine employees of the Thai Agricultural Bank, who spent twelve months in the country beginning in November 1987, dividing their time between two *kibbutzim* and two *moshavim* (one of the latter in the occupied lower Jordan Valley).[69] Though funded by the bank, and not directly connected to Pichit's Frontier Settlement Project, support for this trip was discussed by embassy officials in similar terms of transnational developmentalism. In a telegram to tour guide and businessman Uzi Vered, who was handling the group's logistics for a fee, embassy economic attaché Ariel Kerem noted the "traditional connections" between the state-owned Agricultural Bank and MASHAV, as well as "planned future cooperation" with the Israeli Ministry of Agriculture.[70] But Vered's involvement was itself a portent. A private entrepreneur who had spent years cultivating ties in Thailand—including with Pichit—he was to play a crucial role in the story's next few acts. And though official discourse around the Agricultural Bank group remained resolutely developmentalist, participants plainly spent most of their time in Israel working rather than "training." Though treated as "volunteers" by the Interior Ministry, which granted them visas, and the Moshavim Movement, which provided institutional cover, the monthly "allowance" of $250–400 US that they received formed a competitive wage in Thai terms.[71]

In December 1987, General Pichit came to Israel, met with the IDF's chief of staff and other officials, including the defense minister's assistant for settlement affairs, and visited a NAHAL outpost.[72] Sometime during the next year, the next group of trainees arrived, this time directly associated with Pichit, the Thai military, and the Frontier Settlement Project. While I have not been able to find any documentation, interviewees who were directly involved agree that it was composed of between ten and twenty people mobilized by the Thai military for agricultural settlement under Pichit's direction, in Khao Kho and another location on the Cambodian border, and dispatched around Israel by Uzi Vered's agency. Like the Agricultural Bank group, this "Army Group" also worked in *kibbutzim* and *moshavim* throughout the country in return for an "allowance," part of which had to be set aside to repay the fees they were charged.[73]

The evidence for developments over the following two years is no less hazy.[74] However, there is no question that between 1987 and 1989, new groups of "trainees" began arriving from Thailand in rapid succession, under the sponsorship of various public bodies, including the army. According to one report, one of these, composed of "49 Thais, including 10 villagers," was the first to work in the Arabah, in *moshav* Paran, inciting neighboring farmers to begin clamoring for "ninjas"— as they quickly became known for their full-body coverings.[75] The growth of this transnational labor flow, organized by Vered's agency and supervised by the Moshavim Movement, was clearly triggered by economic motivations on both sides: farmers, confronted with the mounting intifada and the disappearance of Western volunteers, needed labor; "trainees" had to pay large fees and forgo alternative employment at home, which only made sense if the trip could provide a net gain. The continuing need to frame the flow in not-for-profit, developmentalist terms provided middlemen in both countries with opportunities for rent-seeking: particularly infamous among the Israelis was a certain Professor Bun, of a university in southern Thailand, whose exploitation of "trainee" students they considered egregious.[76]

This interregnum was the heyday of structural hypocrisy. Actors in Thailand and Israel quickly realized they could supply each other's needs—for labor-power, for a livelihood, for an outlet for "surplus populations," for profits—but still did not possess a legitimizing discourse or an appropriate institutional infrastructure. This gap between practice and ideology was not a merely discursive affair: as we have seen, it provided well-placed institutional actors with opportunities to siphon off arbitrage rents. Though it had no legitimate reason to meddle in for-profit agricultural labor migration, the Thai military would remain involved for a few years longer, and the Frontier Settlement Project would continue living a ghostly half-life as a legitimating cover. Thus on June 7, 1989, a two-page illustrated report in the daily *Yedioth Ahronoth* advertised "New: Volunteers from Thailand." According to the report, which contradicts other accounts in various ways, these numbered "400 people, mostly graduates of agricultural faculties . . . here to gain practical training in agriculture." Uzi Vered, who is quoted extensively and receives ample credit for organizing the groups, is described as "anxious to clarify [that] this is an educational project of the first degree [and that] there is no intention of importing a cheap labor force." The report also devotes special attention to a "very interesting" subgroup

> of 39 demobilized officers and soldiers of the Thai army currently undergoing training in *moshavim* and *kibbutzim* in the north, close to the Lebanese front. When they complete their training, the members

of the group will return to the frontier between Thailand and Laos, where they will establish agricultural villages, something like the Israeli NAHAL, in an attempt to fortify the border and prevent infiltration from Laos. The group is headed by a cousin of King Bhumipol [sic] Rama IX. This is Chi Disakrol Damlondr (28), an armor officer in the Thai army.[77]

This group may be the same one as the third delegation mentioned in a local report by the Hevron family of Hatzeva, comprising "50 demobilized soldiers . . . teachers and coordinators of frontier areas," and supposedly "led by the deputy commander of the Thai Army"—perhaps a reference to Pichit's visit to Israel around the same time.[78] An Israeli interviewee who had been closely involved also recalled that the first Thais who came to work in the Arabah were soldiers linked to Pichit and frontier settlement.

> They were . . . trying to do something like our NAHAL here . . . each one would get a house and a bit of land, and some training, and they were settled on the border with Cambodia. . . . we saw that they had serious intentions, in the same style as us, to settle the border and populate [it]. Some of [the people who came to work in the *moshav*] were soldiers. They came as NCOs, or officers, or something of that sort. . . . [T]hey didn't wear uniforms, and they were nice, nice people. [They were] a very dominant group, they used to do roll calls and drills. . . . General Pichit . . . was the one who gave his blessing. He would always ask me to give his regards to [then deputy chief of the IDF, later prime minister] Ehud Barak. He had taken some course in the United States with Ehud Barak. I imagine Ehud Barak wouldn't be too impressed. But General Pichit was there, we sat down with him.
>
> [Q:] And the people who worked for you went and settled in these villages afterward?
>
> Some did, some didn't.[79]

But the Frontier Settlement Project was on its last legs, at least as far as Israelis were concerned. Around 1990, several of them visited Khao Kho with Pichit and his wife to investigate the possibility of incorporating returned migrants as agricultural settlers there. One of the visitors recounted the following vivid (if possibly quite inaccurate) scene:

> I came to Khao Kho with General Pichit and his wife. . . . And his wife was a particularly nasty woman. . . . [W]e had an idea at some point of doing a program of guys who would come [to Israel], save money and start settlements with it. And then she grabbed me . . . took me somewhere in the dark [and said, in English:] "don't be smart and don't try to change Thailand." Grabbed me and took me aside. "Drop it." [She meant] "we want them like this. Don't think we really want [the project], we're pretending." That's the meaning of what she told me. . . . There was a very, very big contradiction between my naïveté and my point of view, [that] if you're settling someone, . . . you really want to help them get ahead . . . [and] "don't try to change Thailand, we want them like this."
>
> [Q:] So you dropped it then?
>
> Essentially, we dropped it. We realized that we were tilting against windmills, that they don't really want it.[80]

Here hypocrisy emerges from the structural background into discourse, as accusation. Leveled by an Israeli actor against a Thai one, the imputation of hypocrisy casts the accuser as honest, even quixotically naïve, and the accused as duplicitous and conniving as well as paternalistic. Here we are already deep into the racializing (and gendered) discourse that imagines the "Western" Israeli as forthcoming, well-intentioned, egalitarian, and manly while the "Asiatic" Thai is sneaky, mendacious, clientelist, and effeminate. Such racialized and gendered imaginaries continue to play a role in everyday interactions between Israelis and Thais in the Arabah today. But in reality, the demand for such hypocrisy was rooted more at the Israeli pole of the exchange than at its Thai end. Thai elites may have been more interested in skimming rents off migrant earnings and handing out favors to clients than in training peasants to become politically loyal but economically independent settlers on a frontier that had already been more or less pacified. But Israeli farmers and middlemen were, if anything, even more disingenuous in their pretense that the incoming "ninjas" were anything but a cheap, skilled, and handy replacement for the rebellious Palestinian workforce. In Israel, structural hypocrisy peaked at a moment when the ideological and economic conditions for the reproduction of the labor settlement movement were in collision—across the country, but especially in the Arabah, where the highest premium was placed on ideological fidelity. On the Israeli side, this tension between actions and words would soon be resolved as "volunteers" and "trainees" were reclassified as workers and their flow was expanded in an explicitly strategic move toward the permanent displacement of Palestinian workers by migrants.

The transfusion of cheap workers the Israeli agrarian sector was about to receive would render it economically viable once again. But given the Arabah's recent dip into anomie and even localized "intifada" following the retraction of state support for "Hebrew labor," no less significant than these workers' capacity for hard physical work would be their importation of an interaction ideology of legitimate domination into a context where no such ideology was available. Thanks to its commitment to the world market and territorial control, the Thai regime had developed—with the coerced participation of its Isaanite subjects—just the thing: a paternalistic interaction ideology for the regulation of capitalist-colonial relations. Although its incompatibility with LSM ideology would eventually drive paternalism out of the public sphere in the Arabah, it would retain its power to structure relations of production into the time of my fieldwork, some twenty-five years later. In return for its obsolete and apparently useless gift of "frontier settlement" know-how, the Israeli farm sector would receive not only a cheap labor force, but one provided with the interactional tools necessary to help it shift from one mode of agrarian production and social reproduction to the next.

3 THE "THAI REVOLUTION" IN THE ARABAH

OVER THE 1990S, THE ECONOMY and society of the Central Arabah were transformed in such a thoroughgoing manner as to make the hyperbole in economist Marjorie Strom's declaration that the region had undergone a "Thai revolution" entirely forgivable. The Arabah exited the decade as it had entered it, economically peripheral and heavily dependent on agriculture—but everything else about the region changed, from the produce of its farms to its demographic makeup and culinary tastes. In the context of Israel's neoliberal transformation, it is doubtful whether agricultural settlement in the region could have survived without the unexpected contribution of its new Thai workforce. This chapter begins by detailing the enormous political-economic changes that the shift from "Hebrew" to migrant labor brought to the lives of veteran Arabah settlers and their new employees, before analyzing how the paternalist interaction ideology imported by the new workers provided a highly useful rulebook for a relationship that settlers were ill-prepared to navigate. Paternalism encouraged the emergence of a hybrid public culture in which Israeli and Thai elements met, though on unequal terms, but this culture and the "pure settlement" ethos of the LSM remained in contradiction. Prompted by the rise of the xenophobic right in Israeli politics and anticorruption measures, in the 2000s the migration regime shifted in directions that rendered this explosive contradiction moot by collapsing much of the basis for public paternalism. The state's casting of employers as enforcers of their workers' marginal and temporary status undermined the status quo of the 1990s, all but eliminating public expressions of hybridity and pushing paternalism into the intimate sphere where production takes place.

THE "THAI REVOLUTION"

The Thais who entered Israel in the late 1980s and early 1990s, mostly from Isaan, were administratively classed as "trainees" and received the same sort of visas granted to international volunteers. However, their monthly "allowance," pocket money by Israeli standards, was at the time equivalent to a competitive wage in Isaan.[1] The wage differential proved sufficient to draw thousands of migrants to work in Israel, even after accounting for the cut that middlemen in both countries were taking from the very beginning. Groups of Thais began traveling to Israel in rapid succession under the auspices of the Moshavim Movement in partnership with Vered Tours, for periods ranging from three months to over a year, and by March 1991 the Israeli Interior Ministry had a backlog of three thousand visa requests to process. In the same year, under the influence of LSM traditionalist Ora Namir, head of the Knesset's Labor Committee, the governmental Eilat Commission decided to recategorize Thai "trainees" as migrant workers and to cut down substantially on their numbers.[2] But despite Namir's appointment as minister of labor in Yitzhak Rabin's Labor Party–headed government in 1992, her policy was reversed. As part of its gambit to end the First Intifada by shifting away from direct rule over the Occupied Territories through the establishment of the Palestinian Authority, the government planned to wean the economy off Palestinian labor. The unprecedented "great lockdown" of the OPT, first implemented during the Persian Gulf War, would become permanent, and most Palestinian workers would be replaced by guest workers from abroad in an orderly fashion.[3] In addition to agriculture, migrant workers were recruited to supply the labor requirements of the construction industry and those of an entirely new sector, home eldercare.[4] On top of these planned importations of labor-power, undocumented workers, mostly from Christian-majority countries in West Africa and Latin America, entered the country on tourist visas and took a variety of low-wage urban jobs, many of which had also previously been done by Palestinians.

By 1994 there were 5,000 agricultural migrant workers in Israel, and by 1996 their number had risen to nearly 20,000. No region was as totally transformed by the influx as the Central Arabah, which by this time was the only Israeli region to rely primarily on agriculture for its livelihood. From 1989 to 1999 its Israeli population grew imperceptibly, from 2,000 to 2,100.[5] I do not have accurate figures for the region's migrant population over the same period, but taking the national trend as indicative, it seems probable that Thai residents, who numbered nearly zero at the decade's start, were about to outnumber the Central Arabah's Israeli population by the end of the decade.[6] From 1988 to 1999, the total area under cultivation rose by one-third and water use almost doubled, with over 40 percent given over to intensive greenhouse cultivation by the latter date (see Table 3.1). The wide range of

TABLE 3.1

Key agricultural indicators for the Central Arabah—change over the 1990s. A dunam is equal to 1,000 square meters, or about one-quarter of an acre. Calculations by the author from data in Strom, "The Thai Revolution," 13, 25, 27.

	1988	1999
Area under cultivation (dunams)	15,711	20,767
Greenhouse cultivation (of total area)	3.7%	40.7%

	1991	2000
Water use (cubic meters)	15,300	27,000
Pepper cultivation (of total area)	6.1%	26.2%

vegetables that had been produced for the local market was increasingly replaced with an export-oriented monoculture of bell peppers, whose share in the total cultivated area shot up almost fivefold.[7]

Song, whom I met in her Isaan home in 2017, spent most of this period working for the Sadots, one of the first families to settle in Ein Amal. She came to work in the Arabah in 1991, aged thirty-six, and stayed about ten years. A widow and mother of two, she heard about the possibility of going to work in Israel from men she met in the street in the city of Udon Thani, near her village. After a health check-up, a 50 percent down payment of 25,000 baht on the middleman's fee—which her mother financed by selling a piece of land—and a wait of forty-five days, she was on her way. Song arrived in Ein Amal on a cold winter day and set to work growing cucumbers and peppers. At the first farm she worked on, she was the only Thai employee and recalls sharing lodgings with an Israeli woman and a European man (perhaps a volunteer). Before the end of her first year, she asked to be transferred to the nearby Sadot farm, where two Thais were already working. Yehudit Sadot was running the farm, which then specialized in flowers; her son Ya'ir was a military officer, and her husband, Roni, worked as a repairman. Song remembers having a comfortable, air-conditioned room to herself, and working what she considered easy hours: eight hours a day, six days a week, with optional overtime on the day of rest, Saturday. She recalls earning five to seven thousand baht a month and sending most of it home to her mother, who used it for her immediate needs and those of Song's three children, as well as to undertake some repairs on the modest family house.

On the Sadot farm, the trend toward intensification and monoculture played out in the mid-1990s as a generational shift, with Yehudit retiring and Ya'ir taking over. Ya'ir shifted cultivation from flowers to peppers and introduced other changes intended to speed up the labor process and augment output. By this time Song, the veteran among the farm's seven Thai workers, had assumed the role of headwoman (see Chapter 4). She recalls that Ya'ir recognized his dependence on her, calling her "big boss." Nevertheless, he wanted me to work fast because he wanted more work done. He wanted to be rich like his friends. And he also argued with his mother many times. . . . They argued about the product. Normally we would pick only good quality product and send it out to market when I was working for Yehudit. But Ya'ir didn't care about the quality, he just wanted to send all the product to market.

The first migrants in the Arabah, like Song, slipped into the institutional and cultural slot developed for volunteers. They worked alongside volunteers, lived in lodgings that had been assigned to them, and were at first distributed between farms at approximately the same rates—one or two per employer. Long after Thais had been officially designated as migrant workers, *moshav* residents continued to call them "volunteers." Recalling this period, farmers told me that at first, they had attempted to treat the Thais as they had treated their predecessors, inviting them to eat at their tables and to share social activities. Soon, however, they realized that this practice clashed with migrants' culinary tastes and norms of interaction, and they dropped these expectations.[8] Workers, too, were more comfortable among compatriots, as Song's request to move to a farm with other Thai employees indicates. As another worker, Tiam, told researcher Israel Drori: "I don't feel good when my boss invites me to his house. I don't like to eat with his family. I don't feel comfortable. I feel insecure calling him by his first name. I'd rather call him 'mister 'or 'sir.'"[9]

There were other, even more obvious differences. Whereas volunteers had come to the *moshav* mostly to soak up its ambience, the new workers were there to make a living. Unlike the volunteers, who were famously rowdy, the new workers tended to be frugal and modest in their consumption and leisure habits. About one in ten was a woman, often one who had migrated with a partner.[10] Unattached workers sometimes found mates on a temporary basis—"for emotional support, not for getting married," in Song's words.[11] In her view, farmers preferred to employ couples because a female partner's presence would prevent men from "behaving badly" and lower the likelihood of conflict between them.

During this period recruitment was in the hands of manpower agencies in Israel, who worked in partnership with a network of rural middlemen and urban manpower agencies in Thailand that had been established for the purpose of placing migrants in other countries.[12] Through these middlemen, employers could choose to hire particular people via what became known as the "fax system."[13] By cultivating influence with employers, workers could obtain jobs for their relatives and neighbors, building up their status in the home community and sometimes charging commissions or even becoming intermediaries themselves.[14] As a result, Arabah farming families like the Sadots developed long-standing relationships with families in Isaan, like Song's. Such relationships were encouraged by the laxity of migration controls in Israel at the time: like many other workers, Song would go home for a visit every two or three years, giving her a chance to renew local contacts. After a short stay, she would change her official name, acquire a new passport, and return to Israel, thus circumventing the regulations meant to limit migrants' stay. Over the years, as we shall see in Chapter 6, careful maintenance of her relationship with the Sadots enabled Song to secure employment for her younger relatives. In this way, Isaanite kinship structures became key to the continued flow of labor-power to Israeli farms, which were also structured through kinship, and migration to Israel became essential to the reproduction of families in Isaan. These transnational kinship links, modulated by relations of mutual gratitude and personal preference between employers and employees, were navigated by both sides with the help of the paternalistic interaction ideology that the latter imported with them.

PATERNALISM AND KARMIC RECIPROCITY IN THE ARABAH

In the Arabah, as we have seen, latter-day adherence to the LSM's historical commitment to exclude the indigenous population from wage labor in favor of an egalitarian settler collectivity had proved successful for a generation. Here, as opposed to parts of the country where Palestinians had been steadily employed for decades, farmers had little experience of managing hierarchical workplace relations. As deprived of political power in Israel as they were at home, Isaanite migrants would find paternalist ideology useful for making moral claims on social superiors in their new surroundings as well. Doubtless paternalism worked for them in part because the LSM, despite its experiments with communal living (generally limited to the *kibbutzim*), had never really come close to dismantling the patriarchal family.[15] Thus, the appearance of a workforce that was not only cheap, experienced, and politically innocuous but skilled in the complex labor of handling hierarchical relations was a godsend for the Arabah's settler-farmers.

In his controversial history of US slavery, Eugene Genovese remarks that the involvement of members of the ruling class in the reproductive relations of their subordinates, combined with physical adjacency at work and off, encourages the development of paternalistic relations.[16] Despite the many important differences between the modes of agrarian production practiced in the antebellum US South and in 1990s Israel, the latter was also characterized by physical proximity, even intimacy, combined with stark inequality and a racial rule of difference. Stepping into the ideological breach created by the clash between LSM ideology and new economic exigencies, Isaanite migrants instituted a paternalism "from below," often calling their employers *aba* and *ima* (Hebrew for "father" and "mother"), to their initial bemusement. This paternalist idiom clashed awkwardly with the LSM's ambivalent attitude to the patriarchal family as a model for interpersonal relations.[17] Insofar as settlers' anxiety was rooted in the imperative of an unmediated, physical relationship to the land and the maintenance of a purely Jewish community tied together by fraternal bonds, familial intimacy with non-Jewish subordinates could only be a dangerous, corrosive influence. This is how the pioneer parents of the Arabah's first settlers would probably have judged the matter, and indeed how the settlers themselves saw it until the Thais came marching in.

Arabah farmers thus played the part of patrons in a somewhat stilted and institutionalized manner, very different from the spontaneous, gracious munificence of the Thai archetype. The official "volunteer coordinators" of the *moshavim*, almost always women, retained their positions when volunteers were replaced by migrant workers; together with the manpower agencies—also largely staffed by women—they devoted considerable energies to organizing leisure activities for workers, including outings to snowy Mount Hermon, to Eilat or the Dead Sea, and to musical performances and sermons given by musicians and monks flown in from Thailand on special occasions.[18] Celebrations of Thai holidays, organized at a regional or national level and financed by the agencies, were popular events at which Thai culture was packaged for the joint consumption of migrants and their employers, with music, dancing, boxing, and copious amounts of Israeli-friendly Thai food such as *som tam* (papaya salad), grilled fish, soups, and stir fry.[19]

Song was encouraged by what she saw as a growing acceptance of Thai ways over the course of her time in Ein Amal: "At first, they didn't understand our way of life, what we eat," she said. "The later groups of Thai workers had an easier time . . . because Israelis had a better understanding of the nature [*thammachat*] of Thai people." But the "nature" of proletarian Isaanites like Song, as we have seen, was marked by a century of repeated defeats in the class struggle, leading to their hierarchical integration into a paternalistic body politic. Thus, when I asked Song—who ended up working for the Sadots for over a decade—if she had ever known anyone to complain about their wages to the boss, she replied:

> No . . . I've never seen that. I never made any demands [*riakraung*]. They gave of their own accord. If we'd made a lot of demands, they wouldn't have given us more. We worked and let them see [our work]. If they were satisfied, the employers would raise [the wage] themselves. If they were good and if we saw eye to eye [*hen kap*] with our boss, if he was good to us, if we were good to him—the compensation would get better.

Reminiscent of the adage *tham dii day dii*—"do good, get good"—the logic expressed here by Song is akin to the vernacular Buddhist conception of karma, which sees meritorious actions as leading reflexively to felicitous results, and impulsive, aggressive actions as inherently destructive.[20] Though the law of karma can be understood as a metaphysical principle or a psychological observation, in this interactional context it functions primarily as a realistic appraisal of a social situation in which assertiveness is unlikely to achieve anything. However, there is also something more here: a contention that good things come not only to those who do good by others, but especially to those who reciprocate the good done to them. In relationships of domination, this translates into a paternalist expectation—though emphatically not a demand—that dominant parties fulfill their duties to subalterns. Here, specifically, Song expresses an expectation that the Israeli employer "see eye to eye" (literally "see together," *hen kap*) with his workers, bringing the compensation they receive for their labor into harmony with the efforts they expend. This is an interaction ideology of karmic reciprocity.[21]

But whose karma is at issue, the client's or the patron's? As Scott Stonington shows, Thai Buddhists do not conceive of karma necessarily as pertaining to individuals in atomistic fashion.[22] Just as various organs in a human body might carry their own karmic charges, so we might think of what Felicity Aulino calls the "social body" as an entity itself subject to karmic dynamics.[23] When Song insists that the most effective way to influence others' demeanor toward oneself is to behave well toward them and refrain from making demands, she is arguably applying the principle of karma to a social body made of subaltern and superordinate "organs." These organs have different and unequal roles to play, but if each does their part, the totality will benefit, and in any case, there is no point in one organ waging senseless war against another.

This interpretation by reference to Buddhist concepts should be distinguished from culturally essentialist claims of the kind Arabah settlers make when they speak of the Thais "of old" (*shel pa'am*) in barely culturalized racist terms.[24] In this discourse the first migrants are imagined as childlike primitives who, in the words of one settler, had "just come down from the trees," and whose mythical capacity for labor was matched by their deference and gratitude. For farmers, such essentialism is obviously strategic: if workers are conditioned from childhood to accept exploitation and subjugation, there can be nothing wrong with treating them in accordance. But for us there is no reason to interpret Song's phrasing so innocently: what she is doing is expounding, to an Israeli interlocutor, a moral framework that she and others have found useful for dealing with their predicament in Israel.[25] It was useful precisely because Song and her countrypeople had known relations of long-term, intimate domination before migrating, and had learned how to navigate them in situations wherein revolt was precluded. But it was particularly useful because the people who had become their employers themselves had almost no experience with such relations.

It was in part the new Thai workforce's sophisticated management of its managers that enabled the Arabah settlements to make a smooth transition to the new mode of production. Only a decade before, many settlers had voted against allowing their neighbors to host a second volunteer, fearing that this would sound the death knell for the settlement's ideological purity. But now, as the average number of "foreign" laborers per farm rose from one to three to five and beyond, upending the values the *moshavim* of the Arabah had been founded upon, no alarms were rung. One probable cause of this silence was the disintegration of the community's internal cohesion following the collapse of mutual aid arrangements during the credit crisis, which promised great affluence to some farmers while others faced bankruptcy and ejection from the community. It was also a time of rapid change in other aspects of life in the Arabah: Israel's peace treaty with Jordan, signed in 1994, turned the region from a frontier facing a formal enemy into a peaceful borderland, with an agreement that allowed *moshavim* to lease and cultivate fields across the border and growth in the tourist sector.[26] Implicitly, it seems, the settler community understood that it had only been possible to uphold ideological scruples so long as the state was willing to underwrite them, and following the neoliberal turn of the 1980s, though governments continued to offer lip service to the labor settlement ethos, material support dwindled. In the new state of things, the use of migrant labor was a *hekhrah bal yegune*—a necessity not to be deplored—but the work of the "ninjas" was also appreciated as of special quality. As Doron, a veteran manpower agent, told me:

> [E]mployers were impressed with the Thais because they could work under difficult conditions. . . . Especially, for example, in the Arabah, in the [occupied] Jordan Valley . . . in greenhouses, in very high heat . . . [and] with great precision, because a big part of their product went for export . . . and this totally changed their farming. They got approval [to market product] in Japan which was very strict, in . . . Holland in the flower auction . . . a lot of that was because of the Thais.[27]

But the paternalist idiom in which the new employment relation was couched also played an important part in softening the shock of rapid change in the Arabah. Thais could be perceived as, in the words of one recruitment agent, "friends from another planet,"[28] unencumbered by the colonial drama gripping Israelis and Palestinians. Unlike elements of Palestinian culture, which were inherently dangerous to the national project and could be integrated only through aggressive appropriation,[29] pad thai noodles and *mo lam* music were perceived as exotic curiosities that could be consumed without danger of cultural dilution. Analogously, farmers may have imagined that the strangely exotic relationships they developed with their workers could be deployed for profitmaking purposes without having any serious impact on their communities' social fabric. Nevertheless, the glimmerings of a hybrid public culture, as encompassed in the joint celebrations of Thai holidays, ran against the grain of the LSM's exclusionary egalitarianism and the self-image of the Arabah's *moshavim* as homogeneous Jewish-Israeli communities.

Could a hybrid public culture have survived and even developed despite this contradiction? Historically speaking, the question is moot, since developments in the political economy of migration and intra-Israeli political dynamics were rapidly to erase paternalism from the public face of the *moshavim*. As we shall see in Chapter 4, however, paternalism survives in the "private" but economically generative unit of the farm household, where its danger to the community's self-image is contained and diminished while its contribution to the production of vegetables and profits is maximized.

CLOSED SKIES AND BILATERAL AGREEMENTS

The embryonic paternalist culture of the 1990s arose in close connection with the coalescence of a "migration regime," defined by researchers as a set of "principles, norms, rules, and decision-making procedures" governing transnational movement.[30] An emergent outcome rather than the result of any single actor's planning, the migration regime that sprang up in the transnational space between Israel and Thailand in the 1990s was nevertheless dominated by the politically connected owners of manpower companies in both countries, who amassed considerable fortunes. As we have seen, legal strictures designed to prevent permanent settlement in Israel were rendered ineffectual when migrants discovered they could change their official names and return with new documents, bringing spouses and other relatives along. This was in the interest of employers who used the "fax system" to gain leverage over current workers and access to a reliable stream of future ones, as well as of manpower companies and their networks of middlemen and moneylenders, who fostered connections to particular families and villages that provided them with a regular flow of reliable clients and debtors.[31] As Doron explained, agencies

> used to recruit people in villages . . . we brought workers only from Isaan! Now naturally that's the one who has an interest in making a living. Who wants to earn a living for his family, who knows what farming is, and hard farming, with one's feet in the paddy. . . . Who isn't afraid of the heat in the greenhouses, who is here to make a living! . . . The broker from the village . . . knows what your mother does and that your father is so and so. And in order to go you need to take out a loan.[32]

Doron's easy cosmopolitanism was of a piece with the quintessentially "nineties" vision of a New Middle East in which national boundaries and chauvinistic agendas would no longer block the way of the enterprising to great wealth. But this vision had opponents as well as adherents in Israeli society. The "national camp" (ha-mahaneh ha-le'umi), led by Likud, incorporating the religious Zionist settlers of the Occupied Territories, the military apparatus, and most of the Mizrahi-Jewish working class, opposed the neoliberal visions of the "peace camp" (mahaneh ha-shalom) led by the Labor Party under Rabin and his successor Shimon Peres. The "peace camp," meanwhile, comprised a much more fragile coalition of big capital, the largely Ashkenazi-Jewish middle class, and Israel's Palestinian citizens.[33] Following Rabin's assassination in 1995, state power oscillated between the two blocs—Likud won power in 1996, Labor in 1999, then Likud again in 2001. By this time, US-brokered peace negotiations had broken down and the Second Intifada began, scuttling the dream of a New Middle East once and for all. Incoming Likud prime minister Ariel Sharon and his finance minister, the once and future premier Benjamin Netanyahu, seized the opportunity to win big business over for the right through rapacious privatization and demolition of those parts of the welfare state that had been spared by previous bouts of neoliberal reform.[34]

The Sharon government, like its right-wing contemporaries throughout the Global North, took up the claims that immigrants were stealing jobs, committing crimes, and destroying the national culture, adding to these the settler-colonial concern with maintaining a sizable Jewish majority.[35] Unlike the labor settlement movement, though, the Zionist right had never had any compunction about the exploitation of "outsiders." Under Sharon and the returned Netanyahu, control over the privilege of access to employment in Israel became a central strategy for disciplining the Palestinian population of the West Bank.[36] Law enforcement declared open season on undocumented migrants and a "closed skies" policy was announced, limiting the importation of new workers.[37] When thousands of asylum seekers from East Africa also entered the country and the urban low-wage labor market in the following years, punitive measures were applied to keep them from settling down.[38] But none of this translated into any retreat from dependence on migrant labor: rather, the early 2000s were marked by a deterioration in the political and economic status of all such marginalized workers, abetted by a "revolving door" of deportation and reimportation.[39] Though politicians often used Israeli workers' interests as a pretext for scapegoating immigrants,[40] by weakening the political standing of migrant workers, punitive repression has made their exploitation even more convenient, putting downward pressure on all wages. Today the proportion of noncitizens in Israel's workforce, which continues to include Palestinians from the West Bank as well as both documented and undocumented overseas migrants and asylum seekers, remains among the world's highest.[41]

The new political alignment did, however, bring about significant changes in the agricultural migration regime, perhaps because it coincided with a series of corruption scandals involving manpower agencies and government officials, peaking with the conviction of former Labor Minister Shlomo Benizri for trafficking in immigration quotas between 1996 and 2001.[42] In 2004, biometric identification equipment was installed at Ben-Gurion International Airport and the loophole that had enabled workers to change their names and return with new passports was closed.[43] As enforcement of the five-year limit on work in Israel began in earnest, veteran workers who had assumed important responsibilities on farms were obliged to go home. And as joint migration became practically impossible for couples, the proportion of women began to drop, from 10 percent in 1995 to 6 percent in 2010 and 4 percent in 2017.[44]

In the Central Arabah, these changes met with a continually growing demand for labor-power. As their integration into global markets was completed, the region's family farms were exposed to intense competition, and thus to the need to produce more and more, using ever more land, water, and labor. The institutional architecture of the *moshav* discourages the concentration of landholdings, but such a process nevertheless began, with prosperous farmers leasing land from their retiring or failing neighbors. But this did little to ease the downward pressure on produce prices that resulted from the power imbalance between a handful of wholesale buyers—supermarket chains and exporters—and myriad small producers. Competition was aggravated by the tendency toward specialization in bell peppers, which grew after Spanish growers were caught using illegal pesticides and temporarily banned from EU markets in 2007, generating windfall profits and ski vacations for farmers who had gambled right.[45] In 2011, the government-run export concern Agrexco, which had countered the price-setting power of private exporters by representing growers in aggregate, collapsed and was privatized.[46] Finally, while competition was pressuring employers to hold down wages, economic growth was driving up the cost of living in Isaan and making those wages stagnant in comparative terms.[47]

In this environment, the supports of the Arabah's nascent hybrid public culture fell away one by one. In the early 1990s, a typical farm in the Central Arabah might have employed one or two Thai workers, sometimes a married couple, often for many years on end. Wages were high compared to those in Isaan, and migrants' desire to keep their jobs and secure openings for relatives and friends encouraged them to foster close relations with employers and their children, who would take over the farms as the founding generation reached retirement age. By 2013, the number of workers per farm had shot up to an average of 7.4,[48] and the nested communities of workers on each farm, in each *moshav*, and in the region as a whole, all became both larger and more self-contained. Wages were no longer so high compared to those available in Isaan or in alternative migration destinations such as South Korea and Taiwan. In short, structural conditions were growing less and less conducive to paternalism just as public expressions of paternalist relations, like the joint celebrations of Thai holidays, waned in opulence and visibility under the pressure of the bottom line and the Zeitgeist.[49]

The greatest single blow to the paternalistic mode of relations came in 2012, when, responding to demands from human rights organizations, reform-minded technocrats in the Finance Ministry, and the US State Department's campaign against human trafficking, Israel and Thailand signed the bilateral Thailand-Israel Cooperation agreement (TIC), aimed at removing exploitative middlemen and reducing recruitment fees and the subsequent debt burden.[50] Under TIC,

Thai manpower agencies were cut out of the chain and replaced by a transnational nonprofit, the International Organization for Migration (IOM). The reform was remarkably successful in reducing fees, which fell from an average of US $9,149 before the agreement was signed to $2,191 after its implementation.[51] Though obviously beneficial in its immediate impact on migrants' finances, in the context of upward pressure on wages this reform is perhaps best understood less as an altruistic endeavor to lower the rate of exploitation than as a successful attempt to recuperate some of the value extracted by middlemen for employers' (taxable) profit line.

To cut out illegal mediation, TIC rendered employee placement completely random, destroying the "fax system." Employers could no longer select their own employees, workers were no longer able to secure positions for relatives and friends, and women could no longer count on the protection of partners or male kin.[52] In one swoop, the incentive for workers and employers to maintain long-term personal relations was eliminated, and the mainstay of paternalism withdrawn. As far as Israeli intermediaries are concerned, this has had ruinous effects on labor relations, bringing a new generation of *taylandim* that is urbanized, unskilled, insolent, and disobedient. Doron, the manpower agent, appraised the reform's effect as follows.

> In retrospect, this bilateral agreement only did us harm, though maybe it did [the workers] good. . . . Without a doubt, it did harm here . . . since these workers have no obligations. . . . They can do whatever they want to the farmer, however they want. Even the vetting of these workers . . . is minuscule. It's something random where you stand in line, it doesn't matter whether you're a taxi driver or a ladyboy or whatever, you stand in line, the only criterion is age, male or female. . . . That's no way to recruit a workforce that's supposed to work in agriculture. Naturally 50% of them are middle to low level . . . people who come here [now], they're not the people who came to work . . . you go and sign up at the Labor Ministry . . . nobody knows anything . . . no gatekeepers.[53]

Some of this rhetoric is spurious. "Today's *taylandim*" do not differ greatly from their predecessors in regional and occupational origin;

in fact, they come from similar Isaan backgrounds, though Isaan itself has undoubtedly changed in the last thirty years.[54] The drop in the up-front cost of migration may have encouraged people of lower economic standing to apply for work in Israel, but even these have other options: in recent decades, the most common destination for Thai labor migrants has been Taiwan, and travel to South Korea has also been growing, recently surpassing Israel and Japan.[55] Among the Isaanites I met, there was a general consensus that Taiwan and South Korea were preferable to Israel as migration destinations, since they offered similar wages for easier work under less isolating conditions; however, the South Korean alternative requires a high school diploma and a language qualification, which in turn requires expensive language classes.[56]

ISRAEL'S CAPITALIST-COLONIAL MIGRATION REGIME

The Thailand-Israel migration regime in place today is made up of a bewildering array of actors. Following the 2012 bilateral reform, recruitment in Thailand was taken out of the hands of for-profit intermediaries and placed in those of the nonprofit International Organization for Migration (IOM), an intergovernmental organization providing migration-related services to states around the world.[57] On the Israeli side, manpower agencies retain a residual role, handling bureaucratic and disciplinary issues and taking a cut of workers' earnings. A quasi-nongovernmental organization, the Center for International Migration and Integration (CIMI), is officially tasked with oversight, while a veteran human rights NGO, Workers' Hotline (with which I have collaborated closely—see Chapter 5), advocates and lobbies on behalf of Thai migrants and provides them with free legal advice. Several other human rights organizations play more circumscribed roles, and the Thai embassy also sometimes deigns to affect an interest in workers. The interests of employers are represented by umbrella organizations including the Moshavim Movement, the Kibbutz Movement, and the Farmers' Federation of Israel, as well as the Ministry of Agriculture. Immigration law is enforced by the Ministry of the Interior's Population and Immigration Authority (PIBA), and occupational health and safety law falls under the jurisdiction of the Ministry of Labor, Social Affairs and Social Services, though on this front enforcement is very feeble.

Despite its internal complexity, which is covered exhaustively in the work of Yahel Kurlander,[58] the regime confronts migrants in predictable ways. Thus, in 2016, the legal minimum wage was 25 New Israeli Shekels an hour (US $6.33 at January 2016 rates), 31.25 NIS ($7.91) for overtime between eight and ten hours a day, and 37.50 NIS ($9.49) for each of the next two hours—with work of over twelve hours a day prohibited.[59] The workers I knew were aware of this, but they also knew that the prevailing wage in Ein Amal was much lower, around 18 NIS ($4.56) per hour and 22 NIS ($5.56) for all overtime, including on days that stretched much longer than allowed by law.[60] Deductions of dubious legality were made from wages, and required peripherals such as pension payments usually withheld. Of the nine annual vacation days guaranteed by the contract, only four were observed: the King's and Queen's birthdays (December 5 and August 12 at the time), the calendrical New Year (January 1), and Songkran, the Thai New Year (April 13). Health and safety regulations that require that employers provide proper masks and other protective gear for work with pesticides and let workers shower after such work were widely flouted, with possibly serious effects on workers' health. Similarly, the few female workers could not expect to be protected from sexual assault by employers and coworkers.[61] Workers on different farms in Ein Amal were aware of the uniformity of wage and safety standards across the *moshav* and the region. Implicitly recognizing that in practice these standards were set independently of the law, the workers I knew judged employers as "good" or "bad" not by the baseline and overtime wage rates they provided, but rather by their demeanor toward workers and the degree of trust they fostered.[62]

In contrast to its bald-faced neglect of labor law enforcement, since the institution of the "closed skies" policy at the turn of the millennium the Israeli government has taken a newly proactive stance on the enforcement of regulations intended to prevent the settlement of migrants. On its own terms, this move was successful, at least at first:

according to the immigration authorities, until the COVID-19 pandemic the number of Thai migrants living in the country without documentation was very small,[63] and the number who have settled permanently and legally through marriage with Israelis is negligible.[64] The success of the policy, however, has depended on delegation of its enforcement to employers, placing the responsibility for migrants' actions squarely on their shoulders.

The legal basis for this delegation was laid in the 1990s, in the arrangement that "bound" migrant workers in the country to a particular employer—an arrangement later officially banned by the courts, but still in effect in practice.[65] Since that decade, employers have been assigned a yearly number of "visas"—that is, a quota of workers—based on the size of their holdings and the crops they cultivate. The state reserved the right to dock the quota when workers abandoned their employers or overstayed their visas, but at first these quotas were generous, and as we have seen, violations were roundly ignored. Under the "closed skies" policy enacted at the turn of the millennium, quotas were tightened, making the sanction represented by the docking of visas more economically damaging for employers.[66] Legally, employers are not allowed to impound passports, limit workers' freedom of movement, or forcibly deport them; in practice, however, they have avoided the cost of losing a visa by arrogating such powers to themselves, surveilling workers' movements, and applying pressure to those who leave their workplaces to return.[67] The violation of workers' rights to freedom of movement and contract, then, is just as prevalent and structural a part of the regime as the violation of their rights to the minimum wage and decent living conditions.

In the interest of controlling the migrant population, the state has created an extremely rigid migration regime that makes it very difficult for workers to change their workplace; at the same time, however, it makes it almost impossible to dismiss them. An employer who wishes to let a worker go has two alternatives. The first is to make a formal request for repatriation, which will generally be granted only if the worker is suspected of a crime. The second option is to find another employer willing to take the worker off his boss's hands; however, other farmers will usually be unwilling to use up one of their "visas" on a worker considered problematic. In practice, workers themselves usually initiate such exchanges by leaving their employers to become "runaways" (*barhanim*) at another farm where they prefer to work, whether because they have relatives or friends there, because relations with the boss are better, or because more overtime is available.[68] The situation is then sometimes regularized by the two employers, often through the intervention of the relevant manpower agencies.

The role assigned to farmers by the migration regime is doubly contradictory. As the next chapter will demonstrate, the near impossibility of sacking workers and their solidarity combine to grant them a considerable degree of control over the labor process, with economic consequences for employers. In one sense, then, the latter would be better served by a more flexible labor market, which would enhance their freedom to select workers by deploying social networks in Isaan and to dismiss incompetent or insubordinate workers at will. This interest is sometimes expressed in the language of economic liberalism, with employers arguing that both TIC and the policy that punishes employers for their workers' infractions constitute punitive government intervention.[69] But the severe restrictions on workers' freedom of contract and movement also entail economic advantages for employers, which compound and fortify the indirect subsidy afforded by the non-enforcement of labor law. In a free labor market wages would probably rise, since the prevailing wage in agriculture is not only lower than the legal minimum, but also far lower than the prevailing wage for "unskilled" work in competitive, urban sectors of the Israeli economy, such as housecleaning and food delivery. This wage differential, pocketed as profit by the bosses, would be impossible to sustain if workers were allowed to sell their labor-power to the highest bidder within the agrarian sector, not to mention other economic sectors.

The farmers of the Arabah also embody conflicting positions insofar as they are both individual businessmen and members of a community whose collective identity remains invested in the ideology of "pure settlement" and in denying membership to non-Jews. Their representatives loudly support the state's objective of preventing the permanent settlement of migrants, publicly highlighting their own commitment to making sure no *taylandi* is left behind. Thus, in a lobbying brochure arguing for the enlargement of employment quotas, the Central Arabah Regional Council declared that "the behavioral norms characteristic of workers in the Arabah, unlike other parts of the country, do not include intermarriage, childbirth and lengthy periods of illegal residence in the country."[70] This is not simply a matter of outward-facing rhetoric; while some employers allow particularly valued workers to overstay their visas and continue working without documentation, farmers share in the general anxiety about the danger that Thais might settle down in Israel, and during my fieldwork this this privilege was only granted rarely.[71]

One method for understanding the situation can be extracted from the parallel Marxist analyses of labor migration under racist regimes in midtwentieth-century Africa and the US, developed by Michael Burawoy and Claude Meillassoux.[72] Both scholars observed that wage differentials between itinerant black and permanent white workers were sustained by legal and ideological systems that segregated the two groups at work and their families at home. To explain these differentials, Burawoy developed a distinction between two aspects of the reproduction of labor-power: the day-to-day "maintenance" labor of keeping laborers fed, clothed, and otherwise prepared to work, and the intergenerational "renewal" involved in raising new generations of workers. Assuming that the wage covers the costs of reproduction, Burawoy showed that such differentials could be upheld only so long as the renewal of white and black labor-powers was separated in space to prevent the reproductive costs of the two groups from converging through the use of common infrastructure and adoption of similar consumption practices. Maintenance posed a greater challenge, since in many sectors—including construction and fresh-produce agriculture—production and consumption could not be greatly separated in space. Here institutionalized systems like apartheid and Jim Crow played their roles by segregating activities such as food preparation and recreation, in order to stably maintain black labor-power at a lower price despite its physical proximity to white labor. Meillassoux proposes a model similar to Burawoy's, with two important differences: first, he theorizes the possibility that the labor-power of migrant workers is reproduced in part through nonmarket activities like subsistence farming (as remains the case in Isaan), and second, he raises the grim possibility that the wage does *not* actually cover the costs of maintaining and renewing labor-power; in such cases of hyperexploitation, labor-power is not reproduced but depleted, with migrant workers and their families gradually pushed into destitution.[73]

The analyses offered by Burawoy and Meillassoux can help us better understand the harmonization of Arabah settlements' colonial interests and their capitalist ones. If Thai migrants were to permanently settle in the Arabah and raise families there, rather than residing in barracks where much of the maintenance of labor-power is undertaken on the cheap, the costs of renewing labor-power would rise steeply.[74] But even if their families were to stay in Thailand, the adoption of Israeli-style consumption habits among migrants would lead to a rise in maintenance costs. In either case, there would be strong upward pressure on wages.

I was already thinking along these lines while doing fieldwork in the Arabah and was glad for a chance to test my ideas on Eitan, a farmer who once picked me up as I was hitchhiking to Ein Amal. Hearing about my research objectives, he immediately suggested that I come to his farm, on another *moshav* in the Arabah, to undertake some applied fieldwork. Why, he wanted to know, were his workers remitting less and less of their money, and spending more and more of it in Israel? Increasing drunkenness was one result, but he seemed more disconcerted by such activities as keeping pet dogs. How could they afford to feed them, why would they want to, given that this wasn't (in his opinion) something they did at home, and how could they be talked out of it? Eager to test my intuition, I asked him if he thought the problem was that the Thais were starting to become like Israelis. "Yes!" he agreed. "That's exactly it." Seven years later, Doron announced to me in the same scandalized tones that some Thais were now starting to buy cars.

Like most studies of the interaction between political modes of repression like racism and economic exploitation, so far this investigation has proceeded on the assumption that forms of difference that find an expression in economic phenomena such as split labor markets essentially arrive at the work site fully formed, whether by prejudice, by the effects of history, or both. But consistent application of capitalist coloniality as a unitary analytic requires that we question this assumption. The workplace itself is a site of domination and an active participant not only in the classed violence of abstraction, but also in the racialized violence of misplaced concretion. This is all the truer of workplaces like the farms of the Arabah, which are at the same time units of residence and of the reproduction of labor-power. To find out how these farms reproduce difference at the same time as they produce peppers, it is necessary to enter them ethnographically.

4 PRODUCING VEGETABLES AND REPRODUCING DIFFERENCE

IN A FAMOUS PASSAGE OF *Capital,* Marx dramatizes the encounter between the capitalist and the proletarian as a movement from the sunlit public sphere, "the exclusive realm of Freedom, Equality, Property and Bentham" where the two meet, into an infernal "abode of production," where naked domination rules and the hapless worker can expect nothing but a hiding. The scene is a caustic illustration of the gap between the formal, juridical equality that (sometimes) unites employer and employee and the substantive power differential between them, predicated on the primitive accumulation that takes place offstage before the curtain goes up.[1] However, the scene also has racial and gendered aspects that seem to escape its author's critical eye. Historically, even the tentative and contradictory freedom of the wage laborer has been predicated on masculinity, which entails mastery over wife and children, and on the full citizenship and racial privilege (paradigmatically coded as whiteness) that entitle him to juridical parity and political representation.[2] The opposition between formal equality and substantive domination embodied in the violence of abstraction is most evident for those workers who are lucky enough to become eligible for a "decent" job thanks to such accidents of birth. But for most other proletarians, including Thai workers in Israel, the violence of abstraction is inextricably bound together with the violence of concretion, which reifies their status as badly paid, socially marginalized agrarian laborers, making it appear as a natural condition.[3]

The role of the division between public and private spheres in the drama of capitalist domination breaks into a kaleidoscope of specific arrangements as we move away from the experience of the fully en-franchised, racially privileged male worker, who is compensated for his submission in the productive domain of the workplace by being allowed to dominate the reproductive domain of the home. In Ein Amal, where production as well as reproduction take place within the "private" sphere of the family farm, employers concede a signif-icant degree of collective autonomy to their workers in fields as well as barracks, while keeping them isolated from their surroundings. As opposed to Marx's scenario, this sphere is not an amoral inferno juxtaposed to a public sphere governed by liberal decency, but rather the locus of a steeply hierarchical but stable and morally legitimized division of powers and labors. Ironically, the means that workers use to retain control over the labor process serve to amplify their other-ness, facilitating their public erasure and enabling settlers to continue exploiting them without outside interference. By helping to reproduce the racial rule of difference, this locally atypical pattern of labor rela-tions conduces not only to settler employers' objectives of maximizing output and minimizing costs, but also to the *moshav*'s collective polit-ical mission of shoring up Jewish sovereignty.

But though the reproduction of difference on the farm contributes both to the profits of Arabah farmers as individual businessmen and to their peace of mind as members of the settler community, these contributions are not, for the most part, deliberately engineered. This ideological effect, like many others that support the reproduc-tion of capitalist relations, is produced behind the backs of the actors. The qualities of material entities, as Webb Keane writes, "cannot be manifest without some embodiment that inescapably binds [them] to some other qualities as well, which can become contingent but real factors in [their] social life."⁴ We might like, for analytical or political reasons, to distinguish the qualities that constitute Ein Amal's migrant workers as a class, such as their working conditions or pay, from those imputed to the racialized figure of the *taylandi*. But in reality, dense, two-directional links of causality and proximity bundle these signifying qualities together.⁵ The processes that reproduce exploitation are, to a great extent, the same ones that reproduce exclusion. Through the bundling that links these forms of violence, race, gender, and citizenship become the modalities through which class is lived.

This chapter explores these modalities in a loosely narrative manner, turning on the cycle of a day—a reproductive rhythm with natural as well as social determinants. After sketching the contours of the Sadot farm as the sun rises on a winter morning, we meet the boss, Ya'ir Sadot, sipping coffee and weighing duties to his movement's past against responsibility for his children's future. The gaze then shifts to the flurry of reproductive labor that Ya'ir's workers must get done before heading out for their paid work. Following the workers into the fields, I observe how they maintain collective control over the labor process, contextualizing their effort by reference to another ethnographer's discussion of the value attached by Isaanites to autonomy at work, and discussing a rare refusal and consequent flareup of tensions at lunchtime. In the heat of the afternoon, I show how two of the most salient forms of racial difference, language and bodily appearance, are reproduced as elements of the labor process. First, I demonstrate how the limited pidgin spoken on the farm fulfills linguistic functions requisite to the labor process while precluding contact with Israelis outside it. Then I show how acquired differences in bodily appearance, including not only skin color but also clothing, body hexis, and working pace, play a role in the labor process while indexing the racial difference between Thais on one hand, and both Jews and Arabs on the other. Finally, as the sun sets and the temperatures drop, I follow the team as it heads home to replenish its powers for the next day, and the next.

MORNING

At 6 a.m. in January, the sky above Ein Amal is still dark and the air chilly. If one looks away from the floodlights ringing the fenced perimeter of the *moshav*, into the desert, the constellations are blindingly clear. In the east, the steep mountains over the Jordanian border loom black against the navy blue sky. As the light grows, the mountains will begin to take on the dark red hue suggested by their biblical name, "Edom." Within the *moshav*, too, lights are turning on. Heading from my rented room to the farmhouse, I pass through a pedestrian lane from which the desert has been banished. Here dogs and cats doze under leafy trees, along lawns and flower beds generously fed with water sucked from the salinizing aquifer. From this path a trail branches to the front door of the Sadot family home—a spacious four-bedroom whose large kitchen windows look onto a small private yard on the opposite side.

The farmhouse can also be approached via the *moshav*'s perimeter road, whose outer edge is defined by a featureless stretch of scrub. This is the route the trucks take on their way to the packinghouse and cold-storage room to pick up produce, and it presents a rather different aspect of Ein Amal, industrial and disheveled. Both the newish family SUV and the beat-up pickup with one shattered window that is used for work are parked here, next to the tall metallic wall of the farm's packinghouse and a shed that shares its corrugated metal roof. Two tractors are parked in the shed, an ancient blue Massey-Ferguson and a shiny new red Yanmar. Behind the shed there is a small open space with a wooden picnic table and overflowing trash cans in which a brilliant-feathered cock is foraging. Crates of empty beer bottles line a short hallway, opening onto a kitchen where rice cookers stand next to heavy-duty gas ranges on stainless-steel tables encrusted with cooking oil. At the end of the hallway is the workers' living room, featuring two castaway sofas, more empty bottles, and a clutter of cigarette butts, wastepaper, and food debris. A television, a tower of jerry-rigged speakers, and a karaoke microphone slump at the end of the room. Side doors open onto small bedrooms, each housing two to four residents. Another door gives access to decrepit shower stalls, toilets with broken seats, and an outdoor laundry area with a washing machine and clotheslines.

The planners of the *moshav* envisioned the household as an amalgam of integrated but distinct economic functions, residential and agro-industrial, to be carried out by the farming family according to a division of labor based on gender and age; hence the designation of an operational area within each homestead.[6] Nowadays, this spatial distinction separates Israelis from Thais: Ya'ir's wife, Miri, and their children do not enter the quarters, except on special occasions like Thai holidays. Thai employees similarly steer clear of the family home, though they are invited into the backyard on other special occasions, such as a worker's going-away party. When Ya'ir's son Uri celebrated his bar mitzvah, the farm's Thai and student workers (see note 14) were not invited to the religious ceremony, which took place at the local synagogue during work hours, but were welcomed at the evening party in the spruced-up packinghouse and participated enthusiastically, dressed in their best clothes. Uri himself is a regular in the quarters, often asking Mike, the youngest of the Thais, to make him pad thai or spring rolls—tourist "Thai food" that the workers never prepare for themselves. Miri, who is distant with most of the other workers, has a lot of affection for the long-haired, baby-faced Mike. Freest to come and go are the male Israeli workers, David and me: in the mornings we are encouraged to come into the house to make ourselves coffee and snacks, and in the evenings we sometimes hang out in the workers' quarters, drinking beer and singing karaoke.

THE CARES OF A FAMILY MAN

It might be 6:10 by now. Miri and the children are asleep in rooms darker than the desert, but in the kitchen the light is on and Ya'ir is drinking his black Turkish coffee, not brewed patiently in the traditional style but mixed hastily with kettle-boiled water, forming the thick sediment at the bottom that gives the drink its Hebrew name *botz,* "mud." Ya'ir is fifty years old, a father of three and employer of nineteen. At this moment, as he sips his coffee and stares out the window into the well-kept yard and the stark metal of the packinghouse beyond, his mind is on how best to fill the orders for vegetables that he needs to deliver today.

Past and future generations haunt his musings; Ya'ir is concerned with conserving the legacy bequeathed to him by his parents for his children. The *moshav* has not accepted newcomers in years, but one "continuing son" (*ben mamshich*) from each family may join the community and receive an allocation of land. As a "continuing son" of a founding family, Ya'ir's responsibility is not only to his parents but to the *moshav* and the entire labor settlement movement. In a way, he would be failing all of them if he were to give up cultivation. Granted, he could sublease his allotment to a neighbor, but the income would not be large or stable enough to maintain his family. Unlike farmers in central parts of the country, Ya'ir cannot bank on the prospect of his land being rezoned for residential use and snapped up by developers, nor can he assume that his home's value will rise as the suburban real estate market continues to overheat.[7] His responsibilities to the next generation, then, weigh at least as heavily as the debt he owes to his forebears.

Ya'ir's daughter and two boys, like most of their peers, are uninterested in farming; as the local cliché goes, they "don't even know where Dad's fields are." Like most parents in the *moshav*, Ya'ir accepts his children's predilections. He suspects that the future of Israeli agriculture lies in concentration, corporatization, and mechanization, and that family farmers like himself are on the way out. As regards the next generation, then, Ya'ir's concern is not to reproduce a particular occupation or lifestyle, but rather a class position: as secular Ashkenazim of LSM extraction, or *ahusalim*,[8] his children have cultural and social capital that gives them a head start in the mobility game; but unlike their maternal cousins, they will not inherit an apartment in central Israel. To remain in the middle class, they must deploy this capital through military service and higher education, and Ya'ir's hopes and anxieties for them are concentrated in these fields.[9]

The tension between the demands exerted on Ya'ir by past and future is a permutation of the conflict between political commitment and economic exigency to which the entire LSM has been subjected. But while the ties connecting him to preceding generations are largely ideological and emotional, they have a material dimension as well: like all other farmers in the Arabah, Ya'ir depends on state support that is justifiable only in terms of the national role played by settler farming, and, like his neighbors, he is invested in maintaining a public face that harmonizes with the movement's image of itself. While nobody is any longer quite sure what room there might be for this image in the country's future, for the present farmers understand the importance of galvanizing public opinion not only through their hearts but through their pocketbooks.

Ya'ir's pocketbook is also subject to much more immediate stresses. The price of peppers on the European market fluctuates wildly, beyond his control or ability to predict. Among the factors that have shaped fortunes in the Arabah over the last few years are the decline in effective demand in Russia since the imposition of US sanctions and the unprecedented strength of Israel's currency.[10] The intense competition among Arabah farmers since the collapse of their cooperative marketing arrangements amplifies this volatility, producing rapid boom-and-bust cycles. As a vegetable producer, Ya'ir has few avenues for mechanizing labor processes and improving productivity. But due to the rigidity of the migration regime, he also has little hope of boosting production through intensified discipline and tighter control over workers. If he is to secure his profit margin and ensure his children's future, he must employ as many workers as possible for wages as low as possible. In other words, to care for his family and to best fulfil the role assigned to him by the labor settlement movement, Ya'ir must lean into the character of the figure historically most reviled by that very movement: the capitalist employer of cheap, copious, and corrupting "foreign labor."[11]

MEN WITHOUT WOMEN

While Ya'ir sips his *botz* and mulls over generational legacies, his employees are engaged in reproducing the immediate conditions of their own ability to work a ten-to-twelve-hour day in his greenhouses and packinghouse. One of them, Ton, has been up for half an hour, cooking the glutinous rice (*khaw niaw*) that Ya'ir provides free of charge by custom.[12] Now that the rice is ready, it is ladled into little wicker baskets that will keep it moist and chewy for the rest of the day. The men take turns preparing the various meat, fish, and vegetable dishes that they share. They do their best to approximate Isaan cuisine with ingredients available at the local "Thai shop" (see Chapter 5), and the funky aroma of *plaa raa* (fermented fish paste) in hot oil spreads out of the kitchen, blanketing the yard and mingling with similar smells drifting from nearby farms.

Like male migrants around the world who live on their own, Ya'ir's employees find themselves newly responsible for everyday housekeeping, or what Burawoy terms the "maintenance" side of the reproduction of labor-power. In Isaan, though women prepare most of the food, there is no stigma associated with it for men, and many male Thais in Israel take comfort and pride in cooking.[13] In this they are much luckier than the Ethiopian student-workers on the farm, also all men, who have never entered a kitchen at home and are now reduced to eating the rice cooked by the Thais with a tasteless egg-and-tomato stew they have improvised on the spot.[14] The Ethiopians, who will spend only about six months in Israel, are also far more serious than the Thais about maximizing earnings and minimizing expenditures. They work as many hours as possible, usually including Saturdays, which the Thais take off. The Thais, while also aspiring to earn overtime, are glad to have one day off a week and are more relaxed about spending.

This difference between the farm's Thai and Ethiopian workers fits into a pattern identified by Edna Bonacich as characteristic of "ethnically split" labor markets: the tighter the temporal limits on the opportunity to earn a wage higher than that available at home, the more migrants are willing to forgo "maintenance" activities, like eating well and resting, in order to maximize their savings.[15] But in this respect the difference between the Ethiopians and the Thais is only one of degree. The Thais also settle for a lower standard of living than they would be willing to bear at home, consoling themselves with the thought that the hardship will not last forever. For both groups, reproduction of labor-power is a complex relationship between temporalities: circumstances that cannot be endured indefinitely can be tolerated for a delimited time, while the chance of permanent mobility—by way of starting a successful business or getting a child into a lucrative public-sector job—may justify sacrifices that would not be acceptable for short-term gain.[16]

While the workers of the Sadot farm seem to have the culinary side of maintenance down, the hygienic situation is less encouraging. Standards of cleanliness, of course, are culturally variable, but in even the poorest households in Isaan the house is generally swept daily and the outdoor squat toilets are frequently rinsed out with plenty of water. Here the tiny rooms where the workers sleep are relatively tidy, but the shared spaces, including the living room and the yard, are normally a mess, and the bowl toilets are often stopped up and filthy. None of this should be surprising, given the severely limited temporal and spatial resources available to the Sadot farm's workers for upkeep: nineteen men are crowded into a small living space that has to suffice for sleeping, eating, cooking, washing, laundry, and recreation. With workdays at least ten hours long, housecleaning predictably takes on a low priority; when it does take place, every other Saturday, it is directed by the workers' headman or *balabay*, Daeng, whose authority extends over reproductive as well as productive labors.

The role of the *balabay*—I discuss the term's etymology below—is liminal, an uncomfortable middle ground between workers and employer. The most important factor determining eligibility for this role is seniority: this fits in both with the norm in Thailand, where age and its proxies are central to the structuring of hierarchies,[17] and with the demands of work on the farm, where skill is gained on the job. Formally, Daeng was selected by Ya'ir, but both are aware that he serves at the pleasure of his peers, who could make life hell for him and force his resignation if they wished. Short, wiry, constantly harried, Daeng is a closed book to me at this point, though I will later get to know him much better (see Chapter 6). His role does not entitle him to extra wages or any other material perks, though he is proud of his close relationship with Ya'ir and of the respect the other workers afford him.[18]

By 6:20, Ya'ir has finished his coffee and is making his way to the tractor shed. The workers, done with cooking, scoop hot food into plastic boxes, shuffle into their shoes, light their cigarettes, and file blinking into the yard. The sun is still behind the mountains, but the stars have gone and the sky has turned a dry powder blue. As the workers look on, Ya'ir addresses instructions to Daeng, informing him of the orders to be filled so that the workers can be divided into teams and loaded on the pickup and the two tractor-pulled flatbed trailers. The Massey-Ferguson's engine turns several times under Dii's skilled hand, then coughs and hums. The Yanmar starts up right away. The workers grab their five-liter styrofoam containers of ice water and climb onto the trailers as the vehicles putter away from the yard.

AUTONOMY IN THE FIELDS

The tractors exit Ein Amal through a gate in the perimeter fence, with a fresh wind rolling off the crystal-clear mountains ahead. Here they take separate ways; the trailer on which I am riding behind the old Massey-Ferguson makes its bumpy way along a dirt path between greenhouses and passes through a gate that is only locked when the wadi floods, once or twice per winter. On the other side of the dry, rocky bed, only meters from the Jordanian border, is Ya'ir's "far field," where the group will plant vegetable seedlings throughout the morning. At 9:00 work stops for breakfast, the biggest meal of the day. The greenhouse is already getting hot, but outside, fleecy clouds dot the sky and it is still cool, so we set our dishes out there on some discarded netting and a wooden pallet. The plastic boxes filled with food are placed on a flattened piece of cardboard to be shared; the Thais have no interest in anything I can cook, so my contribution is usually fruit— today, a bunch of bananas.

We finish breakfast, clean up, and go off, each to his own shaded corner—one to nap, one to call family in Thailand, where it is already afternoon, another to scroll through his Facebook feed, yet another to watch cockfights on YouTube. At 9:30 someone's alarm goes off, and we make our drowsy way to the Massey. It starts up noisily and takes us to our next destination, a twenty-minute ride to a field at the opposite end of the *moshav*'s territory. When we pull open the greenhouse's drop-down nylon gate, a gust of hot, humid air escapes. The pleasant weather outside is no match for the netting that traps heat and moisture indoors, facilitating the cultivation of summer vegetables in winter as well as the swift dehydration of the unwary visitor. But conditions are better than they will be later in the day, or the year, and work proceeds apace until lunchtime. Chances are Ya'ir will not be seen; he rarely visits the fields unless he has some specific business there, and relays instructions mostly by phone, though he sometimes sends one of his Israeli workers in the pickup to keep an eye on things while shuttling workers or equipment from field to field. Less experienced than Ya'ir in working with Thais, these workers sometime enter conflicts with the workers that he is quick to defuse, as is the case with David. We'll jump ahead in time to May, when the midday heat makes a long siesta indispensable, to witness a particularly instructive clash.

David has no personal interest in lording it over the Thais, but having recently completed his compulsory military service, he has a somewhat rigid respect for hierarchy. At about 11:30 a.m., Ya'ir calls him with instructions: a new order has come in, and the workers are to postpone their lunch break and fill a few more boxes of vegetables. But by the time David gets to the field in the pickup, the Massey has started up and the workers are piling onto the trailer in back, water containers in hand, on their way home to wolf down some leftovers and take a nap in the air-conditioned trailer. David relays Ya'ir's instructions to Dii, who is driving the tractor, but Dii ignores him and steps on the gas. Frustrated, David tries to insist but is again ignored; but when he calls Ya'ir to tell him what has happened, the boss tells him to leave it alone; the order will have to go unfilled.

Today David has learned that the job he thought of as managerial was really nothing of the sort. As both of us have been aware for months, Daeng and ad hoc team leaders like Dii are the ones who really manage the labor process in the fields. The Thais know the work much better than any of the Israeli employees, and while they treat us deferentially, their regard is rooted exclusively in our status as Israelis. We are not their managers; from Daeng's perspective, as he will explain to me later in an interview, we are white-collar employees in charge of paperwork and marketing who occasionally join them in the fields. Any instructions we relay from Ya'ir would be just that—instructions relayed from their real boss—and while they are eager to avoid conflict with us, there are limits to their flexibility. The boss, for his part, recognizes their power by choosing not to retaliate when they defend their right to a full and timely break.

Seeing as migrant farmworkers picking fruit and vegetables in other countries, such as the US, are subject to draconian disciplinary practices, anything inherent in either the work itself or their noncitizen status can be ruled out as a reason for such leniency.[19] Rather, the workers' autonomy hinges on the peculiarities of the migration regime, as described in Chapter 3. The "binding" of workers to employers makes it quite difficult for either side to terminate the arrangement.[20] Barring extreme circumstances such as evidence of crime, migrants and their employers are stuck with each other for the duration of the contract: five years and three months. Dismissal is thus practically unavailable as a disciplinary tool to employers like Ya'ir Sadot. Lacking the "discipline of the sack," farmers like Ya'ir might be expected to rely on piecework and other incentive schemes, as US agribusinesses do to squeeze more labor out of their own migrant workforce. But such schemes are rarely used in the Arabah. A local farmer interested in technological advances in agriculture told me that several of his colleagues were exploring systems for monitoring individual productivity that could easily be used to calculate piece rates. However, he was skeptical about the potential of these schemes, stating baldly that the Thais "would never accept them."

In his seminal *Manufacturing Consent*, Michael Burawoy writes that piece rates represent an attempt by management to extract more labor per unit of time through the manipulation of individualized incentives. After employees have responded to such incentives by intensifying their work, management can reduce them, locking in a more rapid rhythm as the new norm. In the factory where Burawoy worked, workers collectively instituted an informal cap on work speed in order to block management from ratcheting up intensity in this way, while still enabling workers to adjust pace and income to their preferences—a compromise between solidarity and individual choice.[21] If piece rates are rare in the Arabah because employers know that their workers "would never accept them," one probable reason is that the stable, self-organized, and socially isolated community of workers on each farm is much more cohesive than the multiracial workforce of the US factory where Burawoy worked, or that of industrial farms in the US today. Here the informal penalties for "rate-busting" are heavy and solidarity easily trumps individualism.

The difficulty of supervising workers also enhances their autonomy. The small size of farms makes supervisory labor relatively expensive, but the deeper problem is that Israeli workers, like David and me, inevitably arrive for short periods and usually lack agricultural experience. There will always be Thai workers more knowledgeable about the work, and as a cohesive group, speaking a language their "supervisors" do not understand, the workers will always be one step ahead. Under these circumstances, bosses like Ya'ir are better off trusting in their employees' honesty and palpable drive. When I asked Daeng what motivated him and his colleagues to work so hard despite the lack of sanctions at the boss's disposal, he cited *khwaamkrateureuron*— enthusiasm or diligence. "It's in our subconscious [*jittaaysamneuk*], it's not something that can be taught." Invoking an ideology of karmic reciprocity identical to Song's, he added: "when the boss feels good, we feel good." Such "subconscious" diligence was clearly visible not only in the steady pace of work that my coworkers kept up, but also in the proactive approach they took to any problems encountered in the greenhouses, such as burst water pipes or pest infestations.

As we have seen, when applied to hierarchical relationships, this interaction ideology is clearly compatible with the paternalistic presumption that subaltern and superordinate actors have defined roles to play and obligations to one another. Nobody has the right to demand redress through aggressively direct behavior and speech of the kind which Israelis value as "straight talk," as discussed in the next chapter. On the other hand, those in superior positions should be attuned to subtle signals of dissatisfaction on the part of their underlings or face the possibility of a sudden breakdown of the social body—something Ya'ir seemed to understand very well. Mild-mannered, twinkle-eyed, and soft-spoken by Israeli standards, he never raised his voice to a worker in my hearing. His decision to back down in the face of Dii's refusal of David's order, an unusually bold act that he must have interpreted as signaling the imminent possibility of such breakdown, is of a piece with this understanding. While refraining from surveilling his workers certainly saved Ya'ir precious time, it also expressed tact and an implicit trust in their fidelity to the farm's social body.[22]

Ya'ir's manner also embodied a recognition of the high value his workers placed on what I have called autonomy and Claudio Sopranzetti's interlocutors call freedom, *itsaraphaap*. Adun, an Isaanite living in Bangkok, explained what this word meant to him by comparing a previous job in a factory to his new occupation as a motorcycle taxi driver:

> I like my job because it is a free job. They offered to take me back in the company I used to work for, but that job in Bangkok is bad for a countryman [*sic*] like me. The boss always looks down on you, always orders you around, always insults you. The last place I worked, the boss's son kept insulting me, shouting at me: a twenty-year-old kid with no experience, just out of university. I could not accept that. So I am happy now; I am my own boss.[23]

As Sopranzetti acknowledges, the freedom so highly prized by these impoverished proletarians was a negative, residual one. They could only buy liberation from industrial labor, wage relations, and humiliating subordination by taking a cut to their already meager earnings and committing to grueling, dangerous work enmeshed in slightly less direct but no less onerous relations of domination.[24] This choice could be understood in individualist, even masculinist terms. However, the experience of the Sadot farm's workers demonstrates that autonomy at work is not just a negative freedom from interference but a positive achievement of interpersonal trust built up patiently and reciprocally. Significant as this achievement is to the well-being of the farm's social body, though, it is also circumscribed on all sides and bounded in depth by the strict limits to communication between the parts of that body.

LANGUAGE AND THE LABOR PROCESS

All that is in the future, though. We are back in January, when the midday break is a short siesta in the field—no more than an hour, which most workers utilize to nap rather than eat. I am dozing next to Daeng, and wake up to hear Ya'ir's voice emanating from his phone, which he has placed on speaker mode on his chest while remaining prone. When we finish our break, Ya'ir tells him, we are to join Dii's group in another field, where the season's first peppers are being picked.

The conversation between Ya'ir and Daeng takes place in a language they call "English," though little of it would be immediately comprehensible to English speakers. This language, or rather, linguistic code,[25] features a simple syntactic structure as well as a great number of loanwords from Hebrew and both the standard and Isaan dialects of Thai. Its phonology and the selection of such loanwords point to an accommodation of both Hebrew and Thai verbal habits. Thus, for example, the word for "eggplant" is not taken from the English term, whose consonant clusters would be unpronounceable to a Thai speaker, nor from the Thai *makheua*, whose tones and final vowels would be difficult for a Hebrew speaker to produce, or even from the singular Hebrew *hatzil*, whose final *l* would be difficult for a Thai speaker. Rather, the form selected is the Hebrew plural *hatsilim*, easily pronounceable by speakers of Thai, which does not distinguish singular from plural.[26] This code also employs a very simplified syntax: for example, the question "have the eggplants been picked yet?" would be rendered "somebody pick *hatsilim*?"

These features, together with the code's very limited context of use—neither Thais nor Israelis speak it outside of work—make it possible to classify it as a nascent pidgin.[27] I cannot be sure whether the pidgin used on the Sadot farm is sui generis or whether it resembles that spoken on other farms in Ein Amal and the area; while migrants have few linguistic interactions with Israelis other than their employers, they might pick up some of their "English" from Thais on other farms. Interestingly, Thais in Israel share at least one vocabulary item unique to them: the mild expletive *sombae*, literally meaning "pickled goat" in the Isaan dialect. In a visit to an experimental training camp held in Isaan for workers about to depart to Israel, I observed those with friends already there teaching their peers this interjection as a sort of induction ritual. David and I also made liberal use of the term to express our day-to-day frustrations on the farm, and other Israelis I met who have worked with Thais were also familiar with it.[28]

On the Sadot farm, then, language is one of the forces of production.[29] Both employers and workers list the lack of a common language as one of the frustrations of working together, though all in all the pidgin can be learned quickly and seems adequate to its uses.[30] But the lack of a locally spoken language is a major contributor to Thai migrants' isolation. In this context it matters both that English is widely used in Israel, and that farm "English" is not English. My coworker Boy, for example, learned not only to speak the code but to read it in English script so that he could prepare orders for shipment from written slips. But when he wanted to help a friend from a *moshav* in another part of the country make his way to Ein Amal, he was unable to understand the English bus schedules on Israeli websites. The friend was about to pay an exorbitant sum for a taxi when Boy came to me for help; I quickly found a cheap solution via bus, though I do not know if the man ever made it to the Arabah.

English skills, of course, are a form of linguistic capital recognized around the world.[31] Neither Israel nor Thailand is an exception, but despite the well-intentioned illusions of some employers, including the Sadots, speaking "English" rather than Hebrew with their workers does not result in the latter accumulating much in the way of such capital. They return to their homes as they left them, on one of the bottom rungs of the global working class and unfit for work which requires English skills, for example in tourism. In this they are quite different from the Filipina/o and South Asian eldercare workers who come to Israel already speaking English, as well as from the asylum-seeking East Africans and undocumented Latin Americans who gain proficiency in

Hebrew and English while living and working in the country's urban centers.[32] The linguistic isolation imposed on Thai workers plays an important role in cutting them off from Israeli society and trapping them in farmwork, no doubt contributing to the very low rate at which they escape into undocumented but better-remunerated work in the cities relative to other migrant groups (see Chapter 3).

The term *balabay* condenses much that is peculiar about these relations of production and the reproduction of difference. At one and the same time, it "denote[s a] force . . . of production"—the name of a position within the labor process—as well as "index[ing] the relations of production" through its provenance and reshaping.[33] It derives from the Hebrew *ba'al ha-bayit*, literally "master of the house," a term of biblical antiquity commonly used to refer to persons of authority and often run together to sound like *balabayt*. Together with *balagan*, meaning "mess" or "disarray," it is one of the first Hebrew words learned by migrants of all nationalities, part of the core vocabulary of what Alejandro Paz calls "jargon Hebrew."[34] But adapted to the Sadot farm's pidgin phonology as *balabay*, this word has acquired a narrower meaning, referring specifically to the headman role.

Despite the crucial role played by the *balabay* in managing the farm, there is no standard Hebrew term for his position.[35] This absence reflects a more general trend among employers and their representative institutions to avoid any discussion of the internal division of labor on farms, which contrasts starkly with their willingness to agitate and lobby in favor of increased migration quotas.[36] In this terminological vacuum it is not surprising that workers—who may have heard the boss referring to their headman facetiously as *ba'al ha-bayit*—would pick up the term to reflect their respect for the position and the man who holds it.

BODY MARKINGS

The midday break is over; the rattle of the Massey announces that Dii and the trailer are here to take us to the greenhouse where we will spend the afternoon planting tomatoes. On the ride over we do our best to enjoy the pleasant breeze, since we know that inside the

The minimalistic dress sense of early settlers in the Arabah. Above: plowing; below: sorting cucumbers. Courtesy of Ein Yahav Archive.

greenhouse the heat and humidity will already be suffocating. I have shed my outer layers and am now dressed in the way I find best suited to such weather: short, loose clothing that lets the air circulate and the sweat evaporate. In this, I am a typical *ahusal*: Jewish Israelis, and especially Ashkenazim, value such airiness as well as the bronzed skin that indexes an active, outdoor lifestyle. The suntanned look is specifically associated with the labor settlement movement: photos from the early days of Israeli settlement in the Arabah show young settlers working with only shorts to their bodies, in a clear visual contrast to both Orthodox Jews and Arabs, who traditionally wear long garments.[37]

Thais, in contrast, value a light skin, which indexes a life spent indoors, away from the fields.[38] In contemporary Thailand, the archetype of both female and male beauty is the light-skinned East Asian or European, as opposed to the "black" (*dam*) color associated with Isaan, Malay, and African bodies.[39] My coworkers perceived exposure to the sun as affecting the skin's color and consistency not only temporarily, through tanning, but also in the irreversible long term, by creating blotches and wrinkles. In recent years, Israelis have responded to epidemic levels of skin cancer by adopting practices somewhat closer to Thai ones; Israeli workers now wear long pants and hats to minimize the dangers of exposure. But we can still easily be told apart from our Thai colleagues, who will usually also be wearing a long-sleeved shirt (often in two layers) and a broad-brimmed hat, much as they would when doing similar work at home; often, they will also cover their faces with a repurposed T-shirt or a cloth mask.[40] Even standing still, then, Thais cut a very "foreign" figure; seen from afar, to the Israeli eye, they resemble swaddled mummies rather than people.

What Marcel Mauss calls "body hexis" joins dress sense and skin color in creating visible difference between Israeli and Thai workers.[41] Any visitor to the greenhouse could observe obvious differences in how we approach the task of planting: I find it immensely difficult to work so close to the ground. Ya'ir purchases tomato and pepper seedlings in large Styrofoam trays, each containing about two hundred sprouts; the trays are watered before planting and are quite heavy. The task consists of moving ahead while carrying one of these trays, plucking

FIGURES 4.2A–4.2B

A Thai (left) and an Israeli (right) dressed for farmwork. Illustration by Alma Itzhaky.

one seedling at a time while taking care not to rip it from its roots, reaching down every twenty centimeters to a prepunched hole in the earth, placing the seedling in the hole, scooping earth over it, and then gently tamping it down. This process demands spending a great deal of time close to the ground while moving steadily ahead.

The ideal bodily position for achieving this, if one has the requisite musculature and flexibility, is the crouch or deep squat.[42] A stable crouch enables one to work carefully close to the ground and get up easily to walk to the next hole. Alternatively, one can bend one or both knees to the ground, as I do.[43] But kneeling is a demanding and inefficient position to get in and out of; it also cakes my pant legs with mud, causing discomfort and embarrassment. Toward noon, I grow tired and start crawling forward on both knees. My coworkers

A Thai worker (left) and an Israeli worker engaged in planting. The Thai is crouching; the Israeli is kneeling. The planting tray, usually carried in the free hand or placed on the ground, is not pictured. Illustration by Alma Itzhaky.

would never dream of saying anything, but when we break for lunch, I feel a pang of embarrassment for emerging from the same work so much dirtier than they do. In the West, including Israel, the upright stance is valorized, and postures like the deep squat are associated with primitiveness and animality.[44] But in Thailand, as in many other countries, squatting at ground level is normative, and often used in situations where Westerners would prefer to sit, as for eating or chatting with friends.[45] The muscular capabilities developed over a lifetime of squatting allow Thais to carry out ground-level tasks such as planting without touching any part of their body to the earth except the soles of their feet, minimizing discomfort and back pain and while keeping themselves clear of the dirt.

A final difference, which becomes more and more pronounced as the afternoon wears on, is that of pace. By 3:00 p.m. my head is swimming from the heat, and I am planting perhaps one row of tomatoes for every three completed by my coworkers. The difference is in part one of experience: employers and employees agree that it takes at least a year, with its full round of seasonal tasks, to achieve an adequate level of skill. Nevertheless, both parties also think of Thais as particularly fit for agricultural labor. When I asked workers why they thought Israeli employers preferred to hire Thais, some replied that, being agriculturally skilled and accustomed to hot weather, Thais could do the work better than Israelis. Some employers, too, account for their workers' supposed predilection for hard labor by pointing to their upbringing in poor rural areas, which has supposedly steeled them for such work from an early age.[46] Characteristics of strength and forbearance, projected in the self-image that emerges from migrants' cultural productions,[47] were also stressed by a representative of the Ministry of Labor at the orientation for departing workers I attended in Bangkok. In a sense, the racialized image of the resilient, uncomplaining worker can be considered a production of the migration regime as a whole, a theme I will return to in the next chapter.

But employers also hold a more complex and—given the lack of specialized discourse on agricultural labor relations—surprisingly uniform theory about the nature of Thai labor. Several remarked to me that the Thai style of working is superior to that of both Jews and Arabs, not in speed but in aspects of steadiness and care. Workers of the latter two groups may start out quite energetically in the morning, but by midday they will have worn themselves out. From then on, their work is slow, careless, and potentially damaging to product, plant, and structure. Thais, on the other hand, work relatively slowly but maintain a steady pace throughout the day while taking care not to cause damage.[48] This steady pace ensures predictability and enables planning.

The distinction that groups Jews together with Arabs in contrast to Thais is notable, since as we have already seen, Thais are often perceived in Israel as like Arabs in their capacity for physical labor, but like Jews in that their presence on the farm is politically unthreatening. Jewish labor, mostly that of middle-class *ahusal* youth directly before or after their army service, is highlighted in local public relations efforts and subsidized by the state.[49] Meanwhile, the labor of Bedouin Arabs, organized informally through labor contractors who mobilize a workforce with no legal protections, is still considered a severe breach of LSM ideology.[50] But while employers imagine that Arab workers are envious, resentful, and prone to theft and sabotage, they also regard Jewish workers as impatient and insolent, wanting "to run the farm themselves."[51] Despite the great differences between them, then, both Jews and Arabs are suspected of wanting to take the employer's place in one way or another. This attitude reflects the view, touched upon in Chapter 1, of Jews and Arabs as antagonistically united by struggle.[52] It encloses an assumption that both groups aspire to an immediate relationship with the land—that is, to ownership. In this regard Thais are juxtaposed to both Jews and Arabs, leaving employers free to imagine them as possessing a natural predilection for monotonous, backbreaking labor that nevertheless establishes no "sweat equity."[53]

EVENING

At around four in the afternoon, with the sun already low over the Negev massif, the temperature in the greenhouse seems to drop suddenly and a sort of second wind allows me to pick up my flagging pace for one last stretch of work. Soon the light is too weak for planting; we return the unfinished trays to their metal frame, which the tractor has hauled to the center of the greenhouse, and hop on the trailer for the trip back. Outside the greenhouse the wind is blowing hard and the temperature is falling quickly. Soaked with sweat, I pull on a sweatshirt and huddle close to the other workers, who are sitting cross-legged on a pallet in the center of the trailer. I sit facing the mountains, which flare purple in the crepuscular light. Later, in my room, I will struggle against fatigue to write field notes, but right now, like my co-workers, I am stretching aching muscles, anticipating dinner, a beer, a call home, some TV, and bed. The most enjoyable part of the workday, by far, is its end.

Following the daily round from the quarters to the fields and back home, this chapter has shown how the labor process—its organization, its language, its associated bodily practices—all help to reproduce the racial rule of difference that isolates Thai migrant workers from Israeli society and maintains their vulnerability to hyperexploitation. Paradoxically, workers' autonomy and their agency in structuring workplace relationships with the aid of an interaction ideology they have brought from home tend to reinforce their foreignness and isolation. In some respects, the Sadot farm is a microcosm with its own rules, where Ya'ir's concern for profits and his decades of experience working with Thais encourage him to provide workers with a modicum of what they might call *itsaraphaap,* freedom to do things the way they like, spared the boss's disciplining gaze. But the very boundedness of the farm as a self-contained, paternalistic private sphere where both productive and reproductive labors are undertaken also helps to separate and distinguish it from the public sphere. The qualities that define the *taylandi* as a worker become hopelessly entangled with those that construct him as a foreign, temporary presence, forming a semiotic bundle that encourages the reproduction of the public face of Arabah settlements as paragons of Zionist values. But this in itself is not enough, as Thais cannot help entering the public sphere of the *moshav.* The unpaid labor they undertake to maintain its face when they do so is the topic of the next chapter.

5 SAVING THE FACE OF THE ARABAH

LIKE ITS MEMBER HOUSEHOLDS, *MOSHAV* Ein Amal is also starkly divided between "Israeli" and "Thai" spaces. The operational area behind the Sadot household is contiguous with the corrugated metal sheds, dusty tractors, and vegetable-packing facilities of neighboring farms, which present an industrial appearance reminiscent of the *moshav*'s greenhouses, with their dun-colored net coverings and their black fertilizer tanks. But a visitor who restricted her exploration to the palm-lined central avenue, the leafy paths that lead to settlers' front doors, and the modernist slabs of the administrative compound at the center of the settlement would experience the *moshav* quite differently: as a pleasant, verdant place to live, as well as a clearly Jewish and Israeli place, fruit of the Zionist determination to "make the desert bloom." This space is the "on-display" face of the community, and here there is no room for paternalism or reciprocity; here the Thai presence is powerfully marginalized, though it cannot be entirely erased.[1]

Though this marginalization serves the ideological interest of the settler collectivity, it could not be achieved without the active collusion of its migrant employees. In this chapter I argue that among the most valuable services provided to this community by the workers it imports from Isaan is their contribution to the maintenance of its public "face." The bashful discretion that these men display in public space, as they refrain from competing in tournaments of eroticism and consumption, are part of the skilled labor that they put into protecting the "social body" wherein they find themselves implicated. This is a complicated feat to pull off, because the labor settlement ideology that the *moshavim* of the Arabah still purport to uphold heroizes Hebrew labor while deprecating the dark double of Arab labor, whose claim on the land endangers the national project. In this settler-colonial space there is little room through which non-Jews, and especially poor, conspicuous non-Jews like Thai migrant workers, might wriggle their way into the community. On the contrary, when the presence of such non-Jews becomes too obviously persistent it can only be registered as a "demographic threat," that is, as practically equivalent to an Arab presence.[2] But as we shall see, any blurring of the distinction between Thais and Jews is also perceived as endangering the community's integrity; hence the need to maintain Thais as politically neutral and their labor as a nonphenomenon, a "nothing to see here," a widely known fact that is nevertheless only mentioned publicly in cautiously circumscribed contexts, while images which dissemble and disavow it are preferentially disseminated.

The forms of difference generated at the scale of the farm, as discussed in the previous chapter, are of great use in producing this neutrality. But just as crucial is the labor that migrants perform when moving through the *moshav*'s public spaces, where the finely tuned tact they bring from home enables them to pick up on the none-too-subtle cues scattered by Israelis. As we move from the private realm into the brightly lit public sphere, though, it is worth noting how the paternalistic pattern of labor relations works to conceal itself from public view, much as the privacy of family relations functions to conceal domestic violence and legitimize the oppression of women and children.[3] This is the context in which employers of Thai migrants demand that the police "discard or suspend considerations of lawfulness and formality," that is, desist from its feeble attempts at enforcing the law, for the surprising reason that "they are dealing with extremely delicate family relationships to which policing simply does not belong."[4]

Why do migrants collaborate with a social arrangement that demeans them and denies their contribution to the community's well-being? Two possibilities, neither of them adequate, immediately present themselves. The first is that Thai migrants undertake "face-work" for the same reason they undertake waged work: because they must do so to make a living. But while the "dull compulsion" of poverty back home certainly plays a role, by itself it cannot explain migrants' compliance with tasks that neither their contracts nor their bosses have explicitly assigned to them. In fact, the stringencies of the migration regime make it quite difficult to punish workers for behaving in ways that their employers might see as compromising the social fabric of the *moshav*. The second possibility, that "Thai culture" naturally renders migrants obedient and tactful, is eagerly taken up by employers and organizations involved in the migration regime, like the quasi-nongovernmental Center for International Migration and Integration.[5] This interpretation has the advantage of conforming to the ways Israelis (including myself) tend to experience Thai behavior in public space, but it is also woefully inadequate. As the historical discussion in Chapter 2 has shown, Isaanites have been known to rebel frequently and passionately against the predations of the Thai state and its associated elites, and as Chapter 4 has shown, they are willing and able to exercise power in defense of their autonomy at work. Similarly, as we shall see in this chapter, when invited into a public sphere where criticism of their situation in Israel is legitimized, workers take part with alacrity.

There is thus a need for an interpretive middle way between the smug reification of cultural difference and its blanket disavowal, for a hermeneutic that pays attention both to the histories that give rise to such difference and to the material contexts in which it plays out. Care for the social body and attendance to its face are some of the precious skills that have rendered Isaanites such an attractive workforce for the Arabah's employers. But these skills and the interaction ideology that undergirds them are in no sense imponderable: they spring from Isaanite proletarians' history of unequal integration into the "geo-body" of modern Thailand, which has been accompanied by the deliberate, top-down fortification of paternalistic social relations.

On arrival in Israel, migrants encounter a no-less-specific ideology of interaction: the valorization of sincerity and straightforwardness known as the *dugri* attitude, deliberately propagated as an integral part of the labor settlement movement's exclusionary egalitarianism.[6] This interaction ideology allows settlers to misrecognize migrants' skilled face-work as either a spontaneous expression of their upbringing or as a façade—a suspicion anchored in a deep history of Orientalist racialization and reflected in anxieties about the unruly figure of the drunk, violent "nighttime Thai." The meeting between Israeli settlers and Thai migrants is a contingent encounter between interaction ideologies forged independently, as part of the emergence of colonial capitalism in the two countries. While the structural misunderstanding that subtends the "temporary equilibrium" in Ein Amal is in many ways contingent, it is also stabilized and naturalized by the capitalist-colonial migration regime to which migrants are subjected in Israel. Of course, this does not mean that the *taylandim* will carry on obliging their Israeli employers forever.

The chapter begins on a theoretical footing, discussing the analytical notion of "face" and arguing that migrants' contribution to the community in what Max Gluckman calls "the analytic sense" consists precisely in their self-erasure from that community's public visage. This argument is then substantiated through an examination of two potentially explosive realms of public behavior: the purchase of consumption goods, and the display of sexuality. In the first case, I argue, paternalist relations and Israeli sensitivities encourage the segregation of migrant consumption through the institution of the "Thai shop." In the second, epitomized in the informal taboo on Thai entry to the public pool and expressed in the lyrics of migrant songwriter Sanya Hitakun, the sexuality of Thai men is neutralized. I then discuss two discursive artefacts that throw very different kinds of light on the question of migrant acquiescence. In a brochure disseminated by quasi-nongovernmental organization CIMI, instructing employers on how to manage interactions with their workers, the reification of paternalistic "Thai culture" reaches its apogee, while in the Facebook replies to a video series I coproduced with human rights NGO Workers' Hotline, workers emphatically reject the employer-dominated definition of the situation. I conclude by bringing settlers' interaction ideology—the *dugri* stance—into the discussion, demonstrating how this attitude enables settlers to misunderstand the behavior of migrants in a manner conducive to maintaining their own self-image. The chapter ends by tying the local drama back into the backdrop of the capitalist-colonial world system, the ground for both the "dull compulsion" that enjoins workers to comply and the historical development of the two ideologies.

SAVING THE COMMUNITY'S FACE

The concept of "face" is a complex one, encapsulating both apparently universal concerns and the racializing history of the world-system. Its most influential proponent is doubtless Erving Goffman, whose sociological theory is often formulated in global terms but is in fact deeply anchored in the specificities of twentieth-century North America.[7] In presenting the concept, Goffman cites the work of the forgotten anthropologist Hsien-chin Hu (1944) on China.[8] Hu used the term to render two related Chinese terms, *lian* and *mianzi*, which British merchants had been translating to English as "face" since at least 1834.[9] The analysis of "face-work" has since been transported to a variety of cultural contexts with an ease that points at a shared underlying logic, in which the face is perceived as the proudest, most prominent, most representative part of the human body.[10] This logic certainly applies in both Thai and Hebrew usage: the terms for face, *naa* and *panim* or *partsuf* respectively, are used in quite similar metaphorical ways. Nevertheless, the concept of "face" remains marked by its travels, and especially by the Orientalist whiff of a category that frames Asians as invested in appearance rather than essence, at once "servile" and "inscrutable," and thus essentially untrustworthy.[11] Complicating matters further, as Hu points out, collectives—including nations—also possess faces that their individual members are liable to damage:

> Ego almost always belongs to a closely integrated group on which is
> reflected some of his glory or shame. His family, the wider community
> of friends, and his superiors all have an interest in his advancement

or set-backs. So a person does not simply "lose his own face." ... Many Chinese feel particularly embarrassed when meeting Americans in [the US]: they fear that by unwittingly breaking conventions they may "lose the face of their country."[12]

Like the transnational encounter described by Hu, this one too involves the faces of collectives ranging up to the scale of the nation as well as of individuals. The transindividual nature of face in the Chinese context—completely neglected by Goffman—once again recalls Aulino's notion of the social body. If a social body composed of unequal and integrated organs might have its own karma, perhaps it might also have a face? Aulino answers in the affirmative, explaining that the Thai social body

> comprises various parts, all of which have their place based on the rules of social hierarchy. Only certain individuals can act as the "face" of that body, directing its movement, at any given time. The "attention to" this collective requires the active surmising of these various roles and one's own place in the group, a set of perceptions engaged whenever multiple people are gathered together; the "care of" this body then occurs in the maintenance of harmonious relations and the proper following of whoever is in the lead at any given momen. . . . Thai social interactions abound with instances of indirectness and a glossing over of tensions for the maintenance of surface harmony, a way of behaving in public and semi-private arenas that de-emphasizes the individual as such and continually re-inscribes hierarchical positions between people.[13]

Exhortation to save the national body's face begins before migration: in an orientation for outgoing workers that I attended in Bangkok, a government official's promise of consular protection in exchange for good behavior drew on an implicit interpellation of migrants as responsible for maintaining the national image.[14] Upon arrival in the Arabah, migrants must quickly find their bearings in a social body that disdains obvious markers of status hierarchy, such as differences in dress and bodily bearing. For instance, Boy's first memory of Ein Amal was of bewilderment upon meeting Ya'ir, who "was dressed shabbily, like a worker." Workers often insist on maintaining other status distinctions as well, for example by refraining from riding in the front seats of cars or shaking hands with Israelis, behaviors that often disconcert their Israeli counterparts. In the case of Thais traveling for work in Israel, then, the social body iconizes at least two additional forms of social asymmetry, which are superimposed upon the immediate employment relation. First, there is the unequal position the two states each represent within the capitalist-colonial world order: a wealthy, "honorarily white" nation in need of cheap labor,[15] and a middle-income Asian country whose elites are eager to provide such labor in exchange for hard currency and social peace. Second, there is the disparity between the status that migrants and settlers each hold within their respective national collectives. As shown in Chapter 2, both the Israeli and the Thai states have historically valorized agricultural settlement, but whereas in Israel LSM settlers have deftly used the ideological credit acquired in their role as "salt of the earth" to justify their transformation into rural capitalists, the supposedly authentic, self-sufficient Thainess of Isaanite peasants is used rather to justify their entrapment in poverty and deny them the fruits of modernity for which they have repeatedly organized.[16]

The social body that emerges in Ein Amal is thus a semiotic bundle that can be read in different ways: as composed of bosses and workers, "whites" and "Asians," or pioneers and peasants. Regardless of the reading chosen, however, one party occupies the position of the community's "head" and the other plays the role of a lowlier organ—perhaps the back, to borrow an image used by songwriter Sanya Hitakun (see below). Thanks to the iconic connections that link these asymmetrical binaries—Israel/Thailand, white/Asian, settler/migrant, and head/back—an examination of this composite local social body can expose what Michael Herzfeld describes as "the very aspects of the larger worlds . . . that national and international leaders would prefer to suppress."[17]

The term "community" itself is highly polysemic. Often it is used ideologically, to represent a group of individuals as enjoying shared interests and harmonious relations,[18] but in English the word also can also refer more neutrally to a collective defined by proximal habitation. In Israeli Hebrew the semantic field is divided differently: the term *kehila* is used for "community" in the ideological sense, while the generic term for locality is *yishuv*, which can also mean "settlement" in the colonial sense. Moreover, "community" also has an analytical sense, developed by Max Gluckman in explicit opposition to the ruling ideology that denied the possibility of interracial community in South Africa. Whether or not residents of Zululand saw themselves as members of the same community, Gluckman insisted that their relations could "be studied as social norms, as is shown by the way in which Blacks and Whites, without constraint, adapt their behaviour to one another." From this he deduced "the existence of a single Black-White community"[19] evinced by a "temporary equilibrium," in which

> [t]he White group is dominant over the Black group in all the activities in which they co-operate, and this dominance is expressed in some social institutions, while all institutions are affected by it. The unequal opposition between the two Colour-groups determines the mode of their co-operation.[20]

Paradoxically, then, it is only through migrants' participation in the community in the analytical sense that it becomes plausible to exclude them from the community in the ideological sense. But the "superior force" that Gluckman wishes to exclude from his analysis is key to understanding the "temporary equilibrium" achieved in the settlements of the Arabah.

SEGREGATION AND AVOIDANCE IN EIN AMAL

Timothy Pachirat's *Every Twelve Seconds* describes how marginalized people and the stigmatized jobs they do are hidden away from those who enjoy the products and profits of their labor.[21] Like Marx's "abode of production," where the worker goes to be skinned, the Nebraska slaughterhouses in which Latin American migrants butcher cows are ensconced by material and legal screens designed to deflect inquiring eyes. As we have already seen, the situation in Ein Amal is different:

the people doing the labor are marginalized here as well, but the work itself is neither stigmatized nor hidden away, nor can it be so long as the settlement remains dependent on agriculture for its legitimacy as well as its livelihood. This situation requires a subtler "politics of sight" than the one uncovered by Pachirat, a politics in which marginalized workers must collude if it is to successfully achieve its goals. In this section, I show how the segregation of time and space is achieved at the scale of the *moshav*. By and large, this segregation is informal, guided by an interaction ideology that requires migrants to participate in defending the face of the community. Where the maintenance of this face demands invisibility and neutrality, they do their best to become invisible and neutral.

As we have seen, agricultural holdings in Ein Amal are discontinuous: farmhouses, operational areas, and workers' quarters are clustered together on the small homesteads that form the center of the settlement.[22] Fields are scattered around this center, and a farmer like Ya'ir may have greenhouses in several locations around the *moshav*, sometimes as far as five or six kilometers from the homestead and each other. Workers transiting to the fields and back on slow-moving flatbed trailers like the one I rode in the previous chapter must use roads that pass through the center of the *moshav*, becoming visible in its most public spaces. But just because the workers are visible doesn't mean that many Israelis are there to see them: work is structured to make optimal use of cool hours and limited by the darkness of night. Production in the fields begins at sunrise and ends at sunset, though work in packinghouses—some of which are in the operational areas of the homesteads and some in an industrial zone on the outskirts of the *moshav*—can go on into the night. During the broiling days of the long summer, work stops during the hottest hours in the early afternoon. Thus Thais can be seen moving through the streets at dawn and around sunset, as well as—in the summer—around noon and again in the afternoon, on the way to their siesta and back. The movements of the nonfarming population of Ein Amal take place at complementary hours: they leave for work and school in the midmorning and return in the midafternoon.

FIGURE 5.1

Thai and Israeli movements through Ein Amal on a diurnal scale.
Diagram by the author.

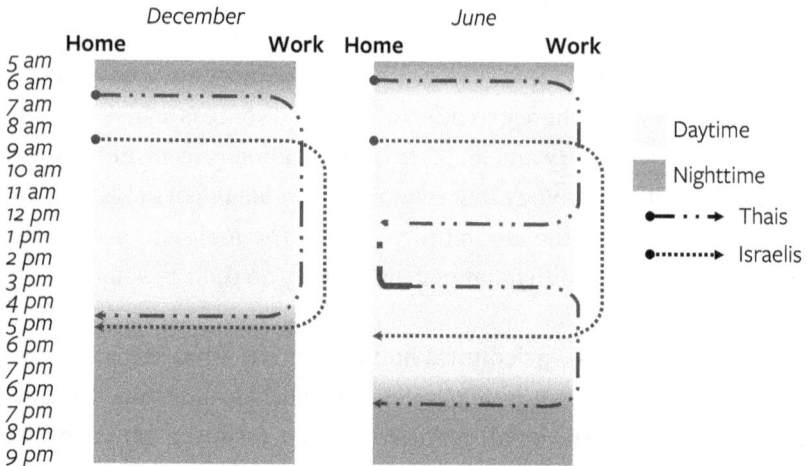

The following diagram represents this diurnal segregation schematically. As it shows, except for a certain amount of overlap on winter afternoons, the different rhythms of Israeli and Thai movements in the *moshav* have the effect of putting each one out of the other's way.

At first glance this result is fortuitous, but a closer look reveals the power relationships involved. Israelis' work and school day is unaffected by seasonal variations because it takes place indoors, where air-conditioning and artificial lighting provide the necessary conditions year-round. Work is limited to eight hours by legal stipulations and the division of reproductive labor that requires women to attend to childcare.[23] But neither labor law (which goes unenforced, as we have seen) nor the need to participate in the intergenerational reproduction of labor-power—a task carried out largely by their female kin in Isaan (see Chapter 6)—restrains the exploitation of migrant workers. Their workday is limited only by heat and light: during the hottest hours in summer, when temperatures in the greenhouses rise above 55 degrees Celsius, it is simply impossible to work, as is also the case before dawn and after dusk. Given the overall shortage of manpower and the illegally low price of Thai labor-power, employers are generally happy to operate overtime, and the workday is almost always over ten hours long, continuing in the packinghouses after it gets dark outdoors.

Thais do, however, have time off in the evenings and on Saturdays, and in the times and spaces of leisure, opportunities for more intensive interaction between Israelis and Thais arise.[24] One instance of relatively harmonious interaction is afforded by the playing field, which was shared equitably, even communally, between young Thai and Israeli men. Many Thais spent free time, especially on Saturdays, playing soccer and *takrau*, the Southeast Asian "kick volleyball." A veteran worker would periodically organize soccer tournaments pitting one farm's workers against another's, and even run-offs featuring the best teams from each *moshav* in the region. These affairs were taken seriously, and workers expected their employers to donate uniforms bearing their logo for the greater glory of the farm.[25]

Such elaborate projects presumed free access to *moshav* playing fields. I do not know whether this resulted from an explicit decision of the *moshav* authorities or from a lack of Israeli demand for the facilities, but Thai use of the playing fields was generally approved of, and Israelis would sometimes congregate to watch them play soccer and especially the more exotic and spectacular *takrau*. Pickup soccer in the evenings and on weekends was probably the most integrated pastime in the *moshav*, regularly featuring spontaneous games with mixed teams of Thais and Israelis. Finally, in a carnivalesque inversion of the norm, on the unusually rainy Songkran of 2016, the Thai New Year's Day traditionally celebrated with much splashing of water, the roadways of the *moshav* were turned over to a procession of soaked Thai revelers on flower-decked tractors and trailers while Israelis made themselves scarce.[26]

But sport as a shared pastime (significantly, involving men only) and the uniquely inverted circumstances of Songkran 2016 are the exception rather than the rule. The only public spaces in the *moshav* that were permanently coded as belonging to Thais were the two shops catering specifically to them, known to Israelis as *taylandiyot*[27] and to Thais simply by the English word *shop* (pronounced *chaup*). Some differences could be noted between the *shop nauy* and *shop yay* ("small" and "big" shop in Thai respectively), each privately owned by an Israeli and operated by Thais: the *shop nauy* was small, dim, and run by a couple who were, by Thai standards, extraordinarily surly and impolite. My Thai colleagues agreed with me that it was worth taking the time to travel to the *shop yay* to get better deals in a more congenial atmosphere. In addition to offering a large selection of culinary merchandise imported especially for Thais and generic groceries, the shops also served as recreational spots featuring billiard tables and shaded outdoor spaces for drinking and socializing. Israelis like me frequented the Thai shops, especially when the *moshav* supermarket was closed, but we had to adjust our sensibilities to sights such as tightly packed live fish and severed pigs' heads, both often stored in makeshift buckets made of recycled paint canisters. If they were to maintain a diet at all like what they were used to, local Thais needed access to affordable products like these, many of which could not be

FIGURES 5.2A–5.2D

Commodities on display in a "Thai shop" in the Arabah. Photographs by Iair G. Or.

sold in the *moshav*'s supermarket due to Jewish dietary restrictions, health regulations, or settler sensibilities (and in the case of the pigs' heads, probably all three).

These shops were quite different in ambience and function from the supermarket, which—despite sporting some signage in Thai—was a markedly Israeli space that Thais generally avoided entering. One colleague at my first job, for example, had a hankering for white bread, and asked me to purchase it for him in the supermarket. The issue could hardly have been the price—he could easily pay 4.5 shekels (around $1.25) for a loaf, and indeed offered to. When I asked him why he did not go to the supermarket to buy the bread himself, he shrugged shyly and refused to answer. I raised this issue in an interview with Ya'ir's worker Mike, who also never entered the supermarket despite living much closer to it than he did to either of the Thai shops. Mike ruled out the explanation I suggested: the prices of commodities available at both the supermarket and the Thai shop were higher in the latter. Rather, he explained, he and his friends preferred to shop there because the owner had an arrangement with Ya'ir to deduct his workers' expenditures directly from their wages, such that they did not have to carry cash. Rather taken aback, I asked Mike if it was difficult for the workers to receive cash advances from Ya'ir. Not at all, he said, but it was better not to, since if workers like himself had cash, they would fritter it away.

Mike's view was counterintuitive to me, since I tend to see credit as more conducive to careless spending than cash, whose waxing and waning are materially palpable and therefore ostensibly more manageable.[28] But Mike was reasoning in terms of a different moral economy, which will be discussed in greater detail in the next chapter. In this economy, the highest moral value is granted to remittances, a form of money that remains virtual until it is withdrawn in Thailand; next come the necessities of life, which, however difficult to define, can be purchased at the Thai shop, at the supermarket, or through the employer's mediation, as electronics like cell phones often were. Finally, there were the illicit or semi-illicit pleasures that Thais in Israel procured from one another—including gambling and drugs. These could be bought only with cash or through risky and expensive informal loans.

Mike, as the reader will recall, was the "baby" of the farm, the youngest of the workers. With no wife or children to take care of at home, both the Sadots and his colleagues considered him prone to wasting money irresponsibly and in need of benevolent direction. Mike supported this view, gratefully accepting both Miri's affection and Ya'ir's "tough love"; thus it is not surprising that he would reiterate his commitment to this paternalistic ideology by presenting the expensive, exploitative arrangement at the Thai shop as more virtuous, precisely because it minimized his freedom to waste money and maximized his employer's control over his consumption. As we shall see in Chapter 6, workers and their relatives at home agreed that such paternalistic control was conducive to their own well-being. For my purposes here, however, two points are important to emphasize: first, that Mike understood his boss, Ya'ir, as responsible for his employees' welfare beyond the bounds of the employment contract and accepted the cost differential between the shop and the supermarket as the price of this benevolence. The second is that this paternalism operates through an institution that caters specifically to Thais. By extending his paternalistic influence over employees through the provision of credit at the Thai shop, Ya'ir helped to pull their potentially irksome consumption off the supermarket's public stage of amoral, one-off transactions and into a semiprivate domain of debt and paternal care, all while minimizing their capacity to damage the community's face.

DAYTIME THAIS AND NIGHTTIME THAIS

In many *moshavim* and *kibbutzim*, the swimming pool is the center of social life during the long summer; indeed, luxurious swimming pools have become a symbol of the labor settlement movement's aristocratic status, since urbanites and especially the Mizrahi residents of the nearby development towns were deprived of such amenities for many decades.[29] The adoration of the near-naked, athletic settler body, which I touched upon in Chapter 4, achieves its zenith with that body's characteristically active repose at the pool. This is particularly true of swimming pools in the Arabah, which are landscaped as verdant, shady oases set against the scorched browns and yellows of the desert, and host lawn games and snack bars. During the hot months in Ein Amal, the pool draws Israelis of all ages, most prominently parents with small children, teenagers, and young Israeli workers.

I never knew a Thai to go to the pool, though. In our interview, Boy told me that he had never set foot there in his four years at Ein Amal. No doubt this is in part because swimming and near-naked sunbathing are not popular pastimes in Thailand, where attitudes to bodily exposure are quite different, as we have seen. Nevertheless, several workers told me that in the past Thais had visited the pool, and others said they would like to go if they could. Workers in another *moshav* in the region told me that Thais were prohibited from entering the pool there, but I never found any official evidence for this. Apparently, like the boss's family house, the pool did not have to be officially forbidden for local Thais to understand that it was off-limits to them. Whatever the reasons, the Israeli residents were far from perturbed by the Thais' absence from this space of intense sociality and erotic display.

More broadly, the sexuality of Thai men appeared to the Israelis I spoke to as at once an issue and a nonissue, a subject of both anxiety and disavowal. Ya'ir's father, Roni, sang the praises of the Thais, telling me that with any other group of workers "there would be much more trouble" of a sexual kind. Thai men could not be perceived as sexually unthreatening without their cooperation, in the form of what Israelis perceive as timidity around local women. Yet my coworkers often expressed their appreciation for Israeli women and even asked, apparently in jest, if I would set them up with my female friends. However, when several of them had an opportunity to meet some of these friends at a party I held, they acted shy and did not make any moves.

Despite this apparent docility, a certain dark border of danger appeared in settlers' comments about Thai workers from time to time. For example, Ya'ir's wife, Miri, told me that at night she preferred her teenage children to drive rather than walk around the *moshav*, "because a lot of men are around." Her comment raises the possibility that Thais are perceived as more threatening at night. In 1999 Erik Cohen wrote that

though Thais and farmers generally live their after-hours lives sepa-
rately, their physical proximity has begun to show Israelis a different
side to their employees, when these remove the protective façade of
a quiet, obedient worker: it turns out that they often get drunk and
subsequently make noise, fight and even hurt each other physically;
sometimes they secretly pilfer chickens, fruit or vegetables from their
employers, and hunt [wild] animals. The positive impression the Thais
initially left on their employers has gradually been tarnished by these
discoveries; as one ['Thai coordinator,' see Chapter 3] commented: it
turns out that there are "daytime Thais and nighttime Thais."[30]

The notion of "nighttime Thais" who reveal the seedy reality be-
neath the docile and submissive veneer is quite compatible with the
Orientalist suspicion that migrants' attention to the social body is a ma-
nipulative dissimulation. Moreover, the connection drawn by Cohen
between nocturnal drinking and the loosening of social norms is not
entirely spurious: I spent a few nights drinking with the Thai workers of
the Sadot farm, and though I never witnessed any form of harassment
or violence, the deference I had gotten used to was entirely dropped.
Likewise, there is evidence that Thais in Israel do hunt and eat wild animals, just as they do at home, though the calumny that accuses them of
eating cats and dogs is almost certainly false.[31] As for violence, though
the isolated rape and murder of an Israeli woman by a Thai worker in
Kibbutz Naan in 1999 is still remembered by some, Thai-on-Thai violence, which is more common, rarely draws public attention.[32]

The danger posed by Thai transgression of invisible boundaries is
brought home in the richly associative lyrics of migrant songwriter
Sanya Hitakun, whose song "Falling in Love with an Israeli Woman"
appears in Phaksornkan Thongkam's English translation in Shahar
Shoham's MA thesis, "Pickers and Packers: Translocal Narratives of
Returning Thai Agriculture Labour Migrants from Israel."

I know I'm just a Thai worker, exposing to the sun (working under the
    sun) and having dark skin
And I'm not brave enough to court you
I'm just a dark skin migrant worker

Looking at your white face

It's so pretty like a peeled egg (you're perfectly white and beautiful)

But look at my back, it's all striped and sloughed

Some of them can be healed but some can't

Just like a cow's back

I want to get close to you

But I'm just afraid that your beauty will be gone (get stained) because
   of me

Yet staying away from you makes me feel discouraged

If my Jewish friends know, they will laugh at me and tease me

I'm afraid of being laughed at and teased that the dark boy falls in love
   with Farang girl

So I have to love you secretly because I don't want to hear the things
   they say

I'm afraid of people comparing you like a swan but I'm just like a
   crow

That's why I'd better not tell you and court the daughter of Jewish
   people.[33]

The song is a gold mine of insight on gender, race, and class relations between Thai migrants and Israelis. Here it will suffice to point out the protagonist's acute awareness of the way the color and texture of his skin, which he compares to that of the *khwaai* or water buffalo (commonly associated with Isaanites—see Chapter 2), forms part of a semiotic bundle that indexes a lifetime of exposure to the sun and thus inferiority to the "perfectly white and beautiful" *face* of the beloved. More than rejection by the woman, he fears the derision of his "Jewish friends," punishment for impudently "staining the beauty" of the beloved's face, and with it the face of the *farang* or white community to which she belongs. Sanya's shame, described as resulting from the imagined response of Israelis to his infatuation, bluntly affirms his subaltern status as well as his understanding of sexual mixing as a severe violation of the social body's integrity.

Romantic relations between a Thai migrant and an Israeli woman might be conducive to the man's permanent settlement in Israel, which we have already mentioned as a possible source of "demographic" anxiety. But the threat to the Jewish community's face goes further than this, as Sanya clearly perceives. As in other colonial contexts, in Israel indigenous men are often imagined as hypermasculine and insatiably attracted to settler women, who are anxiously suspected of reciprocating their affections.[34] In Israel, again as in most such contexts, the settler group is imagined as light-skinned and the colonized group as dark (although in reality both Israeli Jews and Palestinians run the full gamut of skin color). Visible romantic relationships between dark non-Jewish men and Jewish women are thus perceived as a violation of the Jewish community's face, and trigger organized, violent reactions.[35] That Thais are not seen as a threat of this sort, or not unambiguously so, also testifies to a difference between them and Arabs that is salient to settlers. In this light, Sanya's abstention from declaring his love to an "Israeli woman" is an acceptance not of invisibility—he appears in almost all the photos featured in the song's YouTube video, in most of them together with Israeli women—but of neutralization. It is a blunt affirmation of acquiescence to his inferior position in the racial hierarchy and the correlative prohibition of sexual initiative toward women of the dominant racial category.

The work of politically neutralizing Thai men's sexuality is smoothed along by global racial ideologies that helped to frame Asian men as docile and asexual in the Israeli mind long before they became a common sight in the country. In the Atlantic world, where Asian "coolies" were often imported to break the resistance of black and indigenous populations to violent and exploitative relations, and where men of the latter groups were often pictured as hypersexual threats, the former were imagined as effeminate.[36] This global racial imaginary has long been present in Israel, though it has historically taken a back seat to the locally dominant scheme of racialization, wherein the primary opposition is between Jew and Arab.[37] But as the number of non-Jewish, non-Palestinian migrants in the country continues to grow, the two schemes are increasingly becoming articulated, with white supremacy making an appearance beside, and in support of, Jewish supremacy. As the black man, in the form of the East African asylum seeker, joins the Arab man as an anxiety-inducing presence, the Atlantic trope of the Asian man as unthreatening both at work and in the sexual sphere also becomes more discursively available to Israelis—though its dark double, the uncontrollable "nighttime Thai," lingers uneasily.

A STRUCTURAL MISUNDERSTANDING

Few things are easier to ignore than the work other people do for us, and if this applies to the work that the Thais of Ein Amal do on the clock, it is yet truer of the face-work they undertake when off it. But Arabah settlers' exceptional talent for ignoring their employees' face-work also owes something to their own ideology of interaction, which has been incisively analyzed by Tamar Katriel as one of talking and acting "straight," or *dugri* (from Turkish *doğru*, via Palestinian Arabic). Katriel's analysis dates from the 1980s, but the style she describes as prevailing among "the sons and daughters of immigrants of European origin who . . . became a culturally dominant group in the years preceding the establishment of the State"[38]—that is, in and around the LSM—characterizes subsequent generations of the milieu as well. Deliberately developed and promulgated by youth movements and the military, in conjunction with the "religion of labor" and in opposition to refined bourgeois sensibilities, the *dugri* ideology of sincerity, assertiveness, and "anti-style" pragmatism is used to "define the interactional context . . . as involving a conscious, hopefully consensual, suspension of face-concerns."[39] As an interaction ideology, *dugriyut* is defined by "respect for [the] conversational partner as a person who is strong and forthright enough to accept *dugri* talk" and the implication that "[p]eople who are overly concerned with their own face . . . prevent one from treating them with true respect."[40]

From the *dugri* perspective—whose roots might be traced to the Protestant ethic of sincerity and individualism—the Thai sensitivity to face concerns may appear put-on and superficial, in line with the racist tropes depicting Asians as inauthentic and dishonest thrown up by the history of the world-system. Israelis sometimes resort to such rhetoric, but far more often they seem to take Thais' face-work at face value, as an expression of inborn or, less contentiously, acquired character traits. As Katriel explains, the *dugri* sensibility encourages settlers not only to perform frankness themselves, but also to assume transparency in interactional partners as a matter of principle. By interpreting the subservient face presented to them as sincere, settlers can avail themselves of the obverse strand of imagery, which valorizes the Asian laborer on the basis of his supposed tractability. Thus Roni explained that what I had called the migrants' "shyness" around Israelis was caused by a "feeling of inferiority," and interpreted a worker's refusal to shake his hand as exemplifying a "culture of respect for those above" one in the hierarchy. Similarly, Thais' patience and diligence were associated with their Buddhist upbringing, with one farmer even speculating that they approached farmwork as a sort of meditation.[41] As we have seen, even employers' nostalgia for previous generations of workers was couched in language that framed the "Thais of old" as exemplars of cultural purity, uncorrupted by consumerism and urbanization—echoing similar tropes among the Thai elite.[42] The settlers' *dugri* attitude and their workers' attention to the social body thus combine, in an asymmetrical way, to provide settlers with a convenient pretext for structural misunderstanding. They are left free to interpret the obliging, patient, humble behavior of Thai interlocutors not as fulfilling a role within the social body—an interpretation that would entail a recognition of their own responsibilities—but as the unproblematic outcome of an innate or cultivated proclivity to be satisfied with their lot.

Israelis' tendency to slip from empirical observation of the obvious differences in interactional norms between Israelis and Thais into a self-interested reification of "Thai culture" is exemplified in a brochure aspiring to provide employers with tips "for effective work in a multicultural environment," produced in 2017 by CIMI, the quasi-NGO tasked with oversight under the bilateral agreement governing the migration regime (see Chapter 3). The brochure's cover (Figure 5.3) exemplifies its vision of an orderly and harmonious agricultural labor process, with sartorial markings clearly differentiating the Thai and Israeli members of the social body.

FIGURE 5.3

The cover page of "Tools for effective work in a multicultural environment with workers coming from Thailand: A brochure for employers and labor managers in the agricultural sector." CIMI 2017.

"Thai culture," says the brochure,

> places great importance on maintaining dignity[*] and avoiding causing others to lose face[*] at any cost. Insulting someone in public is unacceptable in Thailand and must be avoided. In Thailand it is customary to show great and special appreciation for people in authority, especially older people with a respected role. . . . Thai culture aspires to a state of balance, calm and self-control. Thais do not express feelings in public, especially feelings of anger, sadness or disagreement.[43]

There is something uncanny about this text. As a description of normative behavior among Thais in Israel, it is not particularly inaccurate, and there is much in it that would be of immediate value to Israelis interacting with Thais, naturally including employers. To the latter, the brochure explicitly recommends adapting a paternalistic role:

> [T]he employer is seen as a patron, that is, an adult responsible for the workers, much like a father. . . . Thai workers will find it hard to work faithfully if their employers do not care for their needs and show an interest in them.

As we have seen in the case of the Sadot farm, paternalism is indeed a viable strategy for managing labor relations between Thai workers and Israeli employers, and a skill that the latter must learn. But as we have also seen, in Ein Amal such relations are strictly expunged from the public sphere. Reflecting this disavowal, the CIMI brochure is mostly silent on questions of public culture, only suggesting meekly that workers might "appreciate . . . invitations to participate in events or holidays of the Israeli community," and that it is "possible to visit during workers' holidays and contribute to their activities, for example by . . . providing sports equipment."

CIMI's avoidance of the public sphere in this brochure is striking in comparison to the active involvement of intermediary actors in the migration regime in planning and undertaking public events during the 1990s (see Chapter 3). Today even suggesting such events, not to mention organizing them, may seem like an invitation to xenophobic backlash; better to confine attempts at amelioration to the private sphere, then. But the right to be visible in public and the right to bear rights as a liberal political subject are, of course, intimately related.[44] Thus, whatever its tactical justification in this case, the effacement of Thais from public space strongly reinforces their de facto neutralization as potential members of the community protected by law.

WHEN THE SUBALTERN SPEAKS

The image of the naturally obedient *taylandi* is just an image, as the long history of Isaanites' undeferential political behavior described in Chapter 2 shows. Indeed, masses of Isaanites in Bangkok and throughout the country had participated in resistance against the military coup of 2014, only a year before my fieldwork began.[45] Careful examination of evidence from Israel will also show numerous instances of Thai migrants resisting their exploitation—for example by turning to Workers' Hotline for enforcement of their legal rights, by striking, suing employers, or simply refusing orders, as Dii did in the episode discussed in Chapter 4.[46] And though they are barred from expressing their feelings about life in Israel in the country's public sphere, migrants are in no way reticent about doing so in the alternative public sphere of Facebook groups. Here the language is Thai (Central or the Isaan dialect) rather than Hebrew or English, pseudonyms provide anonymity, and anger at the violation of their rights is voiced freely. I came into contact with this sphere in 2018, when together with Adi Behar of Workers' Hotline, I hosted a four-part web series titled *Cheewit nay Israel*, or "Life in Israel," in which we offered to answer any questions migrants might have.[47]

On the strength of previous experience holding an impromptu Q&A session at an employee training session in Isaan in 2017, I expected some lighthearted or general-interest questions, and planned to interleave responses to these with "serious" information about legal rights and the like. But nearly all the seventy reactions to the video Workers' Hotline posted on Facebook inviting questions were serious in tone. Almost half the questions we received had to do with wages and adjacent issues (such as workman's compensation and taxes), and most of the rest were also work-related; none at all were about Israeli culture or public life. Most respondents seemed painfully aware that their legal rights were not being respected, and many of their comments had a bitter, cynical tone. For example, in response to a worker who wrote that "90 percent of workers are not paid according to the law," another answered: "The Thai government has said in a statement that in fact less than 5 percent are paid below the minimum wage. Unfortunately, we happen to be employed by this 5 percent of employers!" adding "555555," internet slang for laughter.

This collective bitterness—in 2016, *all* the Thai migrants queried by Nona Kushnirovich and Rebeca Raijman reported known violations of their contract[48]—coexists with what the CIMI brochure calls "balance, calm and self-control" by virtue of the constitution of parallel public spheres. The particularities of how face concerns are addressed on social media are beyond my analysis here;[49] nevertheless, one obvious difference between Ein Amal and the Facebook group in which *Cheewit* was publicized is the presence in the former, and absence in the latter, of dominant actors identified with the migration regime.[50] Though I appeared in both, I played very different roles: in Ein Amal, I was an acquaintance and coworker known to be friendly with the boss, who undertook interviews with the help of a locally based interpreter; in *Cheewit*, I spoke (broken) Thai by the side of a fluent Thai speaker in a setting framed explicitly through the defense of migrant workers' rights. In this light it is no surprise that issues like the violation of wage law, which never even came up in my interviews in Ein Amal, could become the object of shared sarcasm.

Cheewit nay Israel offered me a glimpse into a realm of discourse where migrants' anger and frustration at exploitation and hypocrisy are made explicit—approaching what James Scott would term a "hidden transcript."[51] But rather than hidden, it would be more accurate to describe this transcript as discreet: like the migrants of Ein Amal themselves, it pulls out of the way of the hegemonic gaze, but stretches out in relief when it encounters safe and welcoming spaces.[52] After all, domination depends for its stability on the public acquiescence of the dominated, and there are many other situations in which subalterns collude with superordinates to dissemble the coercive nature of the relationship to outsiders, including ethnographers, as well as to themselves.[53] In this case, too, Thais' highly developed talent for discretion might leave them more freedom to act differently when circumstances permit than is available to Israelis of labor settlement background, trapped as we are in our *dugri* ethos of sincerity and "straight talk."[54] For an online social body defined by the role of a human rights organization as host, of workers as rights-bearing participants, and of both the Thai state and Israeli employers as morally legitimate adversaries, workers could tactfully readjust their discourse. Under such circumstances, perhaps, the social body could become less rigidly hierarchical and more reminiscent of a *communitas* of struggle.[55]

———

The interaction ideologies described in this chapter, whether Thai or Israeli in origin, are not deliberately taken discursive positions, but neither are they spontaneous outgrowths of irreducibly particular "cultures," as one might appear from the vantage point of the other. Israelis are more susceptible to this illusion, not only because it serves their interest in self-justification but also because, as Katriel points out, their own ideology of interaction insists on interpreting the discourse of interlocutors as either sincere or duplicitous. In this schema, which leaves no room for a nuanced recognition of context as impacting the truth value of an interlocutor's speech, it makes sense to take migrants' behavior as a straightforward representation of their "culture."

The *taylandim* come to the encounter with a more sophisticated toolbox. The history of their hierarchical integration into the Thai polity endows Isaanite migrants not with a rigid proclivity to deferential patterns of behavior, but with a skill that enables them to implicitly recognize hierarchical social bodies and find their place therein rapidly and smoothly. This skill is as relevant for the ideologically reproductive labor that they undertake in Ein Amal's streets as their embodied skills are for the productive labor they do in its fields. But planting remains work—and hard work at that—even when you know how to squat, and so does keeping the social body together, even when one's tact and grace are well-developed. In other words, face-work *is work*, work that the Thais of the Arabah perform faithfully and without monetary compensation. As such, it is intimately related to the activities of migrants' kinspeople back home—reproductive labor undertaken in Isaan, but essential to the reproduction of Ein Amal.

6 SOCIAL REPRODUCTION AND KARMIC RECIPROCITY

AS WE HAVE SEEN, OVER the past generation Israeli settlements in the Arabah have become dependent on a flow of cheap, docile, and productive labor-power from northeastern Thailand. The reproduction of this flow depends on a constant input of unpaid labor from migrants' kin in Isaan. While much of this labor is invested in what Burawoy calls "renewal"—the production of a new generation of workers to replace those who have finished their tenure in Israel—kinspeople also invest quite a bit of effort into the "maintenance" of migrants' capacity to labor from day to day. Migrants, relatives, and employers all understand that the emotional turmoil engendered by long-term transnational migration can cause workers to lose their motivation, cutting into profits and remittances and triggering further trouble. Here again, as in the "private" space of the farm explored in Chapter 3, it is Isaanites—both in Israel and back home—who set the paternalist framework of relations, and savvy employers like Ya'ir who accept their terms.

This chapter begins with an introduction to the matrifocal Isaan family, which provides women with a degree of control over family life and enables the intergenerational reproduction of labor-power despite the common hazard of divorce. Based on research showing that Isaan families who send their men abroad do so to maintain rather than enhance their class position, I turn to an ethnographic exploration of how these families reproduce themselves through migration. After a brief return visit to Song, who leveraged her ties with the Sadot family to exercise control over the younger generation of her family, I turn to Daeng, whose marriage fell apart while he was in Israel, triggering a spiral of anger, despair, and drug abuse; and to Boy and Moon, who undertook Boy's migration as a joint sacrifice for the sake of their family. The boss's paternalistic intervention plays a role in all these stories, and after relating them I return to karmic reciprocity as an ideology of interaction that makes moral sense of this intervention and enlists it in support of the Isaan family's own reproduction.

ISAAN FAMILIES AND THE REPRODUCTION OF THE MIGRANT FLOW

Though gender relations in Southeast Asia are strikingly different from those prevailing in the "West," recent scholarship, and especially feminist scholarship, has complicated earlier writers' simplistic stipulation that women in the region enjoy high status.[1] As in most parts of the world, in Southeast Asia in general and Isaan in particular women are expected to shoulder the great bulk of reproductive labor without recompense and are exposed to the threat of gendered violence when they resist.[2] As we have seen, female Thai workers in Israel are particularly exposed to sexual violence and pressured to find a sexual patron to minimize their exposure to assault.[3] And as the continued relevance of paternalism as a model of hierarchical relations makes clear, Thai society is fundamentally structured by men's patriarchal oppression and exploitation of women and other nonmen.[4]

Nonetheless, gender and family structures in Isaan sport several features that help women push back against male domination, including bilateral kinship, easy divorce, preference for daughters in inheritance, and a multigenerational kinship structure that revolves around the bond between mothers and daughters. Generally speaking—exceptions are common—the pivot of Isaanite women's lives is their parents' home and village. If they migrate, they expect to return when their parents grow old and require their assistance; if they have children they cannot take care of due to the demands of wage labor, they leave them in their mothers' care and remit income to contribute to their upkeep.[5] These children are considered to belong to both parents' families, but in cases of divorce and conflict over custody, they usually remain with their maternal kin. Similarly, both sons and daughters can inherit at their parents' discretion, but daughters are often rewarded for their care by inheriting more.[6]

Men, especially working-class men, lead a more peripatetic existence, "free to migrate largely unencumbered by domestic responsibilities . . . socialized to be independent, self-determining individuals" with looser ties to natal families and villages.[7] Daughters are considered more economically valuable to their parents than sons, and bridal payments (*khaa sin sot*) are thought of as economic compensation for a daughter's lost services.[8] If men are not to end up alone in their old age—a fate most women do not have to worry about—they must be careful to cultivate relationships with younger people (not necessarily their biological children) who will feel obligated to care for them in turn.[9] Finally, among the working class in Isaan and elsewhere in Thailand the matrimonial bond is relatively weak. Marriages are not always legally registered, and a religious ceremony or simple co-residence can suffice for the community to recognize a couple as married.[10] No-fault divorce can be initiated by either partner, and conflicts over common property and child custody are usually solved informally.[11] Sexual promiscuity is expected and even encouraged in men, and wealthy ones sometimes take second "minor" wives.[12] Female promiscuity carries some opprobrium, but divorcées and women who have had extramarital sex are not shunned as potential wives, and even those known to have undertaken sex work or partnerships of convenience are not necessarily at a disadvantage in starting new relationships.[13]

Many Israelis who come into contact with Thai migrants nurture the notion that "when they go home, they live like millionaires." Even employers who have visited their former workers in Isaan, no doubt encountering the same dirt floors, outdoor toilets, and sparse interiors that I saw, often repeat this contention. This may be an attempt to evade the guilt associated with the unsurprising truth that wages that can only support a low standard of living in Israel do much the same in Thailand; a half-willful naïveté about the supposed mystery of exchange rates also contributes to the obfuscation. But the fantasy also conforms to the perception, common in Israel, of migration as an exceptional windfall that sets lucky migrants apart from their neighbors.

This perception, to be blunt, has no basis in reality. Migration, whether internal or transnational, is a mass phenomenon touching families all over rural Isaan.[14] Many Isaanites spend large sums of money and a great deal of energy trying to get abroad, and many spend much of their adult lives away from home, migrating to several different countries in succession. The cost of living relative to returns from agriculture has grown greatly over the last thirty years, and expenditures that were negligible a generation ago, such as schooling, now weigh onerously on households.[15] The financialization that increasingly forces workers around the world to rely on debt falls especially heavily on rural Thais with no access to bank credit, who often resort to loan sharks who charge exorbitant rates.[16] Migration itself is almost always debt-financed, such that much of its "opportunity benefit"—the difference between what migrants earn abroad and what they could have earned at home during the same period, minus the costs incurred—is swallowed up by interest payments.[17] As we shall see, fraud by migration brokers is also extremely widespread and adds to many families' heavy burden of debt.[18]

An incisive mixed-methods study by a team of sociologists concludes that in Isaan migration is not a pathway to upward class mobility, but rather a move to stave off economic deterioration on which the entire rural community has become dependent. As the authors put it:

> The village continues to function, if not thrive, as a result of the returned migrants. We can speculate that without migration and return, these villages would be less sustainable communities. . . . [I]t is seldom that the migrant experience leads to new economic activity; not only do returnees return to their villages, but they also, largely, return to their old lives.[19]

PATERNALISM AT A DISTANCE

Militating against the sexist dismissal of reproductive work, recent advances in social reproduction theory have emphasized the dependence of capitalist production on unpaid reproductive labor, which takes place outside the workplace. My insistence that agricultural settlement in the Arabah depends on the continued flow of cheap labor from Isaan, which itself depends on unremunerated labor supplied by migrants' kin, is in line with this emphasis. However, the reverse is also true: the reproduction of the migrant family—and of the rural Isaan community itself—also depends on the wages that migrants earn in exchange for their participation in production. Family formations whose roots lie in a precapitalist era of independent subsistence production have become impossible to sustain without the wage and the commodities it can buy: this precisely is the proletarian condition. And while Israelis might be oblivious to the many ways in which reproductive labor undertaken in Isaan supports their way of life, migrants' kin are acutely aware of the role work in Israel plays in their own survival. They thus take an active role in sustaining the wage-labor relationship by inserting themselves—with migrating family members' tacit, sometimes grudging consent—into the latter's paternalistic relations with their employers.

The lax migration regime in place until 2004 was the perfect incubator for such transnational relations of paternalism. As we saw in Chapter 3, by giving favored workers the possibility of leveraging their connections with the employer to secure positions for others, including kin and friends, the "fax system" encouraged the development of a web of paternalistic relations connecting employers with generations of migrants from the same villages and families: in the case of multigenerational farming families like the Sadots, the paternalistic web encompassed kinship structures on the Israeli side as well.

Under this regime, some employers were willing to contribute to the work of stabilizing the intergenerational reproduction of Isaan families, which ensured the continuity of their labor force. Song, for instance, was able to leverage her relationship with the Sadot family farm in this way for a time after her return home. In the late 1990s she was able to secure positions in Ein Amal for her daughter, Jaeng, and her son-in-law, Teun, as well as two or three others from her village. Around 2001 Song finally returned home, after her daughter insisted that she was getting too old to work so hard. Soon after, Jaeng became pregnant, and the couple came home for the birth. They stayed in Thailand for over a year and when Jaeng conceived again, Teun went back to work for the Sadots in Israel. Alone away from home, Jaeng's husband began to neglect his duties. According to Song,

> he stopped sending money back to Thailand because he had a new girlfriend. My money was running out. I had bought a new car at the time and had to pay instalments at 8,000 baht a month. Neither my daughter nor I had money. So, I talked to Yehudit and Ya'ir, [and Teun] was sent home. I didn't let him come into my house, since he had no money, so he went to his mother's house. I told his mother that I didn't need him, I would send my daughter to [work in] Sweden.

At Jaeng's behest and following negotiations with Teun's parents, Song agreed to receive him back into her family, on the condition that the costs of financing the couple's onward migration would be shared by his parents. However, this support was not forthcoming, and Song was again left to cover the costs of the couple's trip. When we met in 2017, they were working in South Korea while Song took care of their two boys. Since they were now undocumented migrants, they could not risk leaving the country, and when I met the children, it had been seven years since they had seen their parents. Overall, Song estimated that the family had managed to save between one and two hundred thousand baht during their stay in Israel, but since Song was diagnosed with cancer, most of the money had been spent on medical fees.

The days of the fax system are long over, and it might be quite difficult for any worker arriving in Israel after the "closing of the skies" to exercise the same sort of influence over employers as Song did by getting Yehudit and Ya'ir to send Teun home. Nevertheless, both migrants and their relatives continue to rely on the moral judgment and practical power of employers to keep familial relationships on track.

It is true that the social costs of failure to maintain such long-distance relationships are not as high in Isaan as they might be elsewhere. Divorced women can draw on the help of their natal families to support their children, while men can go home to their own mothers, and both are free to search for new partners. But even these costs are far from negligible: migrant ex-husbands lose stand to lose savings, access to their children, and claims on their future support, while their ex-wives must find ways to provide for those children on severely reduced incomes. The transnational nuclear family can thus be thought of as a "social body" with its own karma, much like the farming household into which its migrating member is also integrated.

These two social bodies are themselves interconnected by a web of common interests, though tensions can also be observed. As apparent from the cases of the farm "baby" Mike (discussed in the previous chapter) and of Song's absconding son-in-law Teun, migrants' employers and their kin have a shared interest in maximizing workers' productivity as well as the portion thereof that is remitted. In an hourly wage regime, the length of the working day and week determines not only the profits of the employer, but magnitude of the wage to be shared between the migrant and his kinspeople. And the proportion of the wage remitted to those kinspeople is of interest not only to them, but also, as we have seen, to the settler community which is anxious to maintain the racial rule of difference between migrants and locals.

An individualistic reading of the concept, such as comes naturally to Israelis like myself, would lend itself to seeing this interest as common to kin and employers *against* migrants. At times the parties involved might be amenable to such an understanding as well, as Song certainly was when she mobilized Ya'ir to bring Teun to heel. But migrants themselves do not necessarily see things this way: karmic reciprocity enables them to understand both their families and the farms they work on as social bodies whose interest is best served by selfless action. Thus, from the migrant's point of view all three parties—the employer, the kinswoman, and himself—are drawn into a composite social body in which all have responsibilities toward one another, and in which neglect or wrongdoing on anyone's part is a cause not for retaliation but for forbearance. In a conflict between any two parties to the triadic relationship, the third's role is to deescalate tensions, as Ya'ir's role in Daeng's marital woes shall make clear.

DAENG BETRAYED

Daeng's tenure on the Sadot farm ended shortly after mine, and I met him again twice in the spring of 2017: once where he was working, in Sukhothai Province in northern Thailand, and again in his home village in Khon Kaen Province, in central Isaan. Though not far from the Friendship Highway, Isaan's main thoroughfare, the village was only reachable by an unpaved road. Research coordinator Mee and I were entertained in the front yard, surrounded by chicken coops, rather than inside the one-story, dirt-floored home. Daeng was born here in 1981. His parents left the village shortly after, and he was raised by his maternal grandmother as the youngest of her six children. He spent six years of his childhood as a *nen*, or novice, in a temple, where he was schooled and fed, lightening the load on his desperately poor family. As a young man, he found work in a shoe factory near his home village and got engaged. But to marry, Daeng required a bridal payment, and he realized that he could not amass the needed sum of about 150,000 baht while working at the shoe factory. When he met a recruiter looking for potential migrants to Taiwan, Daeng seized the opportunity; after a short interview in Bangkok, he was sent off to an electronics factory on the island, where he made about 23,000 baht (roughly $700) a month.

After more than two years, when he had saved the amount required for the bridal payment, Daeng returned to Isaan and married his fiancée. He spent six more months at the shoe factory, but by this time he had realized that he was a "person who likes challenges" (*khon mak thaathaay*), in search of new experiences (*prasopkan*), and when another recruiter came around, this time looking for men interested in working in Malaysia, he willingly forked over the 45,000-baht fee. But Malaysia was a mistake; the work, in carpentry, was hard, and he was cheated of some thirty or forty thousand baht in

wages. Immediately upon his return, he paid 70,000 baht to a recruiter who promised to get him a job in Israel, but the job never
materialized, and the recruiter disappeared. In the meantime, he returned to the shoe factory, where he progressed to a supervisory position; the owner even sent him on a three-month trip to train workers
in a sister factory in Vietnam. During this period he became a father,
and despite his promotion, his wage was still "only enough for living,
not for saving." When he won 200,000 baht in a lottery, this money,
together with the last of his savings from Taiwan, went toward the
350,000-baht fee that finally got him to Israel.[20] He arrived in Ein
Amal in July 2012. The farm he was assigned to was failing, and he
was often hired out to other farmers in the *moshav*, including Ya'ir
Sadot. Daeng liked Ya'ir, who was patient with his workers and took
care to explain tasks in detail. As work dwindled on the farm he was
posted to, and his income with it, he asked a friend who worked for
him if he might be able to secure a spot on the Sadot farm. After eight
months' wait, he was transferred.

Before his migration Daeng's marriage had been happy, and he felt
no concern when he left home. He sent all his remittances to his wife,
who used them to purchase farmland, a car, and a house. When their
child was old enough, Daeng got her a job in the department he had
supervised at the shoe factory. But when he came home for a three-
month vacation after several years in Israel, he felt that something
was wrong. While out walking, his wife hung back and would not let
him hold her hand. His suspicion grew when she declined to answer
incoming calls on her phone; when he asked who was calling, she insisted it was "just a friend." After his return to Israel, their relationship
grew even colder. His wife would never answer phone calls, and text
messages only rarely. One night in 2015, he hacked her Facebook account and confirmed his suspicions: she was carrying on an affair with
a mechanic he knew from the factory. "Aren't you afraid your husband
will find out?" asked the lover in one of their text exchanges. The next
morning, after breakfast, Daeng called his wife; this time she picked
up. She admitted to the affair and refused to end it. "If you can't take
it," she said simply, "let's break up."

In our first interview, held on the Sadot farm shortly after I had finished working there, Daeng did not go into detail about the affair and its aftermath, and I didn't push him. But when we met again in Isaan, he was candid: discovering his wife's infidelity had sent him into a tailspin. Previously he had been a model worker and husband (closely related roles, as we shall see). But on that day in May, exhaustion and despair fell upon him suddenly. Switching to his limited English, he described his emotional state at the time as "fire in my heart." When he asked Ya'ir for a vacation, so he could go home and confront his wife, the boss, worried that he would kill her, refused—a decision for which Daeng later expressed deep gratitude.[21] He turned to "ice," or methamphetamine, to deal with his pain.[22]

Daeng stayed on the farm for another year, until the end of his contract, but the wind had gone out of his sails. This year included my time on the farm, when he was noticeably jumpy and sullen, though I did not know the reasons for this at the time. Daeng no longer wanted to be *balabay*, resenting the extra work he had to do with no compensation, and claims that he did his best to shirk the role.[23] When Ya'ir suggested that he stay on illegally after the end of his contract, he declined and went home to his grandmother, to whom he had sent remittances over his last year in Israel. When we last spoke, Daeng had not yet attempted to initiate contact with his ex-wife in order to see his son; he was still afraid of how he would react to seeing her. When he started a new family, as he planned to do soon, he thought he would be sure enough of his self-control to attempt a meeting.

Things were tentatively looking up for Daeng when I met him in Thailand. After his return, he got a job driving a truck and delivering animal feed. But he had to carry an unlicensed handgun for protection, and once he was pulled over by police and had to pay a large bribe to stay out of jail. Subsequently he joined his brother, who ran a small business cleaning septic tanks with a specialized truck. Because other operators had monopolized the trade in their home province, Daeng and his brother had to work far afield, in Sukhothai Province in the country's north, where they rented a half-built house and slept in a tent in the living room to avoid the mosquitos. The money was good—about

30,000 baht a month, comparable to what he had earned in Ein Amal—but little remained of the fruits of his labor in Israel.

BOY MEETS MOON

When I met Moon in 2017, she was residing in her natal village together with her mother, a sister, and their children, all living in closely adjacent houses on the same lot. Pooling its income, the extended family managed to furnish the mother's house, on whose veranda we congregated in the evenings, with amenities including a tile floor and washing machine. But debt hung heavily over their heads and cropped up constantly in conversation. Though she was now living at home, Moon's life had been anything but sedentary. She had held a wide variety of jobs, lived all over Thailand, married three men, and given birth to five children, but continued to exude youthful energy. The love story between her and the much younger Boy is unusual, but not surprising once you have met her: Moon is a clear-sighted, sharp-tongued, charismatic woman who knows what she wants and does what she can to get it. In her own appraisal, though, she and her family have not been lucky. Their life, like Daeng's, has been a succession of difficult choices, culminating in Boy's long sojourn abroad, away from her and their children, including one he had yet to meet when I visited.[24]

The second of five children, Moon first left home at age thirteen for work in a textile factory in Bangkok, where at sixteen she met her first husband, an affluent twenty-three-year-old from northern Thailand who was addicted to womanizing, alcohol, and gambling.[25] After giving birth to two children, she found a lucrative quality control job in a factory, paying a generous monthly wage of 10,000 baht; but her husband loafed, spent her money on drink, and eventually turned violent. Moon left him for a new and seemingly more stable partner, who turned out to be just as untrustworthy, leaving her for another woman and disappearing with their son, her third child; Moon located them and took the child back, forcibly but ultimately without contest. Single again, she returned to her home district, where she worked a variety of jobs and started language studies to qualify for work in South Korea. At the end of the course, she accompanied some schoolmates on a merit-making trip to a village in a nearby district, where she met Boy.

Though it lies in the same province, Boy's village is much smaller and more isolated than Moon's. When I visited with Moon and her younger children, elders reminisced about the times when elephants stalked the surrounding forest and the only road out was infested with tigers. Both of Boy's parents are natives of the village, where they cultivated rice and cassava. His father spent some time working in Bangkok, but never went abroad; on his only attempt to do so, a planned trip to Brunei, he was defrauded. Boy, the second of three children, left school at fifteen and worked a succession of factory jobs in the Khorat metropolitan area until he met Moon at age eighteen. It was love at first sight, but only on Boy's end. The stricken youth began visiting Moon at work every week. Thirty-two and wary, she suggested that she could "love him like a big sister," and at first Boy accepted her offer, but as their friendship deepened, he confessed his desire and even kissed her in public, a very daring act. Moon refused to sleep with him and warned him off, making sure he was aware of both her children and her debts. Boy insisted, begging his mother in tears to ask for her hand. After holding out for a few months, his parents relented; filled with compassion (*hen jay*, literally "seeing [his] heart"), Moon agreed to the marriage.

After a three-month engagement, they were wed in a religious ceremony. Moon duly conceived her fourth child as Boy was conscripted into the army. She missed her opportunity to go to South Korea because of the pregnancy, so on his return from the military they hatched a plan to travel together to Israel, where many people from Boy's village had worked. Together with some of his relatives, they met with a recruiter who promised them jobs in return for a fee. But this recruiter was a con man who managed to embezzle over 100,000 baht from the couple; when he demanded another twenty thousand, Moon grew suspicious and went to the police, who confirmed that the couple had been cheated. The story garnered media attention, and Moon appeared on several television shows to tell her story. The cheating middleman was eventually apprehended, but her money was not recovered, and the episode left the growing family in even greater debt, with creditors threatening to repossess her mortgaged house.

Moon's failed business ventures, the couple's commonly shouldered child-raising expenses, and the fraud to which they had fallen victim together all contributed to the debt that pushed Boy onto the airplane bound for Israel. Like other young people in his village, he would have preferred to go to South Korea, where the work is easier and the pay better. He enrolled for work there too but was first selected for work in Israel under the new TIC scheme (see Chapter 3), so he decided not to keep waiting while the family's debt mushroomed, and took his chance.

Boy was picked up at the airport by representatives of the manpower agency which had placed him. His first year was stressful:

> The workers who had come before me said many things that made me anxious. Sometimes, I didn't understand the labor process; sometimes, the employer pressured me, asking me if I understood him; if I didn't understand, I would get yelled at.

But when I met him, near the end of his five-year term, Boy was spending about half of his time in the farm's cold storage room, making up orders from English-language forms filled in by Ya'ir and the Israeli workers. He had picked up far more English, including reading and writing, than the average worker, and was thus especially qualified for this work. He preferred working in the cold storage room because it enabled him to stay out of the sun, but despite his relatively light workload, Boy was the most critical of all my interviewees. He was the only one to venture the opinion that wages were unfairly low, given the tiring nature of the work.

I realized there was something special about Boy's relationship with his wife long before I met her. Whether he was packing vegetables or resting after hours, his phone would usually be propped up somewhere in the room, a video call to Isaan open on its screen, with Moon visible on the other end doing her chores. This level of technologically mediated intimacy was exceptional for the farm; though many of the other migrants called home regularly, none were in such intensive touch with their wives. When I did meet her, Moon made no effort to disguise the fact that this constant contact was partly due to her jealousy and desire to keep Boy in line. When I asked why they had initially wanted to migrate together, Boy explained that they could make more money that way; but Moon was clear that she "was afraid that a woman would deceive him, because to me he [seemed] young, so I wanted to take care of him myself."

This mix of suspicion and concern was quite typical of Moon's attitude to Boy. She took it particularly badly when, a few years back, some "girls from Myanmar" (probably student-workers; see Chapter 4, n. 14) had been employed on the farm. They had been talking on the phone when she heard female voices and demanded that he turn on his camera so she could see who was there, but he refused, kindling her mistrust. By the time we met, she was assured that Boy had "proven himself," and shifted the focus of her concern to his health, and specifically to his chronically runny nose. But whatever the focus of her surveillance, she attempted to recruit everyone who knew Boy to her aid, including his coworkers, his employer, and me.

KARMIC RECIPROCITY AND SOCIAL REPRODUCTION

In interviews, most of my coworkers declined to describe even the physical discomforts they endured in Israel in detail, much less expand on emotions like the sadness aroused by long absence from home, though such sadness was a theme of the music many of them listened and sang along to.[26] It was, however, possible to hear them speak of the effects of suffering on "workers" in general, a figure from which they maintained some individual distance. The migrants I spoke with understood the abuse of alcohol, gambling, and drugs as triggered by the "problems" (panhaa) they had to grapple with. This was not a denunciation of such pastimes: a few beers after work, more on the weekends, and the occasional game for money were standard and played an important role in the sociability of the laboring community. But some people drank and gambled more heavily and more often than others, with direct effects on themselves and their surroundings: they got into fights, lost money, and missed workdays due to hangovers.[27] Workers interpreted such excesses as both proceeding from and contributing to these migrants' unhappiness, usually due to worrying (*khit laay*, literally "thinking a lot") about family, money, or both.[28]

During a discussion of sudden nocturnal death (*laay taay*),[29] which was hypothetical since no one in Ein Amal had died this way for some time, Boy described a tangled web of causes that might conceivably lead to such deaths:

> I don't know, I've never seen it happen here. From what I see these days, Thai workers drink, and go to bed late so that they don't get enough sleep. They do exhausting work. Sometimes they sleep until late because they watch movies and listen to music. Some drink. Some gamble. They gamble all night, so they don't get to sleep. The next day, they go to work. This might be the cause.

Boy's description of how suffering may lead to more suffering and eventually to death—a bad death, far from home—is commonsensical.[30] It also coheres with the Buddhist vernacular understanding of karma. Here the karmic dynamic is ostensibly internal to the individual worker: if he meets his suffering with conditioned, addictive responses, it will spiral into more suffering. But interpersonal relations also prove essential to the process: for example, a migrant who neglects to send remittances may cause his wife to suspect and mistrust him, which could cause him to worry about her fidelity. To distract himself, he might drink, gamble, stay up late, waste money, miss work or work badly, anger his boss, and have even less money to remit in the future, charging the spiral further. Vernacular Thai Buddhism offers a way out of this vicious cycle: the fostering of equanimity and equilibrium, or a "cool heart" (*jay yen*), a quality that Daeng ascribed to Boy.[31]

From this point of view, an unskillful response to suffering can lead to its proliferation and put the relationships that make life possible at such grave risk that death might ensue. Calm and virtuous responses to adversity lead in the opposite direction, and if virtue is maintained, relationships will become stronger and more stable. Karmic reciprocity thus applies as much to marital relationships like Moon and Boy's, which Moon saw as "proven" by her husband's constancy over time and through hardship, as it does to the relations with employers explored in Chapter 4. Meritorious action encourages responses in kind, mitigating suffering and leading to a smoother path in the future.

From migrants' perspective, the exchange of productive labor for wages, of remittances for reproductive labor, and of obedience for paternalistic care all take on a similar kind of affective and ethical charge. The good worker and husband is one who does his duty vis-à-vis his employer and wife; the reverse is also true, but the correct response to violation and disappointment is not retaliation, which brings about further suffering and destabilization, but forbearance and perseverance, which can help to put the relationship back in order. Powerful third parties, such as the employer, will be acting meritoriously if they intervene to make sure this happens. On one hand, this is a potent method for taking responsibility over one's own fate. But on the other, much like the ideologies identified by critical thinkers in the West as "capitalist realism" and "cruel optimism," it absolves and even sanctifies capitalist and patriarchal relations by turning the reproduction of those relations into an ethically praiseworthy goal.[32]

The "good" worker's effort to maintain his own labor-power through frugality, sobriety, and hard work is thus a conscious effort to harmonize his own actions with the interests of his employer and his family. The boss has an interest in getting workers to put in long hours, so as to maximize production and profits, and in keeping their consumption strictly limited, to minimize the disruption of production by drunkenness and other transgressions and to reproduce the racial rule of difference. Kin in Thailand are also interested in maximizing their migrant's time on the clock, so as to enlarge his wage bill, and in minimizing his consumption in order to leave as much of that wage available for remittance as possible.[33] Kin and employers have a common interest in retrieving "runaway" workers, who sometimes cut off contact with their families when they abandon their legal employers. They also share an interest in keeping workers sexually inactive, the former for reasons of marital prerogative and maintaining their monopoly over remittances, and the latter to maintain the rule of difference and its associated sexual taboos (see Chapter 5).

As we have seen, Song used this ideologically framed conjunction of interest to enlist Yehudit and Ya'ir in bringing her son-in-law to heel. Though her position vis-à-vis the Sadots was much weaker, Moon told me that she had made a habit of calling Ya'ir about once a year to inquire about Boy, sounding as distraught as she could to pressure him to make her husband toe the line. In return, she received Ya'ir's assurances in farm pidgin (see Chapter 4): "Boy *naun* [sleeps], Boy *thamngaan* [works], no lady." Not entirely satisfied with these reports, she also asked me to get in touch with the boss to inquire after Boy's health and to petition to have him overstay his allotted time in Israel. When I texted him, Ya'ir ignored the second request, but his reply to the first showed familiarity with the concerns of workers' kin, as well as intercultural frustrations familiar to me:

> I talked to him yesterday because he seemed a little down. I asked if there is any problem, if he misses [home]. He said his leg muscles ache sometimes. It's hard to reach him. I think he's addicted to some computer game. It's true that his nose runs a lot but in that respect [he] seems much better.

When in a later conversation I asked Ya'ir to tell me more about his relations with workers' families, he denied that such contacts were of any importance. This disavowal reflects the norm in Israel, where an employer's interference in such affairs would be frowned upon, as well as the ingrained LSM aversion to paternalism, discussed in Chapter 3. But the migrants I knew, like their relatives, recognized a different norm; when I asked them about this sort of intervention, they indicated that they welcomed it, just as Daeng retrospectively justified Ya'ir's refusal to let him go home on vacation for fear that he would attack his wife, and as Mike preferred that Ya'ir disburse his wages to his family and the shop rather than pay him directly (see Chapter 5).

This is not to say that workers on the Sadot farm conflated their own interests with those of the boss. As we have seen, workers are perfectly able to speak critically, cynically even, of their exploitation when they judge it appropriate and safe to do so. Boy, too, was quite clear that he did not see the wages paid on the farm as fair, and that he worked such long hours only because the hourly pay was so meager. Obviously, more money and more time off would lessen his suffering and that of his family. Indeed, these would probably be the most effective steps toward keeping him within the virtuous cycle of health, happiness, and hard work. But they were not on offer, and he was not inclined to protest to me. Similarly, when Moon inquired about the workman's compensation owed to Boy at the end of his term, I stressed that he might have to speak to Workers' Hotline, the human rights NGO, to make sure he got his fair share. She replied that he would be loath to anger Ya'ir by doing this.

Such expressions of recognition of conflicting interests—part of what in Chapter 5 I called a discreet transcript rather than a secret one—shed a light on the labor involved in reproducing the social body. Neither Daeng nor Boy nor Moon nor Song naïvely believes that "do good, get good" is an accurate description of social reality; each of them knows otherwise from bitter experience. Song, though faithful to the Sadots and skilled at leveraging this fidelity, was nearly as poor after knowing them for three decades as she had been when she first left home. Daeng, by his own lights, had been a good husband up until the moment his wife left him. Misfortune threw him into a spiral of suffering, although he was able to get his bearings back with Ya'ir's help. Boy, too, remained a faithful husband and worker. Nevertheless, his family could not escape the burden of debt and its correlative material deprivation, nor could it overcome the pain of separation.

The confluence of interests between employers, employees, and kin is thus not a given, but an ideal state of the social body, which must be worked toward against a backdrop of steep inequality and insurmountable divisions of race and gender. The interests involved are complex and manifold, but they are also hard facts drawn against the dismal ground of capitalist-colonial relations in Israel, Isaan, and the world-system that links them. As an interaction ideology, karmic reciprocity is almost incapable of taking a stance on such questions. From this perspective, narrowly conceived, any dwelling on the karmic "birth lottery" that makes some of us men and others women, some Israeli and others Thai, some rich and others poor, can only lead to envy, anger, and other destabilizing emotions. Karmic reciprocity enables migrants to negotiate with their employers for such benefits as autonomy in the labor process and personal consideration only in return for an implicit evacuation of any right to question structural issues, such as their de facto exclusion from the protections of Israeli labor law.

For the time being, this state of affairs is quite conducive to the accumulation of capital and the maintenance of colonial control in the Arabah and in Isaan. But this is not a functionalist account: interactional ideologies like karmic reciprocity—or *dugri* egalitarianism for that matter—were not designed with the needs of capitalist-colonial accumulation in mind. As we have seen throughout this book, their accommodation to the demands of the world-system has been a bumpy, uncertain, and incomplete historical process, riven with failures and dead ends as well as successes. Why, then, should we assume that the equilibrium achieved in the Arabah is anything but temporary? Might we uefully ask how the same interaction ideologies could be used to upend this equilibrium—to replace the reproduction of capitalist coloniality with its rupture?

CONCLUSION
ANTHROPOLOGY AND THE
POLITICS OF RUPTURE

ALLOW ME TO BACKPEDAL A little. As used in this book, the concept of reproduction is analytical, not normative. To talk about the reproduction of a social phenomenon is not to assume that said phenomenon is itself either good or bad. But as we have seen, the reproduction of domination usually depends on recruitment of the people involved into upholding the interaction ideologies pertaining to the relevant forms of domination, ideologies which are themselves normative. Such ideologies may cast domination of one sort of another as a positive good or evil, as in the case of the paternalistic ideology that valorizes migrants' relationships with their employers, or the labor settlement movement's anxious denigration of the exploitation of Arab labor, or they may construe it as morally neutral, as the LSM's contemporary ideology does with the labor of Thai migrants. Critical analysis of ideology's role in the reproduction of capitalist-colonial relations is thus rendered tricky, as the unwary theorist might accidentally stumble from simply describing such locally hegemonic ideologies into presenting them as the only reasonable way of appraising the situation and thus, willy-nilly, justifying the status quo as if it were freely chosen by all involved.

For what it's worth, and in case any clarification is needed, I believe that the current form that the employment of Thai migrants in Israeli agriculture takes is very wrong. But my personal opinion is both analytically uninteresting and politically useless. It is uninteresting because it is a "view from nowhere," an ideological dictum shorn of the conditions of its own emergence, and it is useless because there is no reason to suppose that any of the actors in the field might have reason to take it up for themselves. This is a dead end.

However, there is another option. Precisely because interaction ideologies are not parts tooled smoothly to perform a role in the legitimation of domination but previously existing formations, fallibly cobbled together in a contingent assemblage, it may be worthwhile to search for elements of an immanent critique within their logics, and even to look for ways of taking the assemblage apart and putting it back together in such a way that it no longer contributes to the reproduction of domination but rather to its rupture. In doing so, I take inspiration from Eric Cazdyn's argument that a possibility of revolutionary rupture is hidden in the heart not only of Marxism, but also of psychoanalysis and the Buddha-dharma.[1] Incidentally, two interaction ideologies that have been identified as central to the state of affairs in the Arabah, exploitation anxiety and karmic reciprocity, bear an indirect genealogical connection to two of these three bodies of thought. What can be done with this connection?

Let me start with exploitation anxiety, the discomfiting suspicion that exploitative relations are damaging to the spiritual integrity of the exploiting party. This anxiety can be read in the Marxian-psychoanalytic register offered by Slavoj Žižek, as a symptom, and the labor settlement movement's various feints to avoid its consequences might be understood as attempts at repression.[2] But the definitive dimension of exploitation remains the suffering of the exploited, and the goal—the cure—can only be achieved if this "kernel of the real" is confronted and transformed. The desire to refrain from exploiting others is not a problem in itself; the trouble begins when this desire morphs into hostility toward the exploitable subject, who is then punished, either by the violence of expulsion and military occupation meted out to Palestinians, or by the violence of disenfranchisement and exclusion forced on Thai migrants, both of which serve only to further their vulnerability to exploitation. In all its forms, the violence generated by exploitation anxiety prepares the ground for more exclusion and more exploitation, in turn producing more disavowal and more violence. A therapeutic approach along psychoanalytical-Marxist lines would ask how, instead of being reproduced through disavowal and repression, exploitative economic relations can be transformed into equitable, voluntary, and egalitarian relations—socialist ones.

The Buddha-dharma can do an analogous job of immanent critique on karmic reciprocity. This ideology has appeared in this book primarily as a force for stabilizing hierarchical relations, calling upon subaltern subjects to serve superordinates faithfully, expecting recompense but claiming no right to rebel when such is not forthcoming. I have described karmic reciprocity as presenting subjects with a choice between angry and resentful reactions to misfortune, which trigger a spiral of suffering that can lead to family breakup and even death, and calm, acquiescent responses that keep things moving along in a virtuous circle, mitigating suffering somewhat. But the Buddhist logic of karma contains a radical third option, which is neither an outward spiral of painful proliferation nor a circle that seeks merely to keep hardship at a manageable level. The cultivation of qualities of compassion and equanimity, promises the dharma, enables a spiraling motion in the opposite direction, inward. This motion continues gradually to mitigate suffering, all the way to the final horizon of its total extinguishment: liberation, or *nibbana*.

What might happen when we put the retooled wheels of exploitation anxiety and karmic reciprocity together again? What would we get by linking the realization that the best remedy for exploitation is a socialist transformation of the relations of production with an affirmation of the possibility that, through mindful practice and care for others and oneself, suffering can be not only managed but eliminated? We get an ideological orientation capable of seeing Thais, Palestinians, Israelis

and others, employers, employees, kin and bystanders, as inextricably interdependent and potential partners in the project of collectively
realizing the freedom to which all individually aspire. And we get it
not by wholesale importation from the outside, but by drawing logical
conclusions from moral orientations already present in the field.

Certainly, the political implications are daunting. Is it really possible to reconfigure relations in the Arabah such that the interdependence of the various beings involved would be celebrated rather than
disavowed and all given an equal voice in both "political" and "economic" decisions? Perhaps not, but why should we give up in advance?
At their most radical, the philosophies of rupture—psychoanalysis,
dharma, Marxism—insist on not foreclosing this possibility, though
as Cazdyn notes, each one has its own watered-down, blunted form
that gives up in advance on the radical promise: social-democratic
reformism for Marxism, conventional behavioral psychotherapy for
psychoanalysis, and, for Buddhism, "gratuitous spiritual practice or
limited liberal-humanist critique."[3] Giving up in advance is also what
Zionist socialists did when they let their commitment to class struggle curdle into a separatist reformism predicated on the assumption
that capitalist coloniality was inevitable. They then bought into the
corollary—that the egalitarian good life could only be possible within
a strictly policed, homogeneous social space that did not challenge the
powers of the outside world. Academics who limit themselves to giving
policy recommendations to state institutions that proceed along similar assumptions might be guilty of the same failure of imagination.

I speak from experience. In 2014 I coauthored a report with Noa
Shauer, then coordinator for agricultural workers at Workers' Hotline.
The report framed the Israeli state's neglect of Thai migrants' right to
the minimum wage as an indirect subsidy to farmers, which we calculated as adding up to about half a billion NIS per year.[4] In retrospect,
there is something slightly off about the idea of a "subsidy" (which I
also invoke in Chapter 3), since this money is not disbursed from tax
revenues but stolen from workers. Nevertheless, it helped us to make
the rhetorical point that we had no objection to state support for agriculture, a common practice around the world.[5] We simply wanted to

argue that the state should finance this support from its own budget rather than allowing employers to filch it out of the pockets of impoverished migrant workers. Since then, the state's behavior has only grown more shameless: in 2018, Prime Minister Benjamin Netanyahu came out in support of exempting migrant workers from the protection of Israeli labor laws, that is, of legalizing the very robbery we had gently suggested should be curtailed.[6]

Though our approach was unusual, Shauer and I are hardly the only parties to the Thailand-Israel migration regime to demand that labor laws be enforced: a string of governmental and academic commissions have recommended enforcement as a way of ensuring that migrants do not drive down wages for Israelis, as has former minister (subsequently and briefly prime minister) Naftali Bennett.[7] But what all these policy proposals have in common is their implicit definition of Thai migrants as outsiders to the political community. Even the proposal Shauer and I made, in line with dominant strands of human rights discourse, posited migrants merely as subjects worthy of protection, not as ones eligible for full membership in the polity. Such proposals, which accept the legitimacy of the state's "demographic concerns," reinforce the cynical assumption that the political community must vigilantly police its own membership in one way or another, since a commitment to everyone amounts in practice to a commitment to no one.[8] This is the same reef of ethnocentric reformism that the LSM's socialist ideals foundered upon, analogous to the blinkered perspective of conventional psychotherapy and egocentric spiritual practice. This is a vision that gives up on the world outside the nation-state, the racially pure community, or the individual subject, as if it were a desert, a wilderness, an Arabah to be despoiled, turning inward to tend its own carefully demarcated and guarded garden—the aquifer and the acacias be damned.

Perhaps the most serious and sustained attack on this anxious, defensive orientation in the Israeli/Palestinian context is the movement for democratic decolonization, which has achieved some traction among Palestinian and critical Israeli intellectuals at the same time as repression pushes us increasingly into the diaspora. A bilingual collection of speculative short fiction, *Awdah*, which imagines what the return of Palestinian refugees might look like in a variety of modes ranging from the satirical to the utopian, is an impressive exemplar of creative work in this vein.[9] But so far, the democratic decolonial imaginary has been staunchly "binational": there is room in it for Arabs and Jews but not for people of other origins.[10] Keeping in mind the disturbing similarity between the migration regime encountered by migrants in Israel and the *kafāla* system in place in the Gulf states, the recent rapprochement between Israel and some of these states, as well as the historic if brief entry of an Islamist Arab party to an Israeli ruling coalition, the prospect begins to appear of a polity that includes Israelis and (some) Palestinians, but continues to exclude and exploit migrant "others."[11] By and large this imaginary has also ignored questions of class, turning its back on socialism as an ideology demanding the end of exploitation. But what might a democratic, socialist decolonization that welcomes *everyone* look like?

IMAGINING OTHER ARABAHS

"Foreign Hebrew Labor," an rural planning project by landscape architect Adi Elmaliah, can give us an inkling.[12] By asking how communities in the Arabah might be redesigned to better accommodate the needs of Thai migrant workers, and proposing the establishment of attractive housing developments designed with reference to vernacular Isaan architecture, Elmaliah provides an innocuously radical vision of a region where the Thai half of the population has as much of a right to belong as the Jewish half, a right expressed through the built environment. Similarly, Zohar Shvarzberg's research on the vernacular kitchen gardens of Thai migrants in Israel suggests that not only the built environment of the Arabah but its agriculture might become more sustainable, equitable, and indeed beautiful if it were to provide migrants with opportunities to apply their considerable horticultural know-how and refocus production on provision for local needs rather than speculation on faraway markets.[13]

FIGURE C.1

An equitable housing scheme for migrant workers in Moshav Paran.
Figure by Adi Elmaliah.

But why stop here? What might the Arabah look like if the Bedouin
Arabs expelled during the Nakba (see Chapter 1) were welcomed back
and allowed to choose between re-creating their former communities
or joining integrated ones? In addition to its other thrilling perspectives, this scenario may also hold the key to mitigating the ecological
ruin that capitalist colonialization has brought to the Arabah.[14] True,
climate change may have already rendered the unique combination of
pastoralism and agriculture practiced by Bedouin in the region before
1948 impracticable.[15] But the resilience and creativity evidenced by the
Bedouin cultivation of cannabis, forced into illegality while Jewish
growers in the area are licensed as medicinal producers, demonstrates

FIGURE C.2

Thai kitchen gardens, each featuring over twenty edible plants, Sharon region, Israel. Photographs by Zohar Shvarzberg.

that this indigenous population retains an intimate knowledge of local ecological conditions that the settlers of the *moshavim* have never achieved.[16]

Imagine a decolonized, democratic, socialist Arabah shared by Bedouin, Jews, and Isaanites, incorporating agriculture, pastoralism, tourism, and other pursuits and committed to ensuring the long-term conditions of human flourishing rather than those of the colonial, racializing nation-state or the capitalist world-system! Such an imaginative intervention certainly goes beyond the disciplinary boundaries of anthropology as conventionally conceived, and indeed beyond the boundaries of this book. But far-fetched as this speculative vision may seem, my point is that it does not have to come out of nowhere, but can be derived, through a sort of immanent radicalization, from the very ideologies that have contributed to making the Arabah what it is today. If still far from a strategic program for social transformation, a vision of the Arabah's future that builds on these ideologies can at least be said to represent not a "view from nowhere," but the result of careful consideration of the often clashing motivations that a great variety of people have brought to their life in this region: a pioneer spirit of self-sufficiency, yes, but also an attachment to ancient, deeply rooted modes of living, as well as a very modern willingness to make sacrifices for faraway loved ones. Anthropology is not in itself radical politics, but it can help to ground such politics in the most local as well as the most global points of resistance to capitalist coloniality.

NOTES

Preface

1. Nathanel Gams, "'Me'orer Sh'at Nefesh': Gid'on Sa'ar Metzia Lishlol Pitzuyim Mi-Ovdim Zarim She-Rotzim La'azov" ('Revolting': Gideon Sa'ar Suggests Denial of Compensation to Foreign Workers Who Want to Leave), *TheMarker*, October 22, 2023, tinyurl.com/saar-pitzuyim.

2. Simi Spolter, "'Mi-Tokh 30 Elef She-Nirshemu Rak 200 Higi'u': Mashber Ha-Ovdim Ma'amik Vele-Misrad Ha-Hakla'ut En Pitronot" ('Out of 30 Thousand Who Signed up Only 200 Have Arrived': The Labor Crisis Is Deepening and the Agriculture Ministry Has No Solutions), *TheMarker*, December 20, 2023, tinyurl.com/mashber-maamik.

3. Matan Kaminer, "In Israel, Thai Migrant Workers Are Caught in Other People's War," *Jacobin*, December 4, 2023, tinyurl.com/jacobin-kaminer-thais.

Note on Non-English Terms

1. "ISO 11940–2," International Standards Organization, January 28, 2019, www.iso.org/standard/29544.html.

Note on Anonymization

1. "Sadot" is the only pseudonymous last name in the text. Where people outside this family are referred to by their full names, these are the real names of public figures who do not require my protection.

2. See Jason De León, *The Land of Open Graves: Living and Dying on the Migrant Trail* (Berkeley and Los Angeles: University of California Press, 2015), 59–60.

3. Readers familiar with farming in the Arabah may even spot some small incongruities in the description of agricultural labor processes. Rest assured, these are intentional!

Introduction

1. The concept of the capitalist world-system, introduced by Immanuel Wallerstein, has been subjected to productive and wide-ranging critiques. Though I take inspiration from "world-system theory" in Wallerstein's sense, my argument does not hinge on the particularities of his analysis. See Immanuel Wallerstein, *The Capitalist World-Economy* (Cambridge: Cambridge University Press, 1979), and *World-Systems Analysis: An Introduction* (Durham, NC: Duke University Press, 2004); Matan Kaminer, "Connections Yet Unmade: The Reception of Balibar and Wallerstein's *Race, Nation, Class* in Israel," in *"Race, Nation, Class": Rereading a Dialogue for Our Times*, ed. Manuela Bojadzijev and Katrin Klingan (Berlin: Argument-Verlag, 2018), 107–20.

2. Ramón Grosfoguel and Ana Margarita Cervantes-Rodríguez, eds., *The Modern/Colonial/Capitalist World-System in the Twentieth Century: Global Processes, Antisystemic Movements, and the Geopolitics of Knowledge* (Westport, CT: Praeger, 2002). My use of "subaltern" and "superordinate" as generic terms for the two parties to a relationship of domination is taken from the Subaltern Studies literature, and specifically from Ranajit Guha, *Dominance without Hegemony: History and Power in Colonial India* (Cambridge, MA: Harvard University Press, 1997).

3. Loïc Wacquant, "Ethnografeast: A Progress Report on the Practice and Promise of Ethnography," *Ethnography* 4, no. 1 (2003): 5.

4. On multi-sited ethnography as a method for studying the world-system, see George E. Marcus, "Ethnography in/of the World System: The Emergence of Multi-Sited Ethnography," *Annual Review of Anthropology* 24 (1995): 95–117.

5. Pedro Pedreño, "Sustainability, Resilience, and Agency in Intensive Agricultural Enclaves," *Ager: Revista de Estudios Sobre Despoblación y Desarrollo Rural*, no. 18 (April 15, 2015): 139–60.

6. See Pattana Kitiarsa, "The Lyrics of Laborious Life: Popular Music and the Reassertion of Migrant Manhood in Northeastern Thailand," *Inter-Asia Cultural Studies* 10, no. 3 (September 1, 2009): 381–98.

7. Janet L. Abu-Lughod, *Before European Hegemony: The World System A.D. 1250–1350* (Oxford: Oxford University Press, 1991); Abdul Sheriff and Engseng Ho, eds., *The Indian Ocean: Oceanic Connections and the Creation of New Societies* (London: Hurst, 2014).

8. Donald Whitcomb, "Land behind Aqaba: The Wadi Arabah during the Early Islamic Period," in *Crossing the Rift: Resources, Routes, Settlement Patterns, and Interaction in the Wadi Arabah*, ed. Piotr Bienkowski and Katharina Galor (Oxford: Oxbow Books, 2006), 239–42; Porphant Ouyyanont, "Thailand's Northeast 'Problem' in Historical Perspective," ed. Daljit Singh and Malcolm Cook, *Southeast Asian Affairs*, 2017, 367–84.

9. Engseng Ho, "Empire through Diasporic Eyes: A View from the Other Boat," *Comparative Studies in Society and History* 46, no. 2 (April 2004): 210–46.

10. Mike Davis, *Late Victorian Holocausts: El Niño Famines and the Making of the Third World* (London: Verso, 2001); Jan Breman, *Taming the Coolie Beast: Plantation Society and the Colonial Order in Southeast Asia* (Oxford: Oxford University Press, 1989); Lisa Lowe, *The Intimacies of Four Continents* (Durham, NC: Duke University Press, 2015).

11. Onur Ulaş Ince, "Deprovincializing Racial Capitalism: John Crawfurd and Settler Colonialism in India," *American Political Science Review* 116, no. 1 (2022): 5.

12. Harriet Friedmann, "The Political Economy of Food: The Rise and Fall of the Postwar International Food Order," *American Journal of Sociology* 88 (January 1982): S248–86; E. J. Hobsbawm, *The Age of Extremes: A History of the World, 1914–1991* (New York: Vintage Books, 1996), 288–92.

13. Kwame Nkrumah, *Neo-Colonialism: The Last Stage of Imperialism* (New York: International, 1966); Pablo Gonzalez Casanova, "Internal Colonialism and National Development," *Studies in Comparative International Development* 1, no. 4 (April 1, 1965): 27–37; Fayez A. Sayegh, *Zionist Colonialism in Palestine* (Beirut: Palestine Liberation Organization Research Center, 1965), 1.

14. Kalyan Sanyal, *Rethinking Capitalist Development: Primitive Accumulation, Governmentality & Post-Colonial Capitalism* (London: Routledge, 2014).

15. Encarnación Gutiérrez Rodríguez, "The Coloniality of Migration and the 'Refugee Crisis': On the Asylum-Migration Nexus, the Transatlantic White European Settler Colonialism-Migration and Racial Capitalism," *Refuge* 34, no. 1 (June 18, 2018): 23–24.

16. Engseng Ho, *The Graves of Tarim: Genealogy and Mobility across the Indian Ocean* (Berkeley and Los Angeles: University of California Press, 2006); Sarah S. Willen, *Transnational Migration to Israel in Global Comparative Context* (Lanham, MD: Lexington Books, 2007); Crystal A. Ennis and Nicolas Blarel, eds., *The South Asia to Gulf Migration Governance Complex* (Bristol: Bristol University Press, 2022).

17. Partha Chatterjee, *The Nation and Its Fragments: Colonial and Postcolonial Histories* (Oxford: Oxford University Press, 1994); Aníbal Quijano, "Coloniality of Power and Eurocentrism in Latin America," *International Sociology* 15, no. 2 (June 1, 2000): 215–32; Cedric J. Robinson, *Black Marxism: The Making of the Black Radical Tradition* (Chapel Hill: University of North Carolina Press, 2000).

18. Karl Marx, *Capital: A Critique of Political Economy*, vol. 1, trans. Ben Fowkes (Middlesex: Penguin, 1990), 915.

19. For overviews, see Robinson, *Black Marxism*; Tithi Bhattacharya and Liselotte Vogel, eds., *Social Reproduction Theory: Remapping Class, Recentering Oppression* (London: Pluto Press, 2017); Hadas Weiss, "Social Reproduction," in *Cambridge Encyclopedia of Anthropology* (Cambridge: Cambridge University Press, 2021); Sam Ashman, "Combined and Uneven Development," in *The Elgar Companion to Marxist Economics*, ed. Ben Fine and Alfredo Saad-Filho (Cheltenham: Edward Elgar, 2012), 60–65; Max Ajl, "Theories of Political Ecology: Monopoly Capital Against People and the Planet," *Agrarian South: Journal of Political Economy* 12, no. 1 (March 1, 2023): 12–50.

20. See, e.g., Eric Williams, *Capitalism and Slavery* (Chapel Hill: University of North Carolina Press, 1994); Eric R. Wolf, *Europe and the People without History* (Berkeley and Los Angeles: University of California Press, 2010); Jairus Banaji, "The Fictions of Free Labour: Contract, Coercion, and So-Called Unfree Labour," *Historical Materialism* 11 (2003): 69–95; Sanyal, *Rethinking*; Lowe, *Intimacies*.

21. Jairus Banaji, *Theory as History: Essays on Modes of Production and Exploitation* (Leiden: Brill, 2010).

22. Marx, *Capital* vol. 1, chap. 25; Edna Bonacich, "A Theory of Ethnic Antagonism: The Split Labor Market," *American Sociological Review* 37, no. 5 (October 1, 1972): 547–59.

23. This is the approach often taken by Israel's most prominent migration researchers, Adriana Kemp and Rebeca Raijman. For an example, see their "Bringing in State Regulations, Private Brokers, and Local Employers: A Meso-Level Analysis of Labor Trafficking in Israel," *International Migration Review* 48, no. 3 (2014): 604–42.

24. For ideological reproduction, see Louis Althusser, *On Reproduction* (London: Verso, 2014). This has also been the approach of radical researchers inspired by Bourdieu, e.g., Paul E. Willis, *Learning to Labor: How Working Class Kids Get Working Class Jobs* (New York: Columbia University Press, 1977).

25. The literature is voluminous and constantly growing, but for an authoritative introduction, see Bhattacharya and Vogel, *Social Reproduction Theory*. For a review of anthropological approaches, see Weiss, "Social Reproduction."

26. John Bellamy Foster, *Marx's Ecology: Materialism and Nature* (New York: Monthly Review Press, 2000). For links between social reproduction and political ecology, see Maria Mies, *Patriarchy and Accumulation on a World Scale:*

Women in the International Division of Labour (London: Zed Books, 2014); Jason W. Moore, *Capitalism in the Web of Life: Ecology and the Accumulation of Capital* (London: Verso, 2016).

27. See Liron Shani, "Of Trees and People: The Changing Entanglement in the Israeli Desert," *Ethnos* 83, no. 4 (March 30, 2017): 1–19; Matan Kaminer, "The Agricultural Settlement of the Arabah and the Political Ecology of Zionism," *International Journal of Middle East Studies* 54, no. 1 (February 2022): 40–56.

28. The influence of Marxism on theories of ideology in linguistic anthropology is very much recognized, so there is nothing original in the links I draw between them. See Judith Irvine and Susan Gal, "Language Ideology and Linguistic Differentiation," in *Regimes of Language: Ideologies, Polities, and Identities* (Santa Fe: School of American Research, 2000), 25–84.

29. Derek Sayer, *The Violence of Abstraction: The Analytic Foundations of Historical Materialism* (Oxford: Blackwell, 1987).

30. For the role played by the labor process in the racialization of migrant and citizen workers in Israel, see Matan Kaminer, "At the Zero Degree/ Below the Minimum: Wage as Sign in Israel's Split Labor Market," *Dialectical Anthropology* 43, no. 3 (September 2019): 317–32.

31. Anne Pomeroy, *Marx and Whitehead: Process, Dialectics, and the Critique of Capitalism* (Albany: SUNY Press, 2004).

32. Stuart Hall, "Race, Articulation, and Societies Structured in Dominance," in *Black British Cultural Studies: A Reader*, ed. Houston A Baker, Manthia Diawara, and Ruth H. Lindeborg (Chicago: University of Chicago Press, 1996), 16–60.

33. See Barbara Ehrenreich, *Fear of Falling: The Inner Life of the Middle Class* (New York: Twelve, 2020).

34. Webb Keane, "Semiotics and the Social Analysis of Material Things," *Language & Communication* 23, no. 3–4 (July 2003): 409–25.

35. Deeply internalized and partially opaque to conscious reflection, interaction ideologies are similar to the "structuring structures" identified by Pierre Bourdieu under the rubric of *habitus*. However, Bourdieu understood habitus as arising spontaneously over many generations and under relatively unchanging social circumstances, while many aspects of interaction ideology are not only inculcated intentionally, including in adults, but are also amenable to rapid change and, to some extent, to self-reflexive adjustment. See his *Outline of a Theory of Practice* (Cambridge: Cambridge University Press, 1977).

36. Tamar Katriel, *Talking Straight: Dugri Speech in Israeli Sabra Culture* (Cambridge: Cambridge University Press, 1986).

37. Felicity Aulino, "Perceiving the Social Body: A Phenomenological Perspective on Ethical Practice in Buddhist Thailand," *Journal of Religious Ethics* 42, no. 3 (September 1, 2014): 415–41.

38. See Julia Cassaniti, *Living Buddhism: Mind, Self, and Emotion in a Thai Community* (Ithaca, NY: Cornell University Press, 2015); Felicity Aulino, *Rituals of Care: Karmic Politics in an Aging Thailand* (Ithaca, NY: Cornell University Press, 2019); Scott Stonington, "Karma Masters: The Ethical Wound, Hauntological Choreography, and Complex Personhood in Thailand," *American Anthropologist* 122, no. 4 (2020): 759–70.

39. *Rituals of National Loyalty: An Anthropology of the State and the Village Scout Movement in Thailand* (New York: Columbia University Press, 1997).

40. Althusser, *On Reproduction*, 254; see also Claude Levi-Strauss, *The Savage Mind* (Chicago: University of Chicago Press, 1966); Gilles Deleuze and Félix Guattari, *A Thousand Plateaus: Capitalism and Schizophrenia* (London: Continuum International, 2004).

41. Matan Kaminer, "Avoda be-darga efes: Subyektiviyut po'alit be-mahsan ashdodi" (Zero degree labor: Worker subjectivity in an Ashdod warehouse) (MA thesis, Tel Aviv University, 2011).

42. Matan Kaminer, "The Oksana Affair: Ambiguous Resistance in an Israeli Warehouse," *Ethnography* 19, no. 1 (March 2018): 25–43.

43. Timothy Mitchell, "Everyday Metaphors of Power," *Theory and Society* 19, no. 5 (October 1, 1990): 545–77; Susan Gal, "Language and the 'Arts of Resistance,'" *Cultural Anthropology* 10, no. 3 (August 1, 1995): 407–24.

44. Kaminer, "Zero Degree."

45. Rosalind C. Morris, "Failures of Domestication: Speculations on Globality, Economy, and the Sex of Excess in Thailand," *Differences* 13, no. 1 (May 1, 2002): 53.

46. Peter A. Jackson, "The Thai Regime of Images," *Sojourn: Journal of Social Issues in Southeast Asia* 19, no. 2 (2004): 181–218.

47. Jonathan Shapira, *Ilit lelo mamshichim: Dorot manhigim ba-hevra ha-yisre'elit* (An Elite without Successors: Generations of Political Leaders in Israel) (Tel Aviv: Sifriat Po'alim, 1984).

48. See Matan Kaminer, "Mabatim musatim ba-arava" (Averted Gazes in the Arabah), *Hazman Hazeh*, October 23, 2019, hazmanhazeh.org.il/thaiworkers/; Shahar Samooha, "Ben Ha-Moshavnikim Ba-Arava La-Ovdim Ha-Zarim She-Hem Ma'asikim Hitpatha Ma'rekhet Yahasim Murkevet. Doktor Matan Kaminer Hakar et Ha-Tofa'a" (A Complex Relationship Has Developed between the Moshavniks of the Arabah and the Foreign Workers They Employ. Dr. Matan Kaminer Has Researched the Phenomenon), *Globes*, March 14, 2020, tinyurl.com/samooha-globes.

49. This mistake, though common, is particularly egregious given the strong influence of the Isaan-centered forest monk tradition on the *vipassana* practices commonly taught in Israel. See Kamala Tiyavanich, *Forest Recollections: Wandering Monks in Twentieth-Century Thailand* (Honolulu:

University of Hawaii Press, 1997); Joseph Loss, "Buddha-Dhamma in Israel: Explicit Non-Religious and Implicit Non-Secular Localization of Religion," *Nova Religio* 13, no. 4 (May 2010): 84–105.

50. Aulino, *Rituals*; Tamar Katriel, "Kiturim: Griping as a Verbal Ritual in Israeli Discourse," in *Communal Webs: Communication and Culture in Contemporary Israel* (Albany: SUNY Press, 2012), 35–50.

51. Ryan Cecil Jobson, "The Case for Letting Anthropology Burn: Sociocultural Anthropology in 2019," *American Anthropologist* 122, no. 2 (2020): 259–71.

52. See Robert Ovetz, ed., *Worker's Inquiry and Global Class Struggle: Strategies, Tactics, Objectives* (London: Pluto Press, 2020).

Chapter 1

1. See Edwin Ardener, "'Remote Areas': Some Theoretical Considerations," *HAU: Journal of Ethnographic Theory* 2, no. 1 (March 2012): 519–33.

2. This chapter incorporates findings previously published in Kaminer, "Agricultural Settlement."

3. These two terms essentially refer to the same unit of land, whose boundaries were first defined under the British Mandate. Today, this entire unit, plus the Golan Heights taken from Syria, is under the de facto control of the State of Israel, though most of the international community does not recognize Israel's claim to the occupied Palestinian territories (OPT) of the West Bank, including East Jerusalem and the Gaza Strip, or to the Golan. I use "Palestine" to refer to the country prior to 1948 and "Palestine/Israel" thereafter; "Israel" refers to the state and its apparatus, or to the country within its internationally recognized borders. As ethnonyms, "Israeli" refers to Israeli citizens, and "Palestinian" to the indigenous Arabic-speaking inhabitants of the country (about two million of whom are also Israeli citizens).

4. Abu-Lughod, *Before European Hegemony*; Peregrine Horden and Nicholas Purcell, *The Corrupting Sea: A Study of Mediterranean History* (Oxford: Blackwell, 2000).

5. Beshara Doumani, *Rediscovering Palestine: Merchants and Peasants in Jabal Nablus, 1700–1900* (Berkeley and Los Angeles: University of California Press, 1995); Salim Tamari, *Mountain against the Sea: Essays on Palestinian Society and Culture* (Berkeley and Los Angeles: University of California Press, 2008), chap. 2; Ghazi Falah, "The Evolution of Semi-Nomadism in Non-Desert Environment: The Case of Galilee in the 19th Century," *GeoJournal* 21, no. 4 (1990): 397–410; Ghazi Falah, "Dynamics and Patterns of the Shrinking of Arab Lands in Palestine," *Political Geography* 22, no. 2 (February 2003): 179–209.

6. See Kristen Alff, "Levantine Joint-Stock Companies, Trans-Mediterranean Partnerships, and Nineteenth-Century Capitalist Development," *Comparative*

Studies in Society and History 60, no. 1 (January 2018): 150–77; Yael Allweil, "Plantation: Modern-Vernacular Housing and Settlement in Ottoman Palestine, 1858–1918," *Architecture beyond Europe*, no. 9–10 (July 2016), tinyurl. com/allweil; Matan Kaminer, "Behind the Well Houses: The Saknat of Abu Kabir," *Maarav*, no. 30 (June 2021), tinyurl.com/behind-well-houses.

7. Gideon M. Kressel et al., "Changes in the Land Usage by the Negev Bedouin Since the Mid-19th Century: The Intra-Tribal Perspective," *Nomadic Peoples*, no. 28 (1991): 28–55; Reşat Kasaba, *A Moveable Empire: Ottoman Nomads, Migrants, and Refugees* (Seattle: University of Washington Press, 2009).

8. Eugene L. Rogan, *Frontiers of the State in the Late Ottoman Empire: Transjordan, 1850–1921* (Cambridge: Cambridge University Press, 1999); Clinton Bailey, "Relations between Bedouin Tribes on Opposite Sides of the Wadi Arabah, 1600–1950," in *Crossing the Rift: Resources, Routes, Settlement Patterns, and Interaction in the Wadi Arabah*, ed. Piotr Bienkowski and Katharina Galor (Oxford: Oxbow Books, 2006), 251–58; Mansour Nasasra, *The Naqab Bedouins: A Century of Politics and Resistance* (New York: Columbia University Press, 2017).

9. Yair Goldreich and Ora Karni, "Climate and Precipitation Regime in the Arava Valley, Israel," *Israel Journal of Earth Sciences* 50, no. 2 (January 1, 2001): 53–60; H. J. Bruins et al., "Degradation of Springs in the Arava Valley: Anthropogenic and Climatic Factors," *Land Degradation & Development* 23, no. 4 (July 2012): 365–83.

10. In Arabic the word *wadi* has a more expansive meaning, but in English (and Hebrew) wadis have come to be "distinguished from river valleys or gullies in that surface water is intermittent or ephemeral [and that] wadis are generally dry year round, except after a rain." "Wadi," in *Wikipedia*, July 3, 2018, tinyurl.com/wiki-wadi. In keeping with this usage, I distinguish between the valley of the Arabah—which lies between the mountain ranges of the Negev and the Jordanian plateau—and the Wadi Arabah, the ephemeral watercourse that only drains its northern half. The border between Israel and Jordan runs mostly down the middle of this watercourse. See Haim Cerbero, "Gvul Yisrael-Yarden Ba-Arava" (The Israel-Jordan Border in the Arabah), in *Arava En Ketz: Nof, Teva ve-Adam Ba-Arava (The Arava: Landscape, Nature and People in the Arava Valley)*, ed. Yair Giladi et al. (Ein Yahav: Arava, 2012), 286–93.

11. Giora Ilani, *Ma'ale Namer: Zikhronot Zo'olog Yisre'eli* (Leopard Steppe: Memoir of an Israeli Zoologist) (Bnei Brak: Sifriat Po'alim, 2004); Liron Shani, *Shitat Ha-Arava: Antropologia Shel Teva Tarbut ve-Hakla'ut* (The Arava Approach: Anthropology of Nature and (Agri)Culture) (Ra'anana: Lamda, 2021).

12. See the Note on Non-English Terms for my choice of transliteration.

13. HALOT, "עֲרָבָה," in *HALOT Online*, February 2017.

14. HALOT.

15. Andrew Shryock, "History and Historiography among the Belqa Tribes of Jordan" (PhD diss., University of Michigan, 1993), 53–56.

16. Daily maximum temperature averages for July collected between 1995 and 2009 are as follows, from north to south. Havat Eden, near Beit Shean: 38 degrees Celsius; Gilgal, in the West Bank *ghor*: 40; Sdom, just south of the Dead Sea in Israel: 41; Hatzeva and Paran, at the northern and southern ends of the Central Arabah: 41 and 40. Compare Tel Aviv: 32, or Jerusalem: 30. See Israel Meteorological Service, "Erke Temperatura Rav-Shnatiyim, 1995–2009" (Multi-Annual Temperature Values, 1995–2009) (State of Israel, February 2013), tinyurl.com/isratemp1999.

17. Zeev Zivan, *Mi-Nitzana ad Eilat: Sipuro Shel Ha-Negev Ha-Dromi, 1949–1957* (From Nitzana to Eilat: The Story of the Southern Negev, 1949–1957) (Sde Boker: Ben Gurion University Press, 2012), 130.

18. Andreas Hauptmann, "Mining Archaeology and Archaeometallurgy in the Wadi Arabah: The Mining Districts of Faynan and Timna" and Russell Adams, "Copper Trading Networks across the Arabah during the Later Early Bronze Age," both in *Crossing the Rift: Resources, Routes, Settlement Patterns, and Interaction in the Wadi Arabah*, ed. Piotr Bienkowski and Katharina Galor (Oxford: Oxbow Books, 2006), 125–34, 135–42.

19. Michaël Jasmin, "The Emergence and First Development of the Arabian Trade across the Wadi Arabah," in *Crossing the Rift*, 143–50.

20. Yizhar Hirschfeld, "The Nabatean Presence South of the Dead Sea: New Evidence," and Benjamin J. Dolinka, "The Rujm Taba Archeological Project (RTAP): Results of the 2001 Survey and Reconnaisance," both in *Crossing the Rift*, 167–90, 195–214.

21. Piotr Bienkowski, "The Wadi Arabah: Meanings in a Contested Landscape," in *Crossing the Rift*, 7–28; Jasmin, "Emergence and First Development"; Whitcomb, "Land behind Aqaba."

22. Ilan Stavi et al., "Ancient through Mid-Twentieth Century Runoff Harvesting Agriculture in the Hyper-Arid Arava Valley of Israel," *CATENA* 162 (March 1, 2018): 80–87.

23. Bailey, "Relations"; Eveline J. van der Steen, "Nineteenth-Century Travellers in the Wadi Arabah," in *Crossing the Rift*, 243–50.

24. 'Aref el-'Aref, *Toldot Beer Sheva u-Shvatea*, trans. Eliyahu Nawi (Jerusalem: Ariel, 2000), 130–36.

25. Yosef Weitz, "Emeq Ha-Aravah Minekudat Mabat Hakla'it" (The Arabah Valley from an Agricultural Perspective), in *Ha-Ma'avak 'al Ha-Adama* (The Battle over Land) (Tel Aviv: N. Tversky, 1950), 304–5. The last figure is an estimate based on the number of livestock, which suggests that the average "tent" or household comprised about 5 people (Geoffrey Hughes, personal communication).

26. Timothy Mitchell, *Carbon Democracy: Political Power in the Age of Oil* (London: Verso, 2011); Zivan, *Mi-Nitzana*, 27.

27. Nasasra, *Bedouins*, 83–91.

28. The last census carried out by the Mandatory government, in 1931, listed 51,082 residents in the Beersheba subdistrict, which covered the entire Negev less Gaza and its hinterland, out of 1,035,821 residents in all of Palestine. Of these, only 3,101 were "settled," mostly in the town of Beersheba—all the rest being "nomadic" Bedouin. Only 17 Jews and 153 Christians were listed, also almost all in the town. See E Mills, "Census of Palestine: Population of Villages, Towns and Administrative Areas" (Jerusalem: British Mandate for Palestine, 1932), 7–12; Hanina Porat, "Mediniut Rekhishat Karka'ot Veha-Hityashvut Ba-Negev erev Milhemet Ha-Atzma'ut" (Land Purchase and Settlement Policy in the Negev on the Eve of the War of Independence), *Cathedra* 62 (December 1991): 123–54.

29. Samer Alatout, "Bringing Abundance into Environmental Politics: Constructing a Zionist Network of Water Abundance, Immigration, and Colonization," *Social Studies of Science* 39, no. 3 (June 1, 2009): 363–94.

30. Seraje Assi, *The History and Politics of the Bedouin: Reimagining Nomadism in Modern Palestine* (London: Routledge, 2018), 70–71.

31. UNSCOP, "United Nations Special Committee on Palestine Report," 1947, tinyurl.com/unscop-report part 2, sec. "The Jewish State."

32. Zivan, *Mi-Nitzana*, 142; Nasasra, *Bedouins*, 109–10.

33. Sai Englert, *Settler Colonialism: An Introduction* (London: Pluto Press, 2022), chap. 4.

34. Alfred W. W. Crosby, *Ecological Imperialism: The Biological Expansion of Europe, 900–1900* (Cambridge: Cambridge University Press, 2004).

35. Doumani, *Rediscovering Palestine*; Cyrus Schayegh, *The Middle East and the Making of the Modern World* (Cambridge, MA: Harvard University Press, 2017).

36. Brenna Bhandar, *Colonial Lives of Property: Law, Land, and Racial Regimes of Ownership* (Durham, NC: Duke University Press, 2018), chap. 3.

37. John Locke, *The Second Treatise of Government* (New York: Liberal Arts Press, 1952); Gary Fields, *Enclosure: Palestinian Landscapes in a Historical Mirror* (Berkeley and Los Angeles: University of California Press, 2017).

38. Onur Ulaş Ince, *Colonial Capitalism and the Dilemmas of Liberalism* (Oxford: Oxford University Press, 2018), 62 and chap. 2 passim; see also Robert Nichols, *Theft Is Property! Dispossession and Critical Theory* (Durham, NC: Duke University Press, 2020).

39. Bhandar, *Colonial Lives*, chap. 3. It was the British rather than the Zionists who introduced a properly Lockean conception of land tenure into Palestine. Beginning in the 1920s, Mandate authorities undertook systematic

land registration, encouraged the dismantling of *musha'* arrangements, and moved to grant landowners absolute "freehold," encompassing the right to evict tenant cultivators. The colonial authorities encouraged not only the cultivation of "wasteland," but any transformation that would raise land's capacity to produce profitably. Here as elsewhere, the empire sought to encourage "market-oriented development and investment" to achieve "a more efficient revenue system and an enhanced tax base." See Martin Bunton, "'Home,' 'Colony,' 'Vilayet': Frames of Reference for the Study of Land in Mandate Palestine," *Journal of Colonialism and Colonial History* 21, no. 1 (2020): 13.

40. This perverse effect (from the colonizers' point of view) would recur with the employment of West Bank peasants in Israel following the occupation of 1967. See Salim Tamari, "The Dislocation and Re-Constitution of a Peasantry: The Social Economy of Agrarian Palestine in the Central Highlands and the Jordan Valley, 1960–1980" (PhD diss., University of Manchester, 1983).

41. Baruch Kimmerling, *Zionism and Territory: The Socio-Territorial Dimensions of Zionist Politics* (Berkeley: University of California Press, 1983). In Kimmerling's account, "frontierity" is the degree to which land can be freely appropriated by settlers (begging the question of how land came to be free for the taking). The challenge posed to capitalist colonization by low frontierity is clear, as it makes it difficult to appropriate land. However, as Edward Wakefield pointed out in the early 1800s, high frontierity can be equally pernicious to capitalist colonization, as it enables settlers to escape wage-labor by becoming smallholders. See Marx, *Capital* v. I, chap. 33; Ince, *Colonial Capitalism*, chap. 4.

42. Michael Shalev, *Labour and the Political Economy in Israel* (Oxford: Oxford University Press, 1992).

43. Zachary Lockman, *Comrades and Enemies: Arab and Jewish Workers in Palestine, 1906–1948* (Berkeley and Los Angeles: University of California Press, 1996).

44. Avishai Ehrlich, "The Crisis in Israel, Danger of Fascism?" *Khamsin*, no. 5 (July 10, 1978), tinyurl.com/ehrlich-fascism; Beverly Silver, "The Contradictions of Semiperipheral Success: The Case of Israel," in *Semiperipheral States in the World-Economy*, ed. William G. Martin (New York: Greenwood Press, 1990), 161–81.

45. Anita Shapira, *Ha-ma'avak ha-nikhzav: Avoda ivrit, 1929–1939* (The Futile Struggle: Hebrew Work 1929–1939) (Tel Aviv: Hakibbutz Hameuchad, 1977); Gershon Shafir, *Land, Labor, and the Origins of the Israeli-Palestinian Conflict, 1882–1914* (Cambridge and New York: Cambridge University Press, 1989).

46. Derek J. Penslar, *Zionism and Technocracy: The Engineering of Jewish Settlement in Palestine, 1870–1918* (Bloomington: Indiana University Press, 1991).

47. Areej Sabbagh-Khoury, *Colonizing Palestine: The Zionist Left and the Making of the Palestinian Nakba* (Stanford, CA: Stanford University Press, 2023).

48. Daniel DeMalach, "The Political Economy of Communal Life: Zionist Settlement Policy and Kibbutz Collective Practices, 1920–2010," *Communal Societies* 37, no. 2 (May 2018): 129–52; Avi Shnider, *Bimkom Moshavo: Solidariyut Be-Moshav Ha-Ovdim Ha-Mithadesh* (Sense of Place: Solidarity in the Renewed Moshav Ovdim) (Ramat Gan: Yad Tabenkin, 2022), 20.

49. Hizky Shoham, "'Buy Local' or 'Buy Jewish'? Separatist Consumption in Interwar Palestine," *International Journal of Middle East Studies* 45, no. 3 (August 2013): 469–89.

50. Shafir, *Land, Labor.*

51. Shapira, *Elite.*

52. Zvi Ben Dor-Benite, "Satan and Labor: Proletarianization and the Racialization of the Mizrahim," in *Race and the Question of Palestine*, ed. Ronit Lentin and Lana Tatour (Stanford, CA: Stanford University Press, 2025.

53. See Matan Kaminer, "The Rebirth of the 'Natural Worker': Racialisation and Class Formation in Zionist Agriculture," *New Socialist*, September 30, 2023, newsocialist.org.uk/the-rebirth-of-the-natural-worker/.

54. *Liberalism: A Counter-History*, trans. Gregory Elliott (London: Verso Books, 2011).

55. Boaz Neumann, *Land and Desire in Early Zionism*, trans. Haim Watzman (Waltham, MA: Brandeis University Press, 2011), 3.

56. See Neumann, 50–54, 74–99.

57. Neumann, 56–57, 108–11.

58. Neumann, 94.

59. Franz Oppenheimer, *Merchavia: A Jewish Co-Operative Settlement in Palestine* (New York: Co-operative Society Eretz-Israel, 1914), cited in Neumann, *Land and Desire*, 100–101.

60. Neumann, *Land and Desire*, 123–25.

61. Bunton, "Home," 8.

62. Walid Khalidi, *All That Remains: The Palestinian Villages Occupied and Depopulated by Israel in 1948* (Washington, DC: Institute for Palestine Studies, 2006); Michael Fischbach, *Records of Dispossession: Palestinian Refugee Property and the Arab-Israeli Conflict* (New York: Columbia University Press, 2003), ch. 1.

63. Falah, "Dynamics and Patterns"; Geremy Forman and Alexandre (Sandy) Kedar, "From Arab Land to 'Israel Lands': The Legal Dispossession of the Palestinians Displaced by Israel in the Wake of 1948," *Environment and Planning D: Society and Space* 22, no. 6 (December 2004): 809–30.

64. The liturgical distinction between Ashkenazim (literally "Germans") and Sephardim ("Spaniards") has, in Israel, become an ethnic distinction

between those of European and Middle Eastern origin; but not all Middle Eastern Jews are Sephardim, and activists seeking to unite this group in defense of its culture and interests prefer the term *Mizrahim*, literally "Easterners," which I use here. See Sami Shalom Chetrit, *Intra-Jewish Conflict in Israel: White Jews, Black Jews* (London: Routledge, 2010).

65. Moshe Behar, "Palestine, Arabized Jews and the Elusive Consequences of Jewish and Arab National Formations," *Nationalism and Ethnic Politics* 13 (October 1, 2007): 581–611.

66. See Shlomo Swirski and Deborah Bernstein, "Mi Avad Be-Ma, Avur Mi, ve-Tmurat Ma? Ha-Pituah Ha-Kalkali Shel Yisra'el ve-Hithavut Halukat Ha-Avoda Ha-Adatit" (Who Worked at What, for Whom and for How Much? Israel's Economic Development and the Emergence of the Ethnic Division of Labor), in *Ha-Hevra Ha-Yisre'elit: Hebetim Bikortiyim (Israeli Society: Critical Perspectives)*, ed. Uri Ram (Tel Aviv: Breirot, 1993), 120–47; Behar, "Arabized Jews"; Erez Tzfadia and Haim Yacobi, *Rethinking Israeli Space: Periphery and Identity*, 20 (Abingdon: Routledge, 2011).

67. Liron Mor, *Conflicts: The Poetics and Politics of Palestine-Israel* (New York: Fordham University Press, 2023), chap. 5.

68. Tal Elmaliach, *Anshei Ha-Etmol: Ha-Kibbutz Ha-Artzi ve-Mapam, 1956–1977* (Yesterday's People: Ha-Kibbutz Ha-Artzi and Mapam, 1956-1977) (Sde Boker: Ben Gurion Institute, 2018), 71–89; Avshalom Ben Zvi, "Shiluvam Shel Vatikim Ve-olim Bi-Tnu'at Ha-Moshavim Mi-Shilhei Shnot Ha-Hamishim ve-ad Tom Shnot Ha-Shishim" (The Integration of Veterans and Newcomers in the Moshav Movement from the Late 1950s to the Late 1960s) (MA thesis, University of Haifa, 2018), 102.

69. Elmaliach, *Anshei Ha-Etmol*; Ben Zvi, "Shiluvam," 121–23.

70. Elmaliach, *Anshei Ha-Etmol*, 194.

71. Gideon Kressel, "'He Who Stays in Agriculture Is Not a "Freier"': The Spirit of Competition among Members of the Moshav Is Eroded When Unskilled Arab Labor Enters the Scene," in *Perspectives on Israeli Anthropology*, ed. Esther Hertzog, Orit Abuhav, and Harvey Goldberg (Detroit: Wayne State University Press, 2010), 191–216.

72. Zivan, *Mi-Nitzana*, 7, 24, 157; Ilani, *Ma'ale Namer*, 43–47. Hebraization of geographic terms was part of the Zionist settlement project, which staked its legitimacy on a purported link to the ancient kingdoms of Judea and Israel. Though it would be difficult to argue that the far reaches of the new state had ever been part of either kingdom, the granting of Hebrew names, often phonologically or semantically similar to existing Arabic ones, gave entirely new settlements an air of historicity. See Nadia Abu El-Haj, *Facts on the Ground: Archaeological Practice and Territorial Self-Fashioning in Israeli Society* (Chicago: University of Chicago Press, 2001).

73. *Ha-Shkhenim Shelanu—Ha-Bedu'im Shel Ha-Arava* (Our Neighbors—the Bedouin of the Arabah), 2018, tinyurl.com/ha-shkhenim; Gidon Ragolsky, "Al ha-bedu'im ha-hayim ba-arava" (On the Bedouin who live in the Arabah), accessed June 15, 2021, tinyurl.com/ragolsky-bedouin.

74. Ilani, *Ma'ale Namer*, 46.

75. Ilani, 57–58.

76. Nir Kedar, "Ben-Gurion's Mamlakhtiyut: Etymological and Theoretical Roots," *Israel Studies* 7, no. 3 (2002): 117–33.

77. Kedar.

78. See note 28.

79. Nasasra, *Bedouins*; Ahmad Amara, "The Negev Land Question: Between Denial and Recognition," *Journal of Palestine Studies* 42, no. 4 (August 1, 2013): 27–47.

80. Zivan, *Mi-Nitzana*, 52–83.

81. Zivan, 52–83.

82. Ami Shacham, "Mayim Ba-Arava" (Water in the Arabah), in *Arava En Ketz: Nof, Teva ve-Adam Ba-Arava* (The Arava: Landscape, Nature and People in the Arava Valley), ed. Yair Giladi et al. (Ein Yahav: Arava, 2012), 218.

83. Amnon Navon, "Hitpathut Ha-Hityashvut Ba-Arava Ha-Tikhona (The Development of the Settlement of the Central Arabah)," in *Arava En Ketz*, 182–99.

84. Shai Ben-Eliyahu, "Ben-Gurion Mesayea Be-Hakamat Ein Yahav," in *Arava En Ketz*, 172–81.

85. Eitan Bar-Yosef, *Vila Ba-Jungel: Afrika Ba-Tarbut Ha-Yisre'elit* (A Villa in the Jungle: Africa in Israeli Culture) (Jerusalem: Van Leer Institute, 2013), 135–39; Haim Yacobi, Chen Misgav, and Smadar Sharon, "Technopolitics, Development and the Colonial-Postcolonial Nexus: Revisiting Settlements Development Aid from Israel to Africa," *Middle Eastern Studies* 56, no. 6 (November 1, 2020): 937–52.

86. Uri Dromi, "Ben Gurion shel ha-arava: Shai Ben-Eliyahu, ehad mi-mey-asdei Ein Yahav, 1935–2010" (Ben Gurion of the Arabah: Shai Ben-Eliyahu, one of the founders of Ein Yahav, 1935–2010), *Ha'aretz*, July 23, 2010, tinyurl.com/obit-ben-eliyahu.

87. Ben-Eliyahu, "Ben-Gurion Mesayea."

88. Henry Rosenfeld, "The Class Situation of the Arab National Minority in Israel," *Comparative Studies in Society and History* 20, no. 3 (1978): 374–407.

89. The security establishment's estimation that the Central Arabah was too remote to form a military target appears to have been borne out by subsequent events. Apart from a brief period during the early 1960s, when Palestinian guerrillas based in Jordan carried out a few attacks, the Arabah

has been spared the violence of the Israeli-Palestinian conflict (see Shani, *Shitat Ha-Arava*, 54–55). While I was carrying out my fieldwork, in late 2015 and early 2016, Israelis were anxious about the rise in individual attacks by Palestinians (known in the press as the "knife intifada"), but there were no attacks in the Arabah and only distant echoes of the panic that had seized the rest of the country could be heard.

90. Ben-Eliyahu, "Ben-Gurion Mesayea."

91. Avi Navon, "Rishonim Ba-Arava" (First in the Arabah), in *Arava En Ketz*, 156–69.

92. Yeruham Cohen, *Tokhnit Allon* (The Allon Plan) (Tel Aviv: Hakibbutz Hameuchad, 1972).

93. Matan Kaminer, "In the Shadow of the Mountains: The Jordan Valley and Israel/Palestine's Marginalized East," *Jadaliyya*, September 9, 2020, tinyurl .com/kaminer-shadow.

94. Levia Applebaum, "Ha-Shilton Ha-Mekomi Ba-Merhav Ha-Kafri Be-Yisra'el" (Local Government in the Israeli Countryside), in *Ha-Shilton Ha-Mekomi: Ben Ha-Medina, Ha-Kehila ve-Kalkalat Ha-Shuk* (The Local Government: Between the State, the Community and the Market Economy), ed. Yagil Levi and Eti Sarig, vol. 2 (Ra'anana: Open University of Israel, 2014), 618; Shnider, *Bimkom Moshavo*, 38–39.

95. Tsippy Eisenman, "Histaglutam shel moshve ha-arava ha-tikhona li-sviva mishtana" (The adaptation of the moshavim of the Central Arabah to a changing environment) (MA thesis, Ben Gurion University, 1994). These *moshavim* are not the only settlements in the Central Arabah. Sapir (est. 1979) and Tzukim (est. 1983) are non-agricultural settlements; Ein Hatzeva (est. 1960), adjacent to Hatzeva but administratively subordinated to the Tamar Regional Center to the north, is an idiosyncratic *moshav* comprised of only five families; Ir Ovot (est. 1967), now abandoned, was a community of Jewish converts to Christianity. Finally, the Bedouin al-Misk and al-'Amrani families still live near Hatzeva. Without official recognition of their tenure, they are under constant threat of displacement. Adv. Netta Amar, personal communication, June 16, 2021; see also *Ha-Shkhenim Shelanu*.

96. Smadar Sharon, *"Kach Kovshim Moledet": Tihknun ve-Yishuv Hevel Lakhish Bi-Shnot Ha-Hamishim* ("And Thus a Homeland Is Conquered": Planning and Settlement in 1950s Lakhish Region) (Tel Aviv: Pardes, 2017).

97. Shnider, *Bimkom Moshavo*, 41. Hatzeva was settled by "children of *kibbutzim* and *moshavim* from around the country, as well as graduates of agricultural schools" of the LSM; Paran by "youth of the Moshavim Movement and graduates of agricultural schools"; and Tzofar by NAHAL groups and "children of Moshavim and [graduates] of agricultural schools." The youngest of the region's *moshavim*, Idan, has a slightly different profile: it was founded by

Jewish immigrants from the United States, some of whom had Israeli spouses. Eisenman, "Histaglutam," 38, 53, 67, 80–83.

98. Quoted in Shani, *Shitat Ha-Arava*, 41–42.

99. Avi Shnider writes of another *moshav* in the Arabah that the phrase "'Arab labor' was used as an aspersion . . . when a motion opposed to the spirit of the *moshav* was brought up in the general assembly, it was often said . . . 'this will lead to Arab labor.' Employment of Arabs on the family farm was perceived as the deepest moral abyss into which one could fall." Avi Shnider, "Dunam Po Ve-Dunam Sham Regev Ahar Regev: Tahalikh Hafratat Ha-Aguda Ha-Shitufit Be-Moshav Ovdim Ba-Aravah" (A Dunam Here and a Dunam There, One Clod after the Other: The Process of Privatization of the Cooperative Association in a Workers' Moshav in the Arabah) (MA thesis, Ben Gurion University, 2008), 54.

100. Amara, "Negev Land Question"; Marjorie Strom, "The Thai Revolution: The Development of Agriculture in the Arava in the 1990s" (MA thesis, Hebrew University, 2004), 52.

101. Strom gives a figure of 923 million NIS (2000 value, about 227 million US dollars) in state and para-state aid for the Central Arabah for the period from the mid-1970s to 2000. This includes grants for *moshav* infrastructure, including irrigation, and subsidized loans for means of production, but not investment in transport infrastructure such as the Arabah Road. Strom, "Thai Revolution," 45; see also Shani, *Shitat Ha-Arava*, 56.

102. O. Oren et al., "Contamination of Groundwater under Cultivated Fields in an Arid Environment, Central Arava Valley, Israel," *Journal of Hydrology* 290, no. 3 (May 25, 2004): 312–28; Shani, *Shitat Ha-Arava*, 77.

103. Oren et al.

104. Shacham, "Mayim Ba-Arava (Water in the Arabah)"; Shani, *Shitat Ha-Arava*, 56. For future plans, see Kaminer, "Agricultural Settlement," 53–56.

105. Moshe Schwartz, "The Decooperativization of Israel's Moshavim, 1985–1994," in *Rural Cooperatives in Socialist Utopia: Thirty Years of Moshav Development in Israel*, ed. Gideon Kressel, Susan Lees, and Moshe Schwartz (Westport, CT: Praeger, 1995), 223–44.

106. Shnider, "Dunam Po," 53.

107. Avi Shnider, "Gendered Division of Labor in a Post-Privatization Moshav: A Case Study of Moshav Tzin in Southern Israel," *Journal of Rural Cooperation* 42, no. 2 (2014): 181–97.

108. Yael Segev, "Zarim Intimiyim: Hatzayat Gvulot Etno-Le'umiyim Be-Sipur Ha-Mitnadvim Ha-Skandinaviyim Ba-Kibbutz" (Intimate Strangers: Crossing Ethno-National Boundaries in the Story of Scandinavian Kibbutz Volunteers) (PhD diss., Bar-Ilan University, 2022).

109. Shnider, "Dunam Po," 55.

110. See Marcus Addis, "Mistreated Volunteers," Telegram, November 8, 1991, Employees (1991-), 81, Ein Yahav Archive. As for the settlers, Shnider (55) reports, "At the end of the day, when family members wished to sit down together in the living room [where the volunteer was lodged] or watch television together, this family pastime was accompanied by a feeling of unease, due to the intrusion into the volunteer's 'room.'"

111. Shnider, 56.

112. Michael Herzfeld, *Cultural Intimacy: Social Poetics and the Real Life of States, Societies and Institutions*, 3rd ed. (London and New York: Routledge, 2016), 139–46.

113. Eyal Weizman, *Hollow Land: Israel's Architecture of Occupation* (London: Verso, 2007), 77–85.

114. Idith Zertal and Akiva Eldar, *Lords of the Land: The Settlers and the State of Israel, 1967–2004* (Hevel Modi'in: Kinneret Zmora-Bitan Dvir, 2005).

115. Jeff Halper, "The 94 Percent Solution: A Matrix of Control," *Middle East Report*, no. 216 (2000): 14–19; Andy Clarno, *Neoliberal Apartheid: Palestine/Israel and South Africa after 1994* (Chicago: University of Chicago Press, 2017).

116. Shlomo Fox, "The Settlement Department Unsettled," in *Rural Cooperatives in Socialist Utopia: Thirty Years of Moshav Development in Israel*, ed. Gideon Kressel, Susan Lees, and Moshe Schwartz (Westport, CT: Praeger, 1995), 55–62; Gershon Shafir, "From Overt to Veiled Segregation: Israel's Palestinian Arab Citizens in the Galilee," *International Journal of Middle East Studies* 50, no. 1 (February 2018): 1–22.

117. Jonathan Nitzan and Shimshon Bichler, *The Global Political Economy of Israel* (London: Pluto Press, 2002); Danny Filc and Uri Ram, eds., *Shilton ha-hon: Ha-hevra ha-yisre'elit ba-idan ha-globali* (The rule of capital: Israeli society in the global age) (Jerusalem: Van Leer Institute, 2004).

118. Susan Lees, *The Political Ecology of the Water Crisis in Israel* (Lanham, MD: University Press of America, 1997), 136–41.

119. Shnider, *Bimkom Moshavo*, 36; Schwartz, "The Decooperativization of Israel's Moshavim, 1985–1994"; Organisation for Economic Co-operation and Development, "OECD Review of Agricultural Policies: Israel 2010" (OECD, 2010), tinyurl.com/OECD-israel.

120. "Ra'ayon im Yuval Krok al ha-matzav,'" (Interview with Yuval Krok on the situation) *Be'enenu* 99, 20 January 1989, p. 16; Shnider, "Dunam Po," 43, 45.

121. A. Khan, P. Martin, and P. Hardiman, "Expanded Production of Labor-Intensive Crops Increases Agricultural Employment," *California Agriculture* 58, no. 1 (January 1, 2004): 35–39.

122. Leila Farsakh, *Palestinian Labour Migration to Israel: Labour, Land and Occupation* (Abingdon: Routledge, 2005).

Chapter 2

1. This theme of coloniality, often qualified with various prefixes and adjectives, is omnipresent in scholarship on Thailand. For a sample, see Bruce London, "Internal Colonialism in Thailand: Primate City Parasitism Reconsidered," *Urban Affairs Quarterly* 14, no. 4 (June 1, 1979): 485–513; Michael Herzfeld, "The Absent Presence: Discourses of Crypto-Colonialism," *South Atlantic Quarterly* 101, no. 4 (March 3, 2003): 899–926; Hong Lysa, "'Stranger within the Gates': Knowing Semi-Colonial Siam as Extraterritorials," *Modern Asian Studies* 38, no. 2 (2004): 327–54; Peter A. Jackson, "The Performative State: Semi-Coloniality and the Tyranny of Images in Modern Thailand," *Sojourn: Journal of Social Issues in Southeast Asia* 19, no. 2 (2004): 219–53; Thongchai Winichakul, "Siam's Colonial Conditions and the Birth of Thai History," in *Unraveling Myths in Southeast Asian Historiography*, ed. Volker Grabowsky (Bangkok: Rivers Books, 2011), 23–45; Jim Glassman, "Cracking Hegemony in Thailand: Gramsci, Bourdieu and the Dialectics of Rebellion," *Journal of Contemporary Asia* 41, no. 1 (February 2011): 25–46. For a discussion of coloniality beyond formal state structures, see the Introduction.

2. Thongchai Winichakul, *Siam Mapped: A History of the Geo-Body of a Nation* (Honolulu: University of Hawaii Press, 1994); A. Iijima, "The Invention of 'Isan' History," *Journal of the Siam Society*, November 28, 2018.

3. Charles F. Keyes, "Hegemony and Resistance in Northeastern Thailand," in *Regions and National Integration in Thailand, 1892–1992*, ed. Volker Grabowsky (Leipzig: Otto Harrassowitz Verlag, 1995), 154–82; Claudio Sopranzetti, *Red Journeys: Inside the Thai Red-Shirt Movement* (Chiang Mai: Silkworm Books, 2012); Jim Glassman, "Lineages of the Authoritarian State in Thailand: Military Dictatorship, Lazy Capitalism and the Cold War Past as Post-Cold War Prologue," *Journal of Contemporary Asia* 50, no. 4 (August 7, 2020): 571–92.

4. For an overview of the region's geology, hydrology, and ecology, see Harald Uhlig, "The 'Problem-Region' Northeastern Thailand," in *Regions and National Integration in Thailand, 1892–1992*, ed. Volker Grabowsky (Leipzig: Otto Harrassowitz Verlag, 1995), 130–32.

5. Charles F. Keyes, "In Search of Land: Village Formation in the Central Chi River Valley, Northeastern Thailand," in *Population, Land and Structural Change in Sri Lanka and Thailand*, ed. James Brow (Leiden: Brill, 1976), 46–47; Porphant, "Thailand's Northeast 'Problem,'" 327; Abu-Lughod, *Before European Hegemony*, 268–69; Volker Grabowsky, "The Isan up to Its Integration into the Siamese State," in *Regions and National Integration in Thailand, 1892–1992*, ed. Volker Grabowsky (Leipzig: Otto Harrassowitz Verlag, 1995), 110.

6. Grabowsky, "The Isan," 111–14.

7. N. J. Enfield, "How to Define 'Lao,' 'Thai,' and 'Isan' Language? A View from Linguistic Science," *Tai Culture* 7, no. 1 (2002); Charles F. Keyes, *Finding*

Their Voice: Northeastern Villagers and the Thai State (Chiang Mai: Silkworm Books, 2014), 15–28; Porphant, "Thailand's Northeast 'Problem,'" 373–75.

8. Kamala, *Forest Recollections*; Pattana Kitiarsa, "Beyond Syncretism: Hybridization of Popular Religion in Contemporary Thailand," *Journal of Southeast Asian Studies* 36, no. 3 (October 1, 2005): 461–87.

9. J. L. Taylor, "Living on the Rim: Ecology and Forest Monks in Northeast Thailand," *Sojourn: Journal of Social Issues in Southeast Asia* 6, no. 1 (1991): 106–25; Kamala, *Forest Recollections*, 198–225. The Khorat Plateau disturbs the binary distinction often made in the literature on Southeast Asia, between lowlands dominated by intensive rice cultivation and kingdoms adhering to world religions, and forested uplands characterized by slash-and-burn farming, religious heterodoxy, and egalitarian political organization. This middleness is reflected in Isaan's language—Tai, but not quite Thai; in its historic subsistence economy—based on a combination of paddy and forest products; and its religion—Buddhism, but of a sylvan-animistic and egalitarian slant. For classic presentations of the binary see Edmund Ronald Leach, *Political Systems of Highland Burma: A Study of Kachin Social Structure* (Boston: Beacon Press, 1965); Willem van Schendel, "Geographies of Knowing, Geographies of Ignorance: Jumping Scale in Southeast Asia," *Environment and Planning D: Society and Space* 20, no. 6 (December 2002): 647–68; and most prominently, James C. Scott, *The Art of Not Being Governed: An Anarchist History of Upland Southeast Asia* (New Haven, CT: Yale University Press, 2009).

10. Grabowsky, "The Isan"; Porphant, "Thailand's Northeast 'Problem'"; Iijima, "Invention."

11. Porphant, "Thailand's Northeast 'Problem,'" 375–78.

12. Porphant, 378.

13. Iijima, "Invention."

14. Keyes, *Finding Their Voice*, 33–52; see also Yoneo Ishii, "A Note on Buddhistic Millenarian Revolts in Northeastern Siam," *Journal of Southeast Asian Studies* 6, no. 2, (1975): 121–26.

15. David B. Johnston, "Opening a Frontier: The Expansion of Rice Cultivation in Central Thailand in the 1890's," in *Population, Land and Structural Change in Sri Lanka and Thailand*, ed. James Brow (Leiden: Brill Academic, 1976), 40–42; Porphant Ouyyanont, *A Regional Economic History of Thailand* (Singapore: ISEAS-Yusof Ishak Institute, 2017), 306.

16. Porphant, *Regional Economic History*, 310–12.

17. Quoted in Porphant, 313.

18. Porphant, 315.

19. Winfried Manig, "The Taxation of the Agricultural Sector in Thailand: The Effects of the Rice Premium," *Verfassung Und Recht in Übersee / Law and Politics in Africa, Asia and Latin America* 10, no. 2 (1977): 289–317; Jim Glassman,

Thailand at the Margins: Internationalization of the State and the Transformation of Labour (Oxford: Oxford University Press, 2004); Keyes, *Finding Their Voice*, 75–76.

20. For an in-depth case study of the "agrarian transition" in Isaan, see Jonathan Rigg and Albert Salamanca, "Connecting Lives, Living, and Location: Mobility and Spatial Signatures in Northeast Thailand, 1982–2009," *Critical Asian Studies* 43, no. 4 (December 1, 2011): 551–75; Jonathan Rigg, Albert Salamanca, and Michael Parnwell, "Joining the Dots of Agrarian Change in Asia: A 25 Year View from Thailand," *World Development* 40, no. 7 (July 2012): 1469–81.

21. Keyes, *Finding Their Voice*; Porphant, "Thailand's Northeast 'Problem,'" 372; Duncan McCargo and Krisadawan Hongladarom, "Contesting Isan-ness: Discourses of Politics and Identity in Northeast Thailand," *Asian Ethnicity* 5, no. 2 (June 2004): 219–34; Gregory S. Gullette, "Rural-Urban Hierarchies, Status Boundaries, and Labour Mobilities in Thailand," *Journal of Ethnic and Migration Studies* 40, no. 8 (August 3, 2014): 1254–74.

22. David Streckfuss, "An 'Ethnic' Reading of 'Thai' History in the Twilight of the Century-Old Official 'Thai' National Model," *South East Asia Research* 20, no. 3 (September 1, 2012): 305–27; Rigg, Salamanca, and Parnwell, "Joining the Dots," 1477; Keyes, *Finding Their Voice*, 77–78; James Mitchell, *Luk Thung: The Culture and Politics of Thailand's Most Popular Music* (Chiang Mai: Silkworm Books, 2015).

23. Glassman, *Margins*, 57.

24. Thak Chaloemtiarana, *Thailand: The Politics of Despotic Paternalism* (Ithaca, NY: Cornell University Press, 2007), 167–69.

25. Issara Phromma et al., "Protected Area Co-Management and Land Use Conflicts Adjacent to Phu Kao—Phu Phan Kham National Park, Thailand," *Journal of Sustainable Forestry* 38, no. 5 (July 4, 2019): 486–507.

26. Ulrich Scholz, "Deforestation in the Asian Tropics—Causes and Consequences," *ASIEN: The German Journal on Contemporary Asia*, no. 21 (1986): 1–29, cited in Uhlig, "The 'Problem-Region' Northeastern Thailand," 133.

27. Stanley Jeyaraja Tambiah, *The Buddhist Saints of the Forest and the Cult of Amulets: A Study in Charisma, Hagiography, Sectarianism, and Millennial Buddhism* (Cambridge: Cambridge University Press, 1984); Kamala, *Forest Recollections*, 236–37.

28. Kamala, *Forest Recollections*, 236–37.

29. Kamala, 198–99; Taylor, "Living on the Rim."

30. Keyes, *Finding Their Voice*, 122.

31. Saiyud Kerdphol, *The Struggle for Thailand: Counter-Insurgency, 1965–1985* (Bangkok: S. Research Center, 1986); Puangthong Rungswasdisab, "Thailand's Response to the Cambodian Genocide," Case Study, Yale University Genocide

Studies Program (New Haven, CT: Yale University, 2004), gsp.yale.edu/thailands-response-cambodian-genocide.

32. Rigg, Salamanca, and Parnwell, "Joining the Dots," 1474.

33. Mary Beth Mills, *Good Daughters, Modern Women: Modernity, Identity, and Female Labor Migration in Thailand* (New Brunswick, NJ.: Rutgers University Press, 1999); Piya Pangsapa, *Textures of Struggle: The Emergence of Resistance among Garment Workers in Thailand* (Ithaca, NY: ILR Press, 2007); Pattana Kitiarsa, *The "Bare Life" of Thai Migrant Workmen in Singapore* (Chiang Mai: Silkworm Books, 2014); Katie Rainwater, "Gold Diggers and Their Housewives: The Gendered Political Economy of Thai Labor Export to Saudi Arabia, 1975–1990," *Critical Asian Studies* 51, no. 4 (2019): 515–36. The latter statistic is my calculation from Benjamin Harkins, "Thailand Migration Report 2019" (Bangkok: United Nations Thematic Working Group on Migration in Thailand, 2019), 20. The cited figures are for the entire country, but are probably representative of Isaan, which sends more migrants than all other regions together.

34. Rigg, Salamanca, and Parnwell, "Joining the Dots," 1474; Pattana, *Bare Life*.

35. Glassman, *Margins*, 8; see also Alan Klima, "Spirits of 'Dark Finance' in Thailand: A Local Hazard for the International Moral Fund," *Cultural Dynamics* 18, no. 1 (March 1, 2006): 33–60. Except during 1997–98, annual GDP growth in Thailand has consistently been equal to or higher than the world average from 1961 to 2019. See World Bank, "GDP Growth (Annual %)—Thailand, World | Data," accessed December 22, 2022, tinyurl.com/gdp-thai-world.

36. Bowie, *Rituals*; Thak, *Despotic Paternalism*.

37. E. P. Thompson, "The Moral Economy of the English Crowd in the Eighteenth Century," *Past & Present*, no. 50 (1971): 98. Note, however, that Thompson did not see paternalism as a *shared* ideology, "for the popular ethic sanctioned direct action by the crowd, whereas the values of order underpinning the paternalist model emphatically did not." Without denying Thai subalterns' capacity to undertake direct action, I would counter that whenever they are not in revolt—that is, most of the time—they do take part in paternalistic ideology. To assume that the revolting subject is authentic while the acquiescent one is in some way artificial is to take part in the Protestant-inflected methodological individualism assumed by Scott and criticized by Gal and Mitchell (see Introduction).

38. See Naor Ben-Yehoyada, "Transnational Political Cosmology: A Central Mediterranean Example," *Comparative Studies in Society and History* 56, no. 4 (October 2014): 870–901.

39. See Eugene D. Genovese, *Roll, Jordan, Roll: The World the Slaves Made* (New York: Pantheon Books, 1974), 91.

40. See, e.g., Aihwa Ong, "The Family Romance of Mandarin Capital," in *Flexible Citizenship: The Cultural Logics of Transnationality* (Durham, NC: Duke University Press, 1999), 139–57.

41. Thak, *Despotic Paternalism*. Sarit's success at positing both the king and himself as father figures may have to do with his occupation of an additional cultural slot that could never be occupied by the king—that of the *nakleng*, the "tough guy" who is "kind to his friends but cruel to his enemies, a compassionate person, a gambler, a heavy drinker, and a lady-killer." See Thak, 225, 254.

42. Thak, *Despotic Paternalism*, 96.

43. See Andrew Walker, "The Rural Constitution and the Everyday Politics of Elections in Northern Thailand," *Journal of Contemporary Asia* 38, no. 1 (February 1, 2008): 84–105.

44. Paul M. Handley, *The King Never Smiles: A Biography of Thailand's Bhumibol Adulyadej* (New Haven, CT: Yale University Press, 2006), chap. 10; Thak, *Despotic Paternalism*, 234; Bowie, *Rituals*, 105–7.

45. Saiyud, *Struggle for Thailand*; Tom Marks, *Making Revolution: The Insurgency of the Communist Party of Thailand in Structural Perspective* (Chon Buri: White Lotus, 1994); Jeffrey M. Moore, *The Thai Way of Counterinsurgency* (Miami Beach, FL: Muir Analytics, 2014); Puangthong Rungswasdisab (Pawakapan), *The Central Role of Thailand's Internal Security Operations Command in the Post-Counter-insurgency Period* (Singapore: ISEAS—Yusof Ishak Institute, 2017).

46. Thak, *Despotic Paternalism*, 153 n. 14.

47. Bowie, *Rituals*.

48. Puangthong, "Thailand's Response."

49. William Shawcross, *The Quality of Mercy: Cambodia, Holocaust, and Modern Conscience* (New York: Simon & Schuster, 1985).

50. Saiyud, *The Struggle for Thailand*; Arthur J. Dommen, "Laos in 1984: The Year of the Thai Border," *Asian Survey* 25, no. 1 (1985): 114–21.

51. Ann Stoler, "Colony," *Political Concepts* 1 (2011), tinyurl.com/pc-stoler.

52. Suchit Bunbongkan, *The Military in Thai Politics, 1981–86* (Singapore: Institute of Southeast Asian Studies, 1987), 22; Tipparin Panyamee, "A Struggle for Getting Free from Social Exclusion of Tribe-War Volunteers: A Case Study of Ban Khiangfa of Sa Doe Phong Subdistrict in Khao Kho District of Phetchabun Province" (PhD diss., Bangkok, National Institute of Development Administration, 2021); T. Marghescu, "Restoration of Degraded Forest Land in Thailand: The Case of Khao Kho" (UN Food and Agriculture Organization, n.d.), tinyurl.com/fao-degraded.

53. Diplomatic cable from Ambassador Abraham Cohen to MASHAV MASOK, March 11, 1983, File 14/8769-שn, "Tayland: Ksharim mediniyim im Yisra'el

bedereg lo memshalti, 1.1.82-9.7.82" (Thailand: Political relations with Israel at non-governmental level, 1.1.82-9.7.82), pp. 112–113, Israel State Archive Online.

54. Africa Research Group, "Israel: Imperialist Mission in Africa," *Tricontinental* 15 (1969): 39–57; D. V. Segre, "The Philosophy and Practice of Israel's International Cooperation," in *Israel in the Third World*, ed. Michael Curtis and Susan Aurelia Gitelson (New Brunswick, NJ: Transaction Books, 1976), 7–26; Jacob Abadi, *Israel's Quest for Recognition and Acceptance in Asia: Garrison State Diplomacy* (London: Frank Cass, 2004); Rivi Gillis, "Pituah Ha-Zehut: Hakhshara Shel Afrika'im Be-Yisra'el, 1958–1980" (The Development of Identity: Training of Africans in Israel, 1958–1980) (PhD diss., Tel Aviv University, 2017).

55. Bar-Yosef, *Vila*, 129; see also Yacobi, Misgav, and Sharon, "Technopolitics."

56. Magdalena Kozłowska and Michał Lubina, "The Burmese Road to Israeli-Style Cooperative Settlements: The Namsang Project, 1956–63," *Journal of Southeast Asian Studies* 52, no. 4 (December 2021): 712, 710.

57. Kozłowska and Lubina, 721–22; see also Chen Bram and Ran Shauli, "Israel-Myanmar Relations and the Rohingya Mass Killings," in *Israel-Asia Relations in the Twenty-First Century: The Search for Partners in a Changing World*, ed. Yoram Evron and Rotem Kowner (Abingdon: Routledge, 2024).

58. Abadi, *Israel's Quest*.

59. Suchit, *Military*, 56; Handley, *The King*, 190; Shahar Shoham, "The Heroes from Isaan Working in Israel: The Production of Migrants in the Thailand-Israel Migration Regime" (PhD diss., Humboldt-Universität, 2024), chap. 4. Embassy of Israel in Thailand, "Thai-Israel Economic Cooperation," n.d. (probably 1988), File 15/9689-חצ, "Tayland: Yahasim mediniyim im Yisra'el bedereg memshalti, 12.87-1.88" (Thailand: Political relations with Israel at governmental level, 12.87-1.88), pp. 177–180, Israel State Archive Online.

60. L. Laufer, "Country Evaluation: Thailand," Draft, May 1983, File 12/8769-חצ, "Tayland: Ksharim mediniyim im Yisra'el bedereg lo memshalti, 1.11.82-17.6.83" (Thailand: Political relations with Israel at non-governmental level, 1.11.82-17.6.83), p. 5, Israel State Archive Online.

61. Handley, *The King*, 270.

62. Handley, 270. For more on Eisenberg's government connections, his business relations in Asia and his arms trading, see Shlomo Frankel and Shimshon Bichler, *Hameyuhasim: Atzulat Ha-Hon Shel Yisrael* (The Rich Families: Israel's Aristocracy of Finance) (Tel Aviv: CADIM, 1984), 142–52.

63. Shoham, "Heroes," chap. 1.

64. "Siha im sgan SAHAH" (Conversation with Deputy Foreign Minister), March 7, 1985, File 81/0678-חצ, "Tayland: Yahasim mediniyim im Yisra'el

bedereg memshalti, 18.12.84-31.3.85" (Thailand: Political relations with Israel at governmental level, 18.12.84-31.3.85), p. 95, Israel State Archive Online.

65. Suchit, *Military in Thai Politics*, 19.

66. "Pgisha shel MASOK im Avraham Cohen, Shagrir Yisrael leshe'avar be-Tayland" (Meeting of Asia-Oceania Department Head with Abraham Cohen, Former Israeli Ambassador to Thailand), Minutes, May 3, 1985, File 1/1678-חצ, "Tayland: Yahasim mediniyim im Yisra'el bedereg memshalti, 1.4.85-30.9.85" (Thailand: Political relations with Israel at governmental level, 1.4.85-30.9.85), p. 294, Israel State Archive Online.

67. "Pgisha shel MASOK." See also full file on "Tayland: Proyekt hityashvut sfar, 4.86-3.88" (Thailand: Frontier Settlement Project), File 11/0969-חצ, Ibid. In a 1985 meeting former ambassador Cohen predicted that Pichit would soon become prime minister. Though this never happened, his assessment jibes with Suchit Bunbongkarn's sketch of the Thai balance of power at the time. See Suchit, *Military*, 30.

68. "Kvutzat hityashvut ve-homer al filipinim" (Settlement Group and Material on the Philippines), Military Cable from Irit Atzmon, Foreign Relations Division, to Col. Ehud Gross, Military Attaché in Bangkok, March 28, 1987, File 11/0969-חצ, "Tayland: Proyekt hithyashvut sfar," 13, Israel State Archive Online.

69. Interviews, June 2017, May 2023, June 2023; Hevron Family, "Taylandim ba-arava" (Thais in the Arabah), n.d., p. 2, Moshav Ein Yahav Archive. This manuscript, compiled by a couple who served as "Thai coordinators" in their *moshav*, includes quite a bit of information on the first groups of Thais to arrive in Israel. Much of it corroborated by other sources and can thus be viewed as reasonably reliable.

70. "Hishtalmut be-kibbutz le-ovdei bank ha-hakla'ut" (Training in a Kibbutz for Agricultural Bank Workers), Telex from Ariel Kerem, Economic Attaché, to Vered Tours, October 21, 1987, File 4/0969-חצ, "Tayland: Yahasim mediniyim im Yisra'el bedereg lo memshalti" (Thailand: Political relations with Israel at non-governmental level), 229, Israel State Archive Online; Hevron Family, "Taylandim ba-'arava," ibid.

71. Interview, June 2023.

72. "Bikur ha-General Pichit, Sgan Mefaked Tzva Tayland (21.12-24.12)" (Visit of General Pichit, Deputy Head of Thai Army), Letter from Ruth Cahanov to Deputy Chief of Asia-Pacific Branch, Foreign Office, December 24, 1987, File 51/9869-חצ, "Tayland: Yahasim mediniyim im Yisra'el bedereg memshalti 12.87-1.88," pp. 214–216 (Thailand: Political relations with Israel at governmental level 12.87-1.88), Israel State Archive Online.

73. Interviews, May and June 2023.

74. Erik Cohen writes, without providing further references, that "the first Thais who came to agricultural settlements in Israel beginning in 1986 came as trainees and were categorized as volunteers . . . Among them were employees of the Thai Agricultural Bank and military men tasked with establishing new settlements along Thailand's frontiers with neighboring countries." Yahel Kurlander gives 1983 as a starting date, but cites only a 2002 obituary of Vered and a 1988 Interior Ministry document that counts 1,337 Thais in Israel between 1980 and 1987—a number that might include some of the Ovda airport construction workers. See Erik Cohen, "Ovdim Taylandim ba-Hakla'ut ha-Yisre'elit (Thai workers in Israeli agriculture)," in *Ha-po'alim ha -hadashim: Ovdim mi-Medinot Zarot be-Yisra'el* (The New Workers: Wage Earners From Foreign Countries in Israel), ed. Roby Nathanson and Lea Achdut (Tel Aviv: Hakibbutz Hameuchad, 1999), 159–60; Yahel Kurlander, "Mis'hur Ha-Hagira: Al Tzmihata, Sigsuga ve-Shinuya Shel Ta'asiyat Ha-Giyus Veha-Tivukh Le-Hagirat Avoda Le-Hakla'ut Mi-Tayland Le-Yisra'el" (The Marketization of Migration: On the Emergence, Flourishment and Change of the Recruitment Industry for Agricultural Migrant Workers from Thailand to Israel) (PhD diss., University of Haifa, 2019), 77 n. 173.

75. "Taylandim ba-arava," ibid; interview, June 2023. For a discussion of sartorial difference and the racialization of migrants, see Chapter 4.

76. Interviews, May and June 2023.

77. David Regev, "Hadash: Mitnadvim Mi-Tayland" (New: Volunteers from Thailand), *Yedioth Ahronoth*, June 9, 1989. My English transliteration of a Hebrew transliteration of this Thai name is pure guesswork.

78. "Taylandim ba-arava," 2.

79. Interview, January 2018.

80. Interview, May 2023.

Chapter 3

1. Cohen, "Ovdim Taylandim," 160, 165.

2. Kurlander, "Mis'hur Ha-Hagira," 79–81.

3. Leila Farsakh, "Palestinian Labor Flows to the Israeli Economy: A Finished Story?" *Journal of Palestine Studies* 32, no. 1 (October 2002): 13–27; Adriana Kemp and Rebeca Raijman, *Ovdim u-zarim: Ha-kalkala ha-politit shel hagirat avoda le-Yisra'el* (Migrants and Workers: The Political Economy of Labour Migration in Israel) (Tel Aviv: Hakibbutz Hameuchad, 2008).

4. Kemp and Raijman, *Ovdim u-zarim*; Claudia Liebelt, *Caring for the "Holy Land": Filipina Domestic Workers in Israel* (New York: Berghahn, 2011).

5. Central Bureau of Statistics, *Shnaton Statisti Le-Yisra'el* (Israel Statistical Yearbook), vol. 41, 1990, 67; vol. 62, 2000, sec. 2.41.

6. For the national trend in migrant numbers, see Rebeca Raijman and Nonna Kushnirovich, "Labor Migrant Recruitment Practices in Israel" (Jerusalem: JDC, March 2012). By 2013, the first year for which I have been able to find accurate statistics, the *moshavim* of the Central Arabah employed 3,132 migrant workers—about equal to the Israeli population.

7. Rotem Streckman, "Pilpelim Atzuvim: Kach Karas Mikhre Ha-Zahav Shel Hakla'ei Ha-Arava" (Sad Peppers: This Is How the Arabah Farmers' Goldmine Collapsed), *TheMarker*, May 6, 2014, tinyurl.com/sad-peppers.

8. As we have seen (Chapter 1, n. 110), volunteers and their hosts were not always comfortable with these arrangements either.

9. However, Tiam also insisted that the employer not interfere in his domestic life; this attitude contrasts strongly with those of Ya'ir's employees, including Song, as discussed below. See Israel Drori, *Foreign Workers in Israel: Global Perspectives* (Albany: SUNY Press, 2009), 111.

10. Raijman and Kushnirovich, "Practices," 16.

11. For further discussion of norms regarding romantic relationships in Isaan, see Chapter 6.

12. Thanapauge Chamaratana et al., "Connecting the Disconnected: Background, Practices and Motives of Labour Brokers in Isan, Thailand—an Explorative Study," *International Journal of Interdisciplinary Social Sciences* 5, no. 5 (2010): 359–72.

13. Kurlander, "Mis'hur Ha-Hagira," 120–24.

14. Nonna Kushnirovich and Rebeca Raijman, "The Impact of Bilateral Agreements on Labor Migration to Israel: A Comparison between Migrant Workers Who Arrived Before and After the Implementation of Bilateral Agreements" (Jerusalem: CIMI, 2017); Thanapauge et al., "Connecting the Disconnected."

15. See Matan Boord, "Creating the Labor-Zionist Family: Masculinity, Sexuality, and Marriage in Mandate Palestine," *Jewish Social Studies* 22, no. 3 (2017): 38–67.

16. Genovese, *Roll, Jordan, Roll*, 5.

17. See Boord, "Labor-Zionist Family."

18. Cohen, "Ovdim Taylandim," 194; Nurit Bretsky, "Yom Huledet Sameah Bhumipol" (Happy Birthday Bhumipol), *Ma'ariv*, December 24, 2001; Drori, *Foreign Workers*, 109.

19. Bretsky, "Yom Huledet." See also Central Arava Regional Council, "Anu mazminim etkhem le-hagigat yom ha-huledet le-melekh Tailand" (We Invite You to a Celebration of the Birthday of the King of Thailand), Circular, November 29, 1993, Ein Yahav Archive.

20. Cassaniti, *Living Buddhism*, 149–74.

21. I borrow this phrase from Reiko Ohnuma, who uses it in a different (but related) context. See her "Gift," in *Critical Terms for the Study of Buddhism*, ed. Donald S. Lopez (Chicago: University of Chicago Press, 2005), 103–23.

22. Stonington, "Karma Masters."

23. Aulino, "Social Body."

24. See Étienne Balibar, "Racism and Nationalism," in *Race, Nation, Class: Ambiguous Identities*, ed. Immanuel Wallerstein and Étienne Balibar (London: Verso, 1991), 37–68.

25. Note that the pronouns that I have translated as "we" and "they" in the above quote, *haw* and *khaw*, can also mean "I," "he," or "she," depending on context.

26. Haim Levita, "Hilufei Shtahim Ba-Arava" (Territory Swaps in the Arabah), in *Arava En Ketz*, 294–97; Cerbero, "Gvul Yisra'el-Yarden"; Gil Slavin and Ya'ir Giladi, "Tayarut Ba-Arava" (Tourism in the Arabah), in *Arava En Ketz*, 232–43.

27. Interview, June 2023.

28. This is a tongue-in-cheek reference to the Hebrew subtitle of the 1982 hit film *E.T. the Extra-Terrestrial*.

29. Dafna Hirsch, "'Hummus Is Best When It Is Fresh and Made by Arabs': The Gourmetization of Hummus in Israel and the Return of the Repressed Arab," *American Ethnologist* 38, no. 4 (November 1, 2011): 617–30.

30. See Stephen D. Krasner, "Structural Causes and Regime Consequences: Regimes as Intervening Variables," *International Organization* 36, no. 2 (1982): 185–205, cited in Anna Boucher and Justin Gest, "Migration Studies at a Crossroads: A Critique of Immigration Regime Typologies," *Migration Studies* 3, no. 2 (July 2015): 2–3.

31. Cohen, "Ovdim Taylandim," 191; Thanapauge et al., "Connecting the Disconnected."

32. Interview, June 2023.

33. Yoav Peled, "Profits or Glory? The Twenty-Eighth Elul of Arik Sharon," *New Left Review* 29 (October 2004); Uri Ram, *The Globalization of Israel: McWorld in Tel Aviv, Jihad in Jerusalem* (New York: Routledge, 2008).

34. Peled, "Profits or Glory?"; Filc and Ram, *Shilton ha-hon*.

35. See Ferruh Yılmaz, "Right-Wing Hegemony and Immigration: How the Populist Far-Right Achieved Hegemony through the Immigration Debate in Europe," *Current Sociology* 60, no. 3 (May 1, 2012): 368–81; Ian S. Lustick, "Israel as a Non-Arab State: The Political Implications of Mass Immigration of Non-Jews," *Middle East Journal* 53, no. 3 (1999): 417–33; Yossi Yonah, "Israel's Immigration Policies: The Twofold Face of the 'Demographic Threat,'" *Social Identities* 10, no. 2 (March 1, 2004): 195–218.

36. Yael Berda, *Living Emergency: Israel's Permit Regime in the Occupied West Bank* (Stanford, CA: Stanford University Press, 2018).

37. Sarah S. Willen, "Toward a Critical Phenomenology of 'Illegality': State Power, Criminalization, and Abjectivity among Undocumented Migrant Workers in Tel Aviv, Israel," *International Migration* 45, no. 3 (2007): 8–38.

38. Barak Kalir, "The Jewish State of Anxiety: Between Moral Obligation and Fearism in the Treatment of African Asylum Seekers in Israel," *Journal of Ethnic and Migration Studies* 41, no. 4 (March 21, 2015): 580–98.

39. Kemp and Raijman, *Ovdim u-zarim*, 117–25; Kurlander, "Mis'hur Ha-Hagira," 198.

40. Matan Kaminer, "Giving Them the Slip: Israeli Employers' Strategic Falsification of Pay Slips to Disguise the Violation of Thai Farmworkers' Right to the Minimum Wage," *Journal of Legal Anthropology* 3, no. 2 (2019): 124–27.

41. Berda, *Living Emergency*; Willen, *Transnational Migration*; Maya Shapiro, "The Development of a 'Privileged Underclass': Locating Undocumented Migrant Women and Their Children in the Political Economy of Tel Aviv, Israel," *Dialectical Anthropology* 37, no. 3/4 (2013): 423–41.

42. Shmuel Diklo and Galei Tzahal, "HAK Shlomo Benizri Hursha Be-Kabalat Shohad Meha-Kablan Moshe Sela Uve-Hafarat Emunim" (MK Shlomo Benizri Convicted of Taking Bribes from Contractor Moshe Sela and of Breach of Trust), *Globes*, April 1, 2008, tinyurl.com/globes-benizri; Kurlander, "Mis'hur Ha-Hagira," 113–14.

43. Yahel Kurlander and Matan Kaminer, "Ovdim Kvu'im Me-Ahorei Ha-Bayit: Ha'asakat Mehagrei Avoda Mi-Tayland Ba-Hakla'ut Ba-Merhav Ha-Kafri" (Permanent Workers in the Backyard: The Employment of Migrant Workers from Thailand in Agriculture in the Countryside), *Horizons in Geography* 98 (2020): 131–48; Yahel Kurlander, "On the Establishment of Agricultural Migration Industry in Israel's Countryside," *Geography Research Forum* 41, no. 1 (July 15, 2022): 19–34.

44. Raijman and Kushnirovich, "Practices," 16.

45. Streckman, "Pilpelim."

46. Ron Stein, "Ha-Mosdiyim Sakhru et ROAH Barlev Lahkor Nefilata Shel Agrexco (Institutionals Hire CPA Barlev to Investigate the Fall of Agrexco)," *Globes*, August 25, 2011, tinyurl.com/globes-agrexco; Shnider, *Bimkom Moshavo*, 69–72.

47. Since the wages of Thai migrants in Israel are illegally low, there is no publicly available time-series of their evolution. Using the Israeli minimum wage as a rough and very generous proxy, however, one can arrive at an estimate. The ratio of this minimum wage to average income in Isaan went from 9.2 in 1995 to a peak of 18.2 in 2001, following the Thai financial crisis of the late 1990s, but then dipped down to 8.4 in 2015. My calculations from NSOT

(National Statistics Office of Thailand), "Per Capita Income of Population, New Series by Region and Province: 1995–2011" (Bangkok), accessed August 22, 2018, tinyurl.com/nso-income; NII (National Insurance Institute of Israel), "Skhar minimum" (Minimum wage), accessed March 30, 2018, tinyurl.com/nii-miniwage.

48. My calculation from IIM (Israel Interior Ministry), "Reshimat Haktza'ot Le-Ha'asakat Ovdim Zarim Be-anaf Ha-Hakla'ut Li-Shnat 2013" (List of Allocations for the Employment of Foreign Workers in the Agricultural Sector for the Year 2013), 2012, tinyurl.com/alloc-2013.

49. During my fieldwork, the Thai holiday of Songkran was celebrated by Ein Amal's Thai workers without any Israeli participation whatsoever (myself excepted). See Matan Kaminer, "A Lonely Songkran in the Arabah," *Middle East Report* 279 (2016): 34–37.

50. Kurlander, "Mis'hur Ha-Hagira," 126–65.

51. Kushnirovich and Raijman, "Impact," 18; Yuval Livnat and Hila Shamir, "Gaining Control? Bilateral Labor Agreements and the Shared Interest of Sending and Receiving Countries to Control Migrant Workers and the Illicit Migration Industry," *Theoretical Inquiries in Law* 23, no. 2 (July 26, 2022): 65–94.

52. Shahar Shoham and Yahel Kurlander, "Niyar Avoda Be-Nose Alimut Minit Klapei Mehagrot Avoda Be-Anaf Ha-Hakla'ut Be-Yisra'el" (Working Paper on Sexual Violence Directed at Female Migrant Workers in the Agricultural Sector in Israel) (Tel Aviv: Trafflab, October 2021), tinyurl.com/shoham -kurlander-women.

53. Interview, June 2023.

54. Between 2012 and 2016, according to data furnished to me by the IOM office in Bangkok, 82.2 percent of TIC applicants were of Isaan origin, and 10.8 percent were from the North, while only 6 percent came from the Central region, which includes Bangkok.

55. This summary is based on my calculations from national-scale fig-ures provided by Rosalia Sciortino and Sureeporn Punpuing, "International Migration in Thailand 2009" (Bangkok: International Organization for Migration, Thailand Office, 2009), 17; and Harkins, "Thailand Migration Report 2019."

56. See Chapter 6. See also Min Ji Kim, "The Republic of Korea's Employment Permit System (EPS): Background and Rapid Assessment," International Migration Papers (Geneva: International Labour Organization, 2015); Seonyoung Seo, "Temporalities of Class in Nepalese Labour Migration to South Korea," *Current Sociology*, October 4, 2018. See also Supang Chantavanich, "Thailand's Responses to Transnational Migration during Economic Growth and Economic Downturn," *Journal of Social Issues in Southeast Asia* 14, no. 1 (April 1999): 159–77; Shahar Shoham, "Pickers and Packers: Translocal

Narratives of Returning Thai Agriculture Labour Migrants from Israel" (MA thesis, Humboldt-Universität, 2017), 47–51; Katie Rainwater and Lindy Brooks Williams, "Thai Guestworker Export in Decline: The Rise and Fall of the Thailand-Taiwan Migration System," *International Migration Review* 53, no. 2 (June 2019): 371–95.

57. Antoine Pécoud, "What Do We Know about the International Organization for Migration?" *Journal of Ethnic and Migration Studies* 44, no. 10 (July 27, 2018): 1621–38. In 2019, after its request that some of the fees still paid by migrants be assumed by their employers was denied, the IOM announced its departure from the arrangement beginning in July 2020. The task of recruitment then reverted to the Thai Ministry of Labor. See Reuters, "Labor Abuse Fears Rise for Thai Migrant Workers in Israel under New Deal," *Jerusalem Post*, July 21, 2020, tinyurl.com/jpost-iom; Yahel Kurlander and Avinoam Cohen, "BLAs as Sites for the Meso-Level Dynamics of Institutionalization: A Cross-Sectoral Comparison," *Theoretical Inquiries in Law* 23, no. 2 (July 19, 2022): 260.

58. "Mis'hur Ha-Hagira"; "On the Establishment"; Kurlander and Cohen, "BLAs."

59. For minimum wage rates and exchange rates, see, respectively: NII, "Skhar minimum (Minimum wage)" and BOI (Bank of Israel), "Foreign Currency Market—Average Exchange Rates," accessed March 30, 2018, tinyurl .com/boi-rates.

60. My anecdotal figures are corroborated by those of Kushnirovich and Raijman, based on a survey of 25 Thai migrants in Israel carried out in 2016. They found that the average worker earned 4,792 NIS a month after taxes, worked 9.3 hours a day, and had 3.7 days off a month (thus working 26.74 days in an average month). From this I calculate an average hourly wage—including overtime hours—of 19.27 NIS. See Kushnirovich and Raijman, "Impact," 27–28.

61. Given the trust vested in me by the Sadots, I did not see fit to collect data pertaining to legal issues on their farm. The findings in this section are not based on my participant observation in Ein Amal, but on quantitative and qualitative research I undertook with Noa Shauer of Workers' Hotline and secondary sources. However, my personal experience roughly corroborates these findings, excepting those on women workers, as I did not interact with any. For additional evidence on the violation of wage laws as well as on living conditions and other violations, see Noa Shauer and Matan Kaminer, "Below the Minimum—Violation of Wage Laws in the Employment of Migrant Farmworkers" (Tel Aviv: Kav LaOved, 2014), tinyurl.com/below-min; Human Rights Watch, "A Raw Deal: Abuses of Thai Workers in Israel's Agricultural Sector," 2015, tinyurl.com/hrw-raw-deal; Kushnirovich and Raijman, "Impact"; Kaminer, "Giving Them the Slip." For sexual assault and harassment, see Fallon Wexler, "Female Migrant Agricultural Workers in Israel and

Gender-Based Violations of Labor Rights" (Tel Aviv: Kav LaOved, December 2013), tinyurl.com/fallon-klo; Janan Bsoul, "Hithananti Lalekhet La-Rofe, Aval Ha-Bos Lo Hiskim (I Begged to Go to the Doctor, but the Boss Didn't Agree)," *TheMarker*, September 19, 2016, tinyurl.com/bsoul-thai; Shoham and Kurlander, "Niyar Avoda."

62. Violation of minimum wage laws may have come as no surprise to workers, as such violations are also very prevalent in Thailand. See Glassman, *Margins*, 106, 129.

63. In September 2016, there were 22,226 foreign agricultural workers in Israel, almost all of them from Thailand, less than 3 percent of whom were undocumented; compare this to 26 percent in the caregiving sector, 14 percent in construction, and 25 percent among "expert" workers; my calculations from PIBA (Population and Immigration Authority) and CIMI (Center for International Migration and Integration), "Labor Migration to Israel," 2016, 7–8, tinyurl.com/labmigisr. However, in May 2023 PIBA announced that a much larger number of 7,000 workers was employed illegally, implying that measures instituted to facilitate recruitment during the pandemic were being abused. See Inbal Mashash, "Hozer Rosh Minhal 123202: Hakla'im Ba'alei Heterim Le-Ha'asakat Oved Zar" (Authority Director's Circular 123202: Farmers with a Permit to Employ a Foreign Worker) (Population and Immigration Authority, May 31, 2023), tinyurl.com/mashash-hozer.

64. I have been unable to find data on the number of male Thais living in Israel legally through marriage to Israeli citizens, and though I have met some "mixed" couples of this kind, my impression is that they are rare. Somewhat more common are marriages between Thai women and Israeli men, usually contracted following the men's tourism in Thailand. (This is not necessarily sex tourism, but for that phenomenon, see Guy Brucker, "Tayare min yisre'elim be-Tailand" (Israeli male sex tourists in Thailand) (MA thesis, University of Haifa, 2007)). Due to their bilingualism and legal status, many Thai women formerly or currently married to Israelis participate in the migration regime as interpreters, for example in manpower agencies and NGOs.

65. Kemp and Raijman, *Ovdim u-zarim*, 90–98; Kemp and Raijman, "Bringing In."

66. Kemp and Raijman, *Ovdim u-zarim*, 123.

67. In the early days of the "closed skies" period, illegal practices such as passport confiscation and even the kidnapping and forced deportation of workers were common, but according to Workers' Hotline and Human Rights Watch, who mounted a campaign against such practices, they are no longer prevalent. Orit Ronen, Workers' Hotline, personal communication; see also

Ido Efrati, "Tofa'a: Hakla'im megarshim atzma'it ovdim zarim" (Phenomenon: Farmers independently deporting foreign workers), *Ynet*, August 29, 2005, tinyurl.com/indy-deport; HRW, "Raw Deal."

68. Thai workers in Israel are not slaves according to any scholarly definition, nor (more importantly) in their own opinion. That said, Israeli officialdom's casual use of slavery-redolent vocabulary—*kvila*, usually translated as "binding," literally means "shackling"—is remarkable. See also Hila Shamir and Maayan Niezna, "An Alternative Anti-Trafficking Action Plan: A Proposed Model Based on a Labor Approach to Trafficking," SSRN Scholarly Paper (Rochester, NY, November 1, 2020), doi.org/10.2139/ssrn.3835710; Shoham, "Heroes," chap. 2.

69. For an employer's expression of such views, See Shauer and Kaminer, "Below the minimum," 11.

70. Central Arava Regional Council, "Ze Pashut Lo Oved Bli Yadayim Ovdot" (It Just Doesn't Work without Working Hands), August 2006, 4. The language about "other parts of the country" seems to refer not to Thais living in other regions, but rather to migrants of other national origins, who have been targeted as "demographic threats" since the turn of the millennium.

71. Again, this situation appears to have changed—see note 63 above.

72. Michael Burawoy, "The Functions and Reproduction of Migrant Labor: Comparative Material from Southern Africa and the United States," *American Journal of Sociology* 81, no. 5 (March 1976): 1050–87; Claude Meillassoux, *Maidens, Meal and Money: Capitalism and the Domestic Community* (Cambridge: Cambridge University Press, 1981).

73. Meillassoux, *Maidens*, 95, 127–36; see also Harold Wolpe, "Capitalism and Cheap Labour-Power in South Africa: From Segregation to Apartheid," *Economy and Society* 1, no. 4 (November 1, 1972): 425–56. Another influential theory of "split labor markets" has been proposed by Edna Bonacich, who suggested that such markets are the result of a compromise between capital and powerful sectors of the working class. There is ample evidence for this dynamic in historical situations such the white labor movement's push for Chinese exclusion in the US West in the late nineteenth century and apartheid South Africa, as well as in the early history of the LSM. However, the labor movement in Israel has been weak for decades, since before the mass importation of migrant workers began, and has played only a marginal role in designing the migration regime they face. See Bonacich, "Ethnic Antagonism," 555–56; Sai Englert, "Hebrew Labor without Hebrew Workers: The Histadrut, Palestinian Workers, and the Israeli Construction Industry," *Journal of Palestine Studies* 52, no. 3 (July 3, 2023): 23–45.

74. It is a common trope among employers, and in the literature, that Thais and other migrants "do not aspire" to settle down permanently

in Israel. See Cohen, "Ovdim Taylandim," 202; cf. Galia Sabar, *Lo banu le -hisha'er: Mehagrei avoda me-Afrika le-Yisrael uve-Hazara* (We're Not Here to Stay: African Migrant Workers in Israel and Back in Africa) (Tel Aviv: Tel Aviv University Press, 2008). The migrants I spoke to tended to agree, but treated the question as a wildly hypothetical one, as they realized such a chance was not likely to ever materialize. Shahar Shoham's interlocutors were more willing to entertain the scenario: one remarked that "many, many people would like to move" permanently if it were possible. The political-economic stakes were clear to another interviewee, who remarked: "I am not sure the Israeli people will accept Thais. Israeli people have a lot of money, they are the employers, and we are just workers. . . . If they will employ Israelis they will have to pay them more money, this is why they hire Thai workers." Shoham, "Pickers," 66–67.

Chapter 4

1. Marx, *Capital* vol. 1, 279–80; see also William Clare Roberts, *Marx's Inferno: The Political Theory of Capital* (Princeton, NJ: Princeton University Press, 2018).

2. The literature that sympathetically corrects Marx on gender and race is voluminous and constantly growing, but key references include Guha, *Dominance without Hegemony*; Robinson, *Black Marxism*; Walter Johnson and Robin D. G. Kelley, *Race Capitalism Justice* (Cambridge, MA: MIT Press, 2018); Banaji, *Theory as History*; Himani Bannerji, "Building from Marx: Reflections on Class and Race," *Social Justice* 32, no. 4 (102) (2005): 144–60; Mies, *Patriarchy and Accumulation*; Bhattacharya and Vogel, *Social Reproduction Theory*.

3. Kaminer, "Rebirth."

4. Keane, "Semiotics": 414.

5. For an elaboration of this argument through a comparison of Thai migrants with Israeli citizen-workers, see Kaminer, "Zero Degree."

6. Shnider, "Gendered Division"; Michael Chyutin, *Architecture and Utopia: The Israeli Experiment* (London: Routledge, 2016).

7. Kobi Yisha'ayahu, "Rokhshe Karka'ot Yecholim La'asot Tsu'a Yafa al Ha-Hashka'a" (Land Buyers Can Make a Nice Return on Their Investment), *Globes*, March 18, 2016, tinyurl.com/globes-land; Arik Mirovsky, "Israel Tops World in Increase in Housing Prices," *Haaretz*, March 13, 2017.

8. An acronym coined by sociologist Baruch Kimmerling and standing for "Ashkenazi, secular, socialist, liberal." The "socialist" aspect of this identity is rapidly fading. See Kimmerling, *Ketz shilton ha-ahusalim* (The end of Ashkenazi hegemony) (Jerusalem: Keter, 2001); Matan Kaminer, "Ha-zman she-aharei ha-'Post'" (The time after the "post"), *Hazman Hazeh*, May 11, 2021, hazmanhazeh.org.il/post/.

9. For a classic discussion of cultural and social capital, see Pierre Bourdieu, "The Forms of Capital," in *Handbook of Theory and Research for the Sociology of Education*, ed. John G. Richardson (New York: Greenwood Press, 1986), 241–58.

10. Streckman, "Pilpelim"; Ferry Biedermann, "Strong Shekel Changes Israel's Economy and Makes Investors Think Twice," CNBC, July 7, 2017, tinyurl.com/strong-nis.

11. The Hebrew term *avoda zara*, literally meaning "foreign labor" and used in that sense as well, is also the term for "idol worship," carrying a strong connotation of danger to the nation due to its association with the destruction of the First and Second Temples and the end of Jewish sovereignty. This connotation dovetails with exploitation anxiety. See Kemp and Raijman, *Ovdim u-zarim*, 95.

12. Erik Cohen observed this practice over twenty years ago. See "Ovdim Taylandim," 174.

13. In *Textures of Struggle*, her study of female factory workers in Bangkok, Piya Pangsapa (71) writes that "cultural norms and societal attitudes [regarding household labor] are typically more relaxed and *sabai-sabai* (easygoing) in Thailand than elsewhere, allowing men and women to adapt readily to their particular situations, especially to such practical day-to-day matters as cooking and cleaning. Interestingly, many women mentioned that their own parents had shared equally in household chores, a few women even commenting very casually that their fathers did the cooking and cleaning in the family." See also Drori, *Foreign Workers*, 113.

14. Students from around the Global South come to the Arabah for programs of varying length that combine work and study at the regional Arava International School for Agriculture Training. Programs like these, which may be thought of as a continued manifestation of "structural hypocrisy" (see Chapter 2), have come in for heavy criticism, with students and human rights NGOs alleging that they constitute illegal labor importation at best, fraud and human trafficking at worst. The students I met did not express serious criticism of the program, but evaluating it was not within the scope of my research. See Bar Peleg and Josh Breiner, "They Came to Study in Israel—and Ended Up Victims of Slavery and Trafficking," *Haaretz*, November 28, 2022, tinyurl.com/haaretz-slaves2; Kurlander and Cohen, "BLAs," 261–63.

15. Bonacich, "Ethnic Antagonism," 550–51.

16. The moral dimensions of these trade-offs are explored in Chapter 6. See also Andrew Alan Johnson, "Deferral and Intimacy: Long-Distance Romance and Thai Migrants Abroad," *Anthropological Quarterly* 91, no. 1 (2018): 307–24.

17. Aulino, "Social Body," 427 n. 15; Michael Herzfeld, *Siege of the Spirits: Community and Polity in Bangkok* (Chicago: University of Chicago Press, 2016), 48.

18. In her ethnography of migrants returning from Israel to Isaan, Shahar Shoham comes to slightly different conclusions about this intermediary role. She finds that the employer usually appoints "one of the workers who has basic knowledge of English" to the position of "head of the workers," which sometimes carries extra benefits. Interestingly, she recognizes that one of the job's attractions consists in the opportunity it provides "to become more familiar with the employer through constant communication," a familiarity that one former migrant formulated in paternalistic terms: "after I was there for a long time the other employers didn't think that I am a worker, they say [*sic*] I was the son of my employer." She concludes that "[t]his structure . . . created further isolation and stronger hierarchies between the employers and the rest of the employees, resulting in almost a lack of direct communication between them," leaving the "head of the workers" himself—who is in constant and direct communication with both parties—in an ambiguous position. See Shoham, "Pickers," 45–46; see also Drori, *Foreign Workers*, 112.

19. Comparison with US agriculture also makes it possible to analyze the organization of the labor process as a function of the size and structure of the farm unit itself, which differs greatly in the two countries. American vegetable farming is an industry of "factories in the fields," dominated by large agribusiness corporations, while Israeli agriculture is small-scale. See Carey McWilliams, *Factories in the Field: The Story of Migratory Farm Labor in California* (Boston: Little, Brown, 1939); Robert J. Thomas, *Citizenship, Gender, and Work: The Social Organization of Industrial Agriculture* (Berkeley: University of California Press, 1985); Seth Holmes, *Fresh Fruit, Broken Bodies: Migrant Farmworkers in the United States* (Berkeley and Los Angeles: University of California Press, 2013); Gabriel Thompson, ed., *Chasing the Harvest: Migrant Workers in California Agriculture* (London: Verso, 2017).

20. Kemp and Raijman, "Bringing In."

21. Michael Burawoy, *Manufacturing Consent: Changes in the Labor Process under Monopoly Capitalism* (Chicago: University of Chicago Press, 1979), 46–76.

22. Cohen, writing in the late 1990s, found similar attitudes: "Our impression is that the direct employers, after a short period of experimentation, generally refrain from close supervision of their Thai employees. The employers have found that the Thais are reliable workers [. . .] close supervision or pressure to work faster alienate the workers and damage their relationship with the employer. As a result many work providers grant them independence at work and in many cases leave them alone to work in the field or in packing facilities." "Ovdim Taylandim," 183.

23. Claudio Sopranzetti, "Framed by Freedom: Emancipation and Oppression in Post-Fordist Thailand," *Cultural Anthropology* 32, no. 1 (February 27, 2017): 73.

24. Claudio Sopranzetti, *Owners of the Map: Motorcycle Taxi Drivers, Mobility, and Politics in Bangkok* (Berkeley: University of California Press, 2017).

25. Dell Hymes, "Linguistic Problems in Defining the Concept of Tribe," in *Essays on the Problem of Tribe: Proceedings of the 1967 Annual Spring Meeting of the American Ethnological Society* (Seattle: University of Washington Press, 1968).

26. To be perfectly accurate, the initial consonant of the Hebrew word is not an *h* but a velar or pharyngeal fricative (see Note on Non-English Terms). However, Hebrew speakers are used to this sound being pronounced as [h], for example by native English speakers, and have no trouble parsing such a pronunciation.

27. Sarah Grey Thomason, *Language Contact* (Washington, DC: Georgetown University Press, 2001), 157–95.

28. Likewise, in the Isaan village studied by Shoham, many of whose residents have worked in Israel, the Hebrew word *hamama* has become the local term for "greenhouse." See Shoham, "Heroes," chap. 4.

29. Judith T. Irvine, "When Talk Isn't Cheap: Language and Political Economy," *American Ethnologist* 16, no. 2 (1989): 255.

30. Irvine (251) remarks that "within the linguistic system the study of directives (requests and commands) is especially relevant [to work], because it concerns the verbal management of the flow of goods and services in an economy. . . . in conspicuously task-oriented situations, speech coordinating the tasks is often reduced and simple compared to speech of other kinds, or speech in other settings. (The reduction and 'simplicity' of linguistic form in pidgins and trade languages originating in labor or market settings might be relevant also.)" Incidentally, Ludwig Wittgenstein begins his philosophical investigation of language by imagining a workplace idiom that comprises only such directives; see his *Philosophical Investigations* (Oxford: Basil Blackwell, 1968), 3 ff.

31. Joseph Sung-Yul Park and Lionel Wee, *Markets of English: Linguistic Capital and Language Policy in a Globalizing World* (New York: Routledge, 2012); Jürgen Gerhards, "Transnational Linguistic Capital: Explaining English Proficiency in 27 European Countries," *International Sociology* 29, no. 1 (January 1, 2014): 56–74.

32. Liebelt, *Caring for the "Holy Land"*; Kalir, "Jewish State"; Alejandro Paz, *Latinos in Israel: Language and Unexpected Citizenship* (Bloomington: Indiana University Press, 2018).

33. Irvine, "When Talk," 251.

34. Alejandro Paz, "The Circulation of Chisme and Rumor: Gossip, Evidentiality, and Authority in the Perspective of Latino Labor Migrants in Israel," *Journal of Linguistic Anthropology* 19, no. 1 (2009): 118.

35. The former migrants interviewed by Shahar Shoham used the Thai *hua naa*, meaning "chief," or "leader," for the position the Sadot workers called *balabay*, and *balabay* for the employer, in line with usage elsewhere in Israel. See Shoham, "Heroes," chap. 2.

36. In this, they are quite unlike the mouthpieces of the antebellum American South, which disseminated a copious literature on the management of slaves, employing standardized terms for intermediary positions such as "driver." See Genovese, *Roll, Jordan, Roll*, 365–88; David R. Roediger and Elizabeth D. Esch, *The Production of Difference: Race and the Management of Labor in U.S. History* (New York: Oxford University Press, 2012).

37. Kaminer, "Rebirth." The preference for suntanned skin does not necessarily translate to an appreciation for naturally dark skin, which is often negatively associated with Mizrahi Jews and Palestinians; see Yifat Biton, "Mizrahim Ba-Mishpat: Ha-'ayin' Ke-'yesh'" (Mizrahim and the Law: Absence as Existence), *Mishpatim* 41 (2011): 455–516. However, the difficulty of telling the acquired from the innate introduces an indeterminacy into Israeli ideas about skin tone. Israelis of this group often think of short clothing as "natural" for the hot Israeli climate. The assumption is challenged by the fact that indigenous Palestinians traditionally wear long clothing, not to mention the very high rates of skin cancer in Israel; see T. Sella et al., "Incidence Trends of Keratinocytic Skin Cancers and Melanoma in Israel 2006–11," *British Journal of Dermatology* 172, no. 1 (January 1, 2015): 202–7. Anthropologist Tamar El Or has written on the aesthetics and politics of skin exposure in the case of "biblical" sandals as well as on the sartorial production of difference among Palestinian and ultra-Orthodox women. See her "Ha-Horef Shel Ha-Re'ulot: Kisuy ve-Giluy Be-2007/8" (The Winter of the Veiled Women: Covering and Uncovering in 2007/8), *Theory and Criticism* 37 (Fall 2010): 37–68; "The Soul of the Biblical Sandal: On Anthropology and Style," *American Anthropologist* 114, no. 3 (September 1, 2012): 433–45.

38. Pilapa Esara, "Imagining the Western Husband: Thai Women's Desires for Matrimony, Status and Beauty," *Ethnos* 74, no. 3 (September 1, 2009): 403–26; Amare Tegbaru, "The Racialization of Development Expertise and the Fluidity of Blackness: A Case from 1980s Thailand," *Asian Anthropology* 19, no. 3 (July 2, 2020): 195–212.

39. Pilapa, "Imagining"; Tegbaru, "Racialization."

40. It is difficult to say how functional each of these getups is for the climate in which it is worn. According to J. M. Hanna and D. E. Brown, the optimal choice for heat loss in hot-dry climates such as the Arabah is long, loose-fitting clothing, while in hot-humid climates like Isaan it is best to wear "the least amount possible"; see their "Human Heat Tolerance: An Anthropological Perspective," *Annual Review of Anthropology* 12, no. 1 (1983): 259–84. Ironically,

each group seems to have adopted the clothing best adapted to the other's habitat, but looked at diachronically, things are more complex. Until recently men doing farm labor in Thailand wore only a loincloth, and the indigenous people of the Arabah, the Bedouin, traditionally wear long, flowing robes. Taking into consideration not only heat tolerance but long-term skin health, which requires protection from the sun as well as from irritants like pesticides, covering up as fully as possible when working in the Arabah would appear advisable. On balance, then, the contemporary Thai outfit seems optimal—if one feels comfortable in it, that is.

41. Marcel Mauss, "Techniques of the Body," *Economy and Society* 2, no. 1 (February 1973): 70–88.

42. Postures 114 and 127 in the typology designed by Gordon W. Hewes, "World Distribution of Certain Postural Habits," *American Anthropologist* 57, no. 2 (1955): 231–44.

43. Postures 126 and 102–4, respectively, in Hewes's typology.

44. Sander L. Gilman, "'Stand Up Straight': Notes Toward a History of Posture," *Journal of Medical Humanities* 35, no. 1 (March 1, 2014): 57–83.

45. Hewes, "World Distribution," 238.

46. A. V. Chayanov argues that peasants in land-poor regions work "unimaginably hard and long for the smallest increments in production." Paraphrased in James C. Scott, *The Moral Economy of the Peasant: Rebellion and Subsistence in Southeast Asia* (New Haven, CT: Yale University Press, 1976), 13. Isaan is land-poor, but it has only become so recently; the region's "land frontier," or geographical limit of cultivation, was reached in the mid-1980s (see Chapter 2). For discussions of the political and cultural implications of land availability in Southeast Asia, see Clifford Geertz, *Agricultural Involution: The Process of Ecological Change in Indonesia* (Berkeley and Los Angeles: University of California Press, 1963); Scott, *Art*; Tania Murray Li, *Land's End: Capitalist Relations on an Indigenous Frontier* (Durham, NC: Duke University Press, 2014).

47. See Shoham, "Heroes," chap. 3.

48. Cf. Cohen: "Employers have found that the Thais are reliable workers, who persevere at work and carry it out carefully and responsibly but at a slow pace." "Ovdim Taylandim," 183.

49. On the other hand, one farmer told me that as a rural person, he felt an affinity with Thai workers that he did not share with urban Israelis. This is surprising, since (as I discuss in the introduction) as the Israeli farming class is probably the most socially proximate to the urban, educated middle class of any farming stratum in the world; this farmer himself had close kin in Tel Aviv.

50. Ya'ir hired temporary Bedouin laborers from time to time, but I never had the chance to speak to them or learn much about their experience.

51. Michael Taussig also describes how farmers of a dominant race/ class fraction imagine themselves to be victims of their laborers' resentment through an imaginary redoubling of perspectives; see his *Shamanism, Colonialism, and the Wild Man: A Study in Terror and Healing* (Chicago: University of Chicago Press, 1991), 242–54. On "envying down" more generally, see Geoffrey Hughes, "Envious Ethnography and the Ethnography of Envy in Anthropology's 'Orient': Towards a Theory of Envy," *Ethos* 48, no. 2 (2020): 192–211.

52. This antagonistic unity is also expressed in Kareem Rabie's concept of "mirroring" and in Liron Mor's notion of "severance." One of its most potent metaphors is the patrilineal cousinage relation between Jews and Arabs, as children of Abraham's sons Isaac and Ishmael respectively. See Rabie, *Palestine Is Throwing a Party and the Whole World Is Invited: Capital and State Building in the West Bank* (Durham, NC: Duke University Press, 2021); Mor, *Conflicts*; Matan Kaminer, "The Abrahamic Ideology: Patrilineal Kinship and the Politics of Peacemaking in the Contemporary Middle East," *Millennium: Journal of International Studies*, online first (November 20, 2023).

53. For Palestinian sweat equity in Israel, see Andrew Ross, *Stone Men: The Palestinians Who Built Israel* (London: Verso, 2019).

Chapter 5

1. Andrew Shryock, "Other Conscious/Self Aware: First Thoughts on Cultural Intimacy and Mass Mediation," in *Off Stage/On Display: Intimacy and Ethnography in the Age of Public Culture*, ed. Andrew Shryock (Stanford, CA: Stanford University Press, 2004), 3–28. The current chapter incorporates material previously published in Matan Kaminer, "Saving the Face of the Arabah: Thai Migrant Workers and the Asymmetries of Community in an Israeli Agricultural Settlement," *American Ethnologist* 49, no. 1 (February 2022): 118–31.

2. Paz, *Latinos in Israel*, 13–17, 170–83.

3. Sonya O. Rose, "Class Formation and the Quintessential Worker," in *Reworking Class*, ed. John R. Hall (Ithaca, NY: Cornell University Press, 2018), 133–66.

4. Iair G. Or and Elana Shohamy, "'Youth Should Be Sent Here to Absorb Zionism': Jewish Farmers and Thai Migrant Workers in Southern Israel," in *Sociolinguistic Perspectives on Migration Control: Language Policy, Identity and Belonging*, ed. Markus Rheindorf and Ruth Wodak (Bristol: Multilingual Matters, 2020), 158.

5. As also by elite Thai actors. See the discussion in Shoham, "Heroes," chap. 4.

6. Katriel, *Talking Straight*.

7. Erving Goffman, "On Face-Work," in *Interaction Ritual* (New York: Doubleday, 1967), 5–45.

8. Hsien-chin Hu, "The Chinese Concepts of 'Face,'" *American Anthropologist* 46, no. 1 (1944): 45–64.

9. "Face, n.," in *Oxford English Dictionary* (Oxford: Oxford University Press, 2009) def. P8 h.

10. See George Lakoff and Mark Johnson, *Metaphors We Live By* (Chicago: University of Chicago Press, 2003), 37.

11. Mae M. Ngai, "American Orientalism," *Reviews in American History* 28, no. 3 (September 1, 2000): 408.

12. Hu, "Chinese Concepts," 50.

13. Aulino, "Social Body," 417.

14. For documentation of similar demands made on Bangkok's proletarians (many of them of Isaan origin) by the kingdom's elites, see Mills, *Good Daughters*; Alan Klima, *The Funeral Casino: Meditation, Massacre, and Exchange with the Dead in Thailand* (Princeton, NJ: Princeton University Press, 2002); Sopranzetti, *Owners of the Map*.

15. Kaminer, "Connections," 118–19.

16. McCargo and Krisadawan, "Contesting Isan-ness"; Claudio Sopranzetti, "Burning Red Desires: Isan Migrants and the Politics of Desire in Contemporary Thailand," *South East Asia Research* 20, no. 3 (2012): 361–79; Gullette, "Rural–Urban Hierarchies."

17. Herzfeld, *Cultural Intimacy*, 121.

18. See Miranda Joseph, *Against the Romance of Community* (Minneapolis: University of Minnesota Press, 2002).

19. Max Gluckman, "Analysis of a Social Situation in Modern Zululand," *Bantu Studies* 14, no. 1 (January 1940): 11.

20. Gluckman, 28.

21. *Every Twelve Seconds: Industrialized Slaughter and the Politics of Sight* (New Haven, CT: Yale University Press, 2011).

22. In some *moshavim*, and most *kibbutzim*, migrant workers are all housed together in one segregated neighborhood rather than spread out on their employers' individual lots. See Cohen, "Ovdim Taylandim," 189.

23. Shnider, "Gendered Division."

24. Saturday is the mandated day of rest for Israel's Jewish population, and practically speaking for Thai workers as well. Legally, non-Jews in Israel may select either Friday, Saturday, or Sunday as their weekly day off, and given a choice, I imagine Thais would prefer Sunday, since public services in general and transport in particular are unavailable from Friday afternoon until Saturday evening. But here again, the law is one thing and reality another, and in practice workers have no choice in the matter. It is more convenient

for employers to have their workers rest on the same day as they do, and once more their individual economic interest synergizes with the migration regime's goal of curtailing workers' freedom of movement and their opportunities of interacting with other Thais, as well as with Israelis other than their employers.

25. For a detailed description of Thai migrants' soccer tournaments in Singapore, where employers are also actively involved, see Pattana, *Bare Life*, 63–67.

26. Kaminer, "Lonely Songkran."

27. Sing. *taylandiya*, a compound noun composed of *taylandi*, "Thai person" + suffix *-iya*, used for businesses. I do not have much information on the ownership or management of the *taylandiyot*. Since Thais are not allowed to work outside agriculture, the legality of the arrangement is dubious, and I thought it best not to enquire too much. See also Iair G. Or, "Regime Changes and the Impact of Informal Labor: The Case of Thai Workers in Southern Israel," *Linguistic Landscape* 7 (February 19, 2021): 160–65.

28. On the materiality of cash, see Alaina Lemon, "'Your Eyes Are Green Like Dollars': Counterfeit Cash, National Substance, and Currency Apartheid in 1990s Russia," *Cultural Anthropology* 13, no. 1 (February 1, 1998): 22–55; Maxim Bolt, "The Sociality of the Wage: Money Rhythms, Wealth Circulation, and the Problem with Cash on the Zimbabwean-South African Border," *Journal of the Royal Anthropological Institute* 20, no. 1 (March 2014): 113–30.

29. Eli Ashkenazi, "Semel ha-status ha-mushlam: Kfitzat rosh li-vrekhot ha-s'hiya shel Yisra'el" (The Perfect Status Symbol: Diving Headfirst into Israel's Swimming Pools), *Walla! News*, July 29, 2017, tinyurl.com/israpools.

30. Cohen, "Ovdim Taylandim," 179. For a similarly dichotomous view of Thai migrant workers among employers in Singapore, see Pattana Kitiarsa, "Village Transnationalism: Transborder Identities among Thai-Isan Migrant Workers in Singapore," SSRN Scholarly Paper (Rochester, NY, August 1, 2006), 12.

31. See Cohen, "Ovdim Taylandim," 186; Nir Avieli, "Thai Migrant Workers and the Dog-Eating Myth," in *Food and Power: A Culinary Ethnography of Israel* (Berkeley and Los Angeles: University of California Press, 2017), 178–216.

32. According to the Israeli Health Ministry, homicide was the suspected cause of death of four Thais in Israel between 2015 and 2021. See Miri Cohen, "Ma'aneh MASHHAB Li-Fniyat Ha-va'ada Ha-Meyuhedet Le-Ovdim Zarim Be-Nose Etgarim Be-Ha'asakat Ovdim Zarim Be-anaf Ha-Hakla'ut" (Response of the Health Ministry to the Enquiry of the Special Committee for Foreign Workers on the Challenges of Employing Foreign Workers in the Agricultural Sector) (Israel Health Ministry, November 16, 2021).

33. *Mak Saaw Israel* (Israeli Woman), YouTube, 2011, tinyurl.com/sanya -song. The translation appears in Shoham, "Pickers," 80.

34. Ann Stoler, *Race and the Education of Desire: Foucault's History of Sexuality and the Colonial Order of Things* (Durham, NC: Duke University Press, 2012); Hella Bloom Cohen, *The Literary Imagination in Israel-Palestine: Orientalism, Poetry, and Biopolitics* (London: Palgrave Macmillan, 2016).

35. Ari Engelberg, "Fighting Intermarriage in the Holy Land: Lehava and Israeli Ethnonationalism," *Journal of Israeli History* 36, no. 2 (July 3, 2017): 229–47.

36. Moon-Ho Jung, *Coolies and Cane: Race, Labor, and Sugar in the Age of Emancipation* (Baltimore: Johns Hopkins University Press, 2006); Peter Chua and Dune C. Fujino, "Negotiating New Asian-American Masculinities: Attitudes and Gender Expectations," *Journal of Men's Studies* 7, no. 3 (June 1, 1999): 391–413; Yen Ling Shek, "Asian American Masculinity: A Review of the Literature," *Journal of Men's Studies* 14, no. 3 (June 1, 2007): 379–91.

37. Kaminer, "Connections."

38. Katriel, *Talking Straight*, 18–19.

39. Katriel, 36.

40. Katriel, 47.

41. The use of Orientalist tropes to cast racialized migrant workers as "spiritually" fit for their labors is also a feature of the employment of Indian programmers in Germany. See Sareeta Amrute, *Encoding Race, Encoding Class: Indian IT Workers in Berlin* (Durham, NC: Duke University Press, 2016), 104.

42. Sopranzetti, "Burning Red."

43. CIMI, "Kelim Le-Avoda Ye'ila Bi-Sviva Rav-Tarbutit Im Ovdim Ha-Megi'im Mi-Tayland" (Tools for Effective Work in a Multicultural Environment with Workers Coming from Thailand), 2017. As if to emphasize their academic legitimacy, the words marked here by asterisks appear first in Hebrew and then, in parentheses, in English. For "dignity" the brochure uses *kvod ha-adam*, a legalistic construction used, for example, in the name of Israel's "Basic Law on Human Dignity and Liberty"; for "to make [someone] lose face" it uses an idiom which literally translates as "to make [someone's] face pale." In the interest of transparency, I should mention that I was consulted on the brochure by CIMI staff; however, not all my suggestions were implemented, and I bear no responsibility for its final form.

44. See Jürgen Habermas, *The Structural Transformation of the Public Sphere: An Inquiry into a Category of Bourgeois Society*, trans. Thomas Burger (Cambridge: Polity Press, 2008); Stephanie DeGooyer et al., *The Right to Have Rights* (London: Verso, 2018).

45. Claudio Sopranzetti, "Thailand's Relapse: The Implications of the May 2014 Coup," *Journal of Asian Studies* 75, no. 2 (2016): 299–316. For a migrant's positive appraisal of the Thaksin government, overthrown by a previous coup in 2006, see Shoham, "Heroes," chap. 4.

46. Yael Aberman, "Shvitat me'ot ovdim taylandim be-moshav Ahituv" (Strike of hundreds of Thai workers in moshav Ahituv) (Tel Aviv: Worker's Hotline, July 12, 2011), tinyurl.com/hotline-strike; Telem Yahav, "Arba'a Taylandim She-Putru Tov'im 1.5 Milyon Shekel" (Four Thais who were Fired are Suing for 1.5 Million Shekels)," *Ynet*, March 11, 2011, tinyurl.com/ fired-thais; see also Shoham, "Heroes," chap. 2.

47. For a summary of the project, see Matan Kaminer, "Learning About 'Life in Israel' from Thai Migrant Farmworkers," *Discover Rackham* (blog), November 14, 2018, tinyurl.com/kaminer-learning.

48. "Impact," 23.

49. For such an analysis, see Geoffrey Hughes, "Cutting the Face: Kinship, State and Social Media Conflict in Networked Jordan," *Journal of Legal Anthropology* 2, no. 1 (June 1, 2018): 49–71.

50. This applies to relations within the farm and the interviews I conducted there as well as to public interactions in the *moshav*. I did appear in the video inviting questions for *Cheewit nay Israel*, but speaking (atrocious) Thai rather than English or Hebrew, and we took questions in Central and Isaan Thai.

51. James C. Scott, *Domination and the Arts of Resistance: Hidden Transcripts* (New Haven, CT: Yale University Press, 1990).

52. For conceptual problems involved with the notion of a "hidden" transcript, see Mitchell, "Everyday Metaphors," and Gal, "Language and the 'Arts.'"

53. Kaminer, "Oksana Affair." For the Thai state's attempts to interpellate citizens into responsibility for maintaining the nation's image in the context of tourism and public relations, see Klima, *Funeral Casino*, 31–52; Herzfeld, *Siege of the Spirits*.

54. Katriel, *Talking Straight*, 9–33.

55. For the concept of *communitas*, "an unstructured or rudimentarily structured and relatively undifferentiated . . . communion of equal individuals" which forms in liminal situations, see Victor Turner, "Liminality and Communitas," in *Culture and Society: Contemporary Debates*, ed. Jeffrey C. Alexander and Steven Jay Seidman (Cambridge: Cambridge University Press, 1990), 148.

Chapter 6

1. Anthony Reid, "Female Roles in Pre-Colonial Southeast Asia," *Modern Asian Studies* 22, no. 3 (January 1, 1988): 629–45; Suzanne Brenner, "Why Women Rule the Roost: Rethinking Javanese Ideologies of Gender and Self-Control," in *Bewitching Women, Pious Men: Gender and Body Politics in Southeast Asia*, ed. Aihwa Ong and Michael G. Peletz (Berkeley and Los Angeles: University of California Press, 1995), 19–50; Barbara Watson Andaya, "Studying Women and Gender in Southeast Asia," *International Journal of Asian Studies* 4, no.

1 (January 2007): 113–36; Brenda Yeoh, "Migration and Gender Politics in Southeast Asia," *Migration, Mobility, & Displacement* 2, no. 1 (March 2, 2016).

2. Mills, *Good Daughters*; Amornrat Saito et al., "Effect of Intimate Partner Violence on Postpartum Women's Health in Northeastern Thailand," *Nursing & Health Sciences* 14, no. 3 (2012): 345–51; Ann le Mare, Buapun Promphaking, and Jonathan Rigg, "Returning Home: The Middle-Income Trap and Gendered Norms in Thailand," *Journal of International Development* 27, no. 2 (2015): 285–306.

3. Shoham and Kurlander, "Niyar Avoda."

4. LGBT identities are common in Isaan and elsewhere in Thailand, but to the best of my knowledge they did not play an important part in the lives of my informants. I did meet a few *kathoey* (transgender female) migrants in Israel, but I did not have the opportunity to converse with any. See Ara Wilson, *The Intimate Economies of Bangkok: Tomboys, Tycoons, and Avon Ladies in the Global City* (Berkeley: University of California Press, 2004); Dredge Byung'chu Käng, "Kathoey 'In Trend': Emergent Genderscapes, National Anxieties and the Re-Signification of Male-Bodied Effeminacy in Thailand," *Asian Studies Review* 36, no. 4 (December 1, 2012): 475–94.

5. Mills, *Good Daughters*; Leonora C. Angeles and Sirijit Sunanta, "Demanding Daughter Duty: Gender, Community, Village Transformation, and Transnational Marriages in Northeast Thailand," *Critical Asian Studies* 41, no. 4 (December 1, 2009): 549–74.

6. Leah K. Vanwey, "Altruistic and Contractual Remittances between Male and Female Migrants and Households in Rural Thailand," *Demography* 41, no. 4 (November 1, 2004): 745.

7. le Mare, Promphaking, and Rigg, "Returning Home," 289–90.

8. Charles F. Keyes, "Mother or Mistress but Never a Monk: Buddhist Notions of Female Gender in Rural Thailand," *American Ethnologist* 11, no. 2 (May 1, 1984): 223–41; Mary Beth Mills, "Gendered Encounters with Modernity: Labor Migrants and Marriage Choices in Contemporary Thailand," *Identities* 5, no. 3 (November 1, 1998): 312.

9. Scott Stonington, "Facing Death, Gazing Inward: End-of-Life and the Transformation of Clinical Subjectivity in Thailand," *Culture, Medicine, and Psychiatry* 35, no. 2 (May 15, 2011): 113–33.

10. See Mills, "Gendered Encounters"; Pilapa Esara, "Moral Scrutiny, Marriage Inequality: Cohabitation in Bangkok, Thailand," *Asia Pacific Journal of Anthropology* 13, no. 3 (June 1, 2012): 211–27.

11. Pilapa, "Moral Scrutiny," 213.

12. Jiemin Bao, "Denaturalizing Polygyny in Bangkok, Thailand," *Ethnology* 47, no. 2/3 (2008): 145–61.

13. Mills, "Gendered Encounters"; Johnson, "Deferral and Intimacy."

14. Rigg and Salamanca, "Connecting Lives."

15. Rigg, Salamanca, and Parnwell, "Joining the Dots," 1475.

16. Klima, "Dark Finance."

17. Rosalia Sciortino and Sureeporn Punpuing, "International Migration"; Sudarat Musikawong and Panida Rzonca, "Debt Bondage Scales of Intensity: Thai Overseas Agricultural Workers in the United States," in *On the Move: Critical Migration Themes in ASEAN*, ed. Supang Chantavanich, Carl Middleton, and Michiko Ito (Chiang Mai: Chulalongkorn University Press, 2014).

18. Huw Jones and Tieng Pardthaison, "The Impact of Overseas Labour Migration on Rural Thailand: Regional, Community and Individual Dimensions," *Journal of Rural Studies* 15, no. 1 (January 1, 1999): 35–47; see also Mary Beth Mills, "Engendering Discourses of Displacement: Contesting Mobility and Marginality in Rural Thailand," *Ethnography* 6, no. 3 (September 1, 2005): 396–97.

19. le Mare, Promphaking, and Rigg, "Returning Home," 302–3.

20. This figure is immense even by the exorbitant standards of the pre-TIC migration regime. Daeng repeated it several times, but given that the interview was held more than seven years after the events discussed, it is possible that he erred.

21. Jealous rages like Daeng's should not be interpreted simply as reflexive reactions to betrayal and heartbreak, but also as weapons serving to reproduce a relation of domination through repressive violence. See P. Valentine, "The Gender Distinction in Communization Theory," *LIES: A Journal of Materialist Feminism* 1 (2012): 191–208.

22. I never encountered methamphetamine during my time on the Sadot farm, but when we met in Thailand, Daeng insisted that it was quite common, both for recreation and to give workers energy for work. He identified it as a social problem mainly because of the way it drained incomes, including his own; but he saw no ill effects on his health and insisted that he had no trouble kicking the habit when he returned home. However, he did tell Mee and me disturbing stories about paranoid behavior and a suicide triggered by the drug. The widespread use of *yaa baa*, a mix of caffeine and methamphetamine, has been documented among Thai workers in Israel for many years; according to Daeng, pure meth began eclipsing it in popularity around 2015. See Shimon Ifergan, "Ekstazi La-Aniyim" (The Poor Man's Ecstasy), *Mako*, December 20, 2012, tinyurl.com/ifergan-yaba; HRW, "Raw Deal."

23. When I interviewed Boy in May 2016, he claimed that there was currently no *balabay* on the farm, though I knew Daeng was still "officially" holding the post. At the time I was bewildered, but in retrospect this seems to have been a recognition on Boy's part that Daeng was disinclined to continue in the role.

24. For a more detailed account of Moon's life before meeting Boy, see Matan Kaminer, "By the Sweat of Other Brows: Thai Migrant Labor and the Transformation of Israeli Settler Agriculture" (PhD diss., University of Michigan, 2019), 148–50.

25. On the lives of garment workers in Bangkok during this period, see Piya, *Textures of Struggle*. While more specific terms exist, the word most commonly used to describe romantic partners, *faen*, can be the equivalent of "spouse," "boy/girlfriend," "fiancé/e," or "lover" (see Pilapa, "Moral Scrutiny," 213.). When I met her, Moon considered herself married for the third time, so I refer to her former *faen*, the fathers of her elder children, as ex-husbands.

26. Pattana, "Lyrics."

27. Betting was usually on "high-low," a simple game with dice, and sometimes on soccer games. Some migrants raised cocks and I heard rumors of Isaan-style cockfights being held in Israel, but I never witnessed one—though, for evidence of cockfighting in Israel, see Zohar Shvarzberg, "Landscapes in Migration: The Gardens of Thai Agricultural Migrants in Central Israel" (MA thesis, Haifa, Technion, 2023), 74–77. Incidentally, almost all the workers I knew smoked cigarettes, but if this was ever treated as a problem, it was only due to the expense involved. As related above (note 22), I had no knowledge of illegal drug use on the farm until Daeng raised the issue during my visit to Isaan.

28. For discussion of this idiom (*khit maak* in Central Thai), see Scott Stonington, *The Spirit Ambulance: Choreographing the End of Life in Thailand* (Oakland: University of California Press, 2020), 43–46.

29. See Mary Beth Mills, "Attack of the Widow Ghosts: Gender, Death and Modernity in Northeast Thailand," in *Bewitching Women, Pious Men: Gender and Body Politics in Southeast Asia*, ed. Aihwa Ong and Michael G. Peletz (Berkeley and Los Angeles: University of California Press, 1995), 244–73.

30. For many Thais, death far from home and one's family is a particularly terrible fate, to be avoided at all costs. See Stonington, *Spirit Ambulance*.

31. Cassaniti, *Living Buddhism*, chap. 1.

32. Mark Fisher, *Capitalist Realism: Is There No Alternative?* (Winchester: Zero Books, 2009); Lauren Berlant, *Cruel Optimism* (Durham, NC: Duke University Press, 2011).

33. Except for Daeng, I never heard male migrants bring up any conflict with their families, but as the story of Song's son-in-law makes clear, migrants often express their rejection of a common family interest practically, by cutting off relations with their wives.

Conclusion

1. Eric Cazdyn, "Enlightenment, Revolution, Cure: The Problem of Praxis and the Radical Nothingness of the Future," in *Nothing: Three Inquiries in*

Buddhism, by Marcus Boon, Eric Cazdyn, and Timothy B. Morton (Chicago: University of Chicago Press, 2015), 105–84.

2. Slavoj Žižek, *The Sublime Object of Ideology* (London: Verso, 1989).

3. Cazdyn, "Enlightenment," 207.

4. Shauer and Kaminer, "Below the Minimum."

5. OECD, "Review of Agricultural Policies." Incidentally, as currently practiced such subsidies also wreak havoc on the environment and exacerbate inequality by undercutting producers in the Global South. See FAO, UNDP, and UNEP, *A Multi-Billion-Dollar Opportunity—Repurposing Agricultural Support to Transform Food Systems* (Rome: FAO, UNDP, and UNEP, 2021), doi.org/10.4060/cb6562en.

6. Ariel Vitman, "Netanyahu: 'Livhon bitul skhar ha-minimum le-ovdim zarim'" (Netanyahu: 'Look into abolishing the minimum wage for foreign workers'), *Israel Hayom*, August 12, 2018, tinyurl.com/abolish-wage.

7. Kurlander and Kaminer, "Ovdim Kvu'im," 136; Kaminer, "Giving Them the Slip."

8. As Lucy Mayblin and Joe Turner remark about decolonial perspectives in migration studies more generally: "Do such perspectives allow us to frame our research in terms that accord with the interests of policy makers? No. Are such perspectives policy friendly in the current terms of debate on migration? Rarely." See their *Migration Studies and Colonialism* (Cambridge, UK, and Medford, MA: Polity Press, 2021), 27.

9. Tomer Gardi and Omar Al-Ghabari, *Awdah: Eduyot medumyanot ma-atidim efshariyim* (Awdah: Imagined Testimonies from Possible Futures) (Tel Aviv: Pardes, 2013). See also some of the contributions to Basma Ghalayini, ed., *Palestine +100: Stories from a Century after the Nakba* (Manchester: Comma Press, 2019).

10. A commendable exception is Jeff Halper's *Decolonizing Israel, Liberating Palestine: Zionism, Settler Colonialism, and the Case for One Democratic State* (London: Pluto Press, 2021), which acknowledges the presence of non-Arab, non-Jewish migrants in the country. See also Kaminer, "In Israel."

11. Andrew M. Gardner, "Engulfed: Indian Guest Workers, Bahraini Citizens and the Structural Violence of the Kafala System," in *The Deportation Regime: Sovereignty, Space, and the Freedom of Movement*, ed. Nicholas De Genova and Nathalie Mae Peutz (Durham, NC: Duke University Press, 2010), 196–223; Rebeca Raijman and Adriana Kemp, "The New Immigration to Israel: Becoming a de-Facto Immigration State in the 1990s," in *Immigration Worldwide*, by U. Segal, N. Mayadas, and D. Elliot (Oxford: Oxford University Press, 2010), 227–43; Dana El Kurd, "The Paradox of Peace: The Impact of Normalization with Israel on the Arab World," *Global Studies Quarterly* 3, no. 3 (July 1, 2023): ksad042; Kaminer, "The Abrahamic Ideology."

12. Adi Elmaliah, "Avoda Ivrit Zara" (Foreign Hebrew Labor), *Adrikhalut Nof: The Journal of the Israeli Union of Landscape Architects*, no. 64 (September 2017): 44–45.

13. Shvarzberg, "Landscapes." Certainly, not all or even most migrant workers would remain in the Arabah permanently if given the chance, and many of the possibilities opened up by this imaginative exercise do not hinge on their doing so. Nevertheless, it is quite reasonable to imagine that some Thais would stay in the country, move into other branches of employment, and raise families—with each other and with Israelis. See Chapter 4, n. 74.

14. Kaminer, "Agricultural Settlement."

15. Stavi et al., "Runoff," 86.

16. Roy Galili, "Hitporerut" (Disintegration), *Aravot*, August 2020.

BIBLIOGRAPHY

Abadi, Jacob. *Israel's Quest for Recognition and Acceptance in Asia: Garrison State Diplomacy*. London: Frank Cass, 2004.

Aberman, Yael. "Shvitat me'ot ovdim taylandim be-moshav Ahituv" (Strike of hundreds of Thai workers in *moshav* Ahituv). Tel Aviv: Worker's Hotline, July 12, 2011. tinyurl.com/hotline-strike.

Abu El-Haj, Nadia. *Facts on the Ground: Archaeological Practice and Territorial Self-Fashioning in Israeli Society*. Chicago: University of Chicago Press, 2001.

Abu-Lughod, Janet L. *Before European Hegemony: The World System A.D. 1250–1350*. Oxford: Oxford University Press, 1991.

Adams, Russell. "Copper Trading Networks across the Arabah during the Later Early Bronze Age." In *Crossing the Rift: Resources, Routes, Settlement Patterns, and Interaction in the Wadi Arabah*, edited by Piotr Bienkowski and Katharina Galor, 135–42. Oxford: Oxbow Books, 2006.

Africa Research Group. "Israel: Imperialist Mission in Africa." *Tricontinental* 15 (1969): 39–57.

Ajl, Max. "Theories of Political Ecology: Monopoly Capital Against People and the Planet." *Agrarian South: Journal of Political Economy* 12, no. 1 (March 1, 2023): 12–50.

Alatout, Samer. "Bringing Abundance into Environmental Politics: Constructing a Zionist Network of Water Abundance, Immigration, and Colonization." *Social Studies of Science* 39, no. 3 (June 1, 2009): 363–94.

Alff, Kristen. "Levantine Joint-Stock Companies, Trans-Mediterranean Partnerships, and Nineteenth-Century Capitalist Development." *Comparative Studies in Society and History* 60, no. 1 (January 2018): 150–77.

Allweil, Yael. "Plantation: Modern-Vernacular Housing and Settlement in Ottoman Palestine, 1858–1918." *Architecture beyond Europe*, no. 9–10 (July 2016). tinyurl.com/allweil.

Althusser, Louis. *On Reproduction*. London: Verso, 2014.

Amara, Ahmad. "The Negev Land Question: Between Denial and Recognition." *Journal of Palestine Studies* 42, no. 4 (August 1, 2013): 27–47.

Amornrat Saito, Debra Creedy, Marie Cooke, and Wendy Chaboyer. "Effect of Intimate Partner Violence on Postpartum Women's Health in Northeastern Thailand." *Nursing & Health Sciences* 14, no. 3 (2012): 345–51.

Amrute, Sareeta. *Encoding Race, Encoding Class: Indian IT Workers in Berlin*. Durham, NC: Duke University Press, 2016.

Andaya, Barbara Watson. "Studying Women and Gender in Southeast Asia." *The International Journal of Asian Studies* 4, no. 1 (January 2007): 113–36.

Angeles, Leonora C., and Sirijit Sunanta. "Demanding Daughter Duty: Gender, Community, Village Transformation, and Transnational Marriages in Northeast Thailand." *Critical Asian Studies* 41, no. 4 (December 1, 2009): 549–74.

Applebaum, Levia. "Ha-Shilton Ha-Mekomi Ba-Merhav Ha-Kafri Be-Yisra'el" (Local Government in the Israeli Countryside). In *Ha-Shilton Ha-Mekomi: Ben Ha-Medina, Ha-Kehila ve-Kalkalat Ha-Shuk* (The Local Government: Between the State, the Community and the Market Economy), edited by Yagil Levi and Eti Sarig, 2:613–84. Ra'anana: Open University of Israel, 2014.

Ardener, Edwin. "'Remote Areas': Some Theoretical Considerations." *HAU: Journal of Ethnographic Theory* 2, no. 1 (March 2012): 519–33.

'Aref, 'Aref el-. *Toldot Beer Sheva u-Shvateya* (The History of Beersheba and Its Tribes). Translated by Eliyahu Nawi. Jerusalem: Ariel, 2000.

Ashkenazi, Eli. "Semel ha-status ha-mushlam: Kfitzat rosh li-vrekhot ha-s'hiya shel Yisra'el" (The perfect status symbol: Diving headfirst into Israel's swimming pools). *Walla! News*, July 29, 2017. tinyurl.com/israpools.

Ashman, Sam. "Combined and Uneven Development." In *The Elgar Companion to Marxist Economics*, edited by Ben Fine and Alfredo Saad-Filho, 60–65. Cheltenham: Edward Elgar, 2012.

Assi, Seraje. *The History and Politics of the Bedouin: Reimagining Nomadism in Modern Palestine*. London: Routledge, 2018.

Aulino, Felicity. "Perceiving the Social Body: A Phenomenological Perspective on Ethical Practice in Buddhist Thailand." *Journal of Religious Ethics* 42, no. 3 (September 1, 2014): 415–41.

———. *Rituals of Care: Karmic Politics in an Aging Thailand*. Ithaca, NY: Cornell University Press, 2019.

Avieli, Nir. "Thai Migrant Workers and the Dog-Eating Myth." In *Food and Power: A Culinary Ethnography of Israel*, 178–216. Berkeley and Los Angeles: University of California Press, 2017.

Bailey, Clinton. "Relations between Bedouin Tribes on Opposite Sides of the Wadi Arabah, 1600–1950." In *Crossing the Rift: Resources, Routes, Settlement Patterns, and Interaction in the Wadi Arabah*, edited by Piotr Bienkowski and Katharina Galor, 251–58. Oxford: Oxbow Books, 2006.

Balibar, Étienne. "Racism and Nationalism." In *Race, Nation, Class: Ambiguous Identities*, edited by Immanuel Wallerstein and Étienne Balibar, 37–68. London: Verso, 1991.

Banaji, Jairus. "The Fictions of Free Labour: Contract, Coercion, and So-Called Unfree Labour." *Historical Materialism* 11 (2003): 69–95.

———. *Theory as History: Essays on Modes of Production and Exploitation*. Leiden: Brill, 2010.

Bannerji, Himani. "Building from Marx: Reflections on Class and Race." *Social Justice* 32, no. 4 (102) (2005): 144–60.

Bao, Jiemin. "Denaturalizing Polygyny in Bangkok, Thailand." *Ethnology* 47, no. 2/3 (2008): 145–61.

Bar-Yosef, Eitan. *Vila Ba-Jungel: Afrika Ba-Tarbut Ha-Yisre'elit* (A Villa in the Jungle: Africa in Israeli Culture). Jerusalem: Van Leer Institute, 2013.

Behar, Moshe. "Palestine, Arabized Jews and the Elusive Consequences of Jewish and Arab National Formations." *Nationalism and Ethnic Politics* 13 (October 1, 2007): 581–611.

Ben Dor-Benite, Zvi. "Satan and Labor: Proletarianization and the Racialization of the Mizrahim." In *Race and the Question of Palestine*, edited by Ronit Lentin and Lana Tatour. Stanford, CA: Stanford University Press, 2025.

Ben Zvi, Avshalom. "Shiluvam Shel Vatikim Ve-'olim Bi-Tnu'at Ha-Moshavim Mi-Shilhei Shnot Ha-Hamishim ve-ad Tom Shnot Ha-Shishim" (The Integration of Veterans and Newcomers in the Moshav Movement from the Late 1950s to the Late 1960s). MA thesis, University of Haifa, 2018.

Ben-Eliyahu, Shai. "Ben-Gurion Mesayea Be-Hakamat Ein Yahav." In *Arava En Ketz: Nof, Teva ve-Adam Ba-Arava* (The Arava: Landscape, Nature and People in the Arava Valley), edited by Yair Giladi, Haim Levita, Menahem Marcus, and Amnon Navon, 172–81. Ein Yahav: Arava, 2012.

Ben-Yehoyada, Naor. "Transnational Political Cosmology: A Central Mediterranean Example." *Comparative Studies in Society and History* 56, no. 4 (October 2014): 870–901.

Berda, Yael. *Living Emergency: Israel's Permit Regime in the Occupied West Bank.* Stanford, CA: Stanford University Press, 2018.

Berlant, Lauren. *Cruel Optimism.* Durham, NC: Duke University Press, 2011.

Bhandar, Brenna. *Colonial Lives of Property: Law, Land, and Racial Regimes of Ownership.* Durham, NC: Duke University Press, 2018.

Bhattacharya, Tithi, and Liselotte Vogel, eds. *Social Reproduction Theory: Remapping Class, Recentering Oppression.* London: Pluto Press, 2017.

Biedermann, Ferry. "Strong Shekel Changes Israel's Economy and Makes Investors Think Twice." CNBC, July 7, 2017. tinyurl.com/strong-nis.

Bienkowski, Piotr. "The Wadi Arabah: Meanings in a Contested Landscape." In *Crossing the Rift: Resources, Routes, Settlement Patterns, and Interaction in the Wadi Arabah,* edited by Piotr Bienkowski and Katharina Galor, 7–28. Oxford: Oxbow Books, 2006.

Biton, Yifat. "Mizrahim Ba-Mishpat: Ha-'ayin' Ke-'yesh'" (Mizrahim and the Law: Absence as Existence). *Mishpatim* 41 (2011): 455–516.

Bloom Cohen, Hella. *The Literary Imagination in Israel-Palestine: Orientalism, Poetry, and Biopolitics.* London: Palgrave Macmillan, 2016.

BOI (Bank of Israel). "Foreign Currency Market—Average Exchange Rates." Accessed March 30, 2018. tinyurl.com/boi-rates.

Bolt, Maxim. "The Sociality of the Wage: Money Rhythms, Wealth Circulation, and the Problem with Cash on the Zimbabwean-South African Border." *Journal of the Royal Anthropological Institute* 20, no. 1 (March 2014): 113–30.

Bonacich, Edna. "A Theory of Ethnic Antagonism: The Split Labor Market." *American Sociological Review* 37, no. 5 (October 1, 1972): 547–59.

Boord, Matan. "Creating the Labor-Zionist Family: Masculinity, Sexuality, and Marriage in Mandate Palestine." *Jewish Social Studies* 22, no. 3 (2017): 38–67.

Boucher, Anna, and Justin Gest. "Migration Studies at a Crossroads: A Critique of Immigration Regime Typologies." *Migration Studies* 3, no. 2 (July 2015): 182–98.

Bourdieu, Pierre. "The Forms of Capital." In *Handbook of Theory and Research for the Sociology of Education,* edited by John G Richardson, 241–58. New York: Greenwood Press, 1986.

———. *Outline of a Theory of Practice.* Cambridge: Cambridge University Press, 1977.

Bowie, Katherine A. *Rituals of National Loyalty: An Anthropology of the State and the Village Scout Movement in Thailand.* New York: Columbia University Press, 1997.

Bram, Chen, and Ran Shauli. "Israel-Myanmar Relations and the Rohingya Mass Killings." In *Israel-Asia Relations in the Twenty-First Century: The Search for Partners in a Changing World*, edited by Yoram Evron and Rotem Kowner. Abingdon: Routledge, 2024.

Breman, Jan. *Taming the Coolie Beast: Plantation Society and the Colonial Order in Southeast Asia*. Oxford: Oxford University Press, 1989.

Brenner, Suzanne. "Why Women Rule the Roost: Rethinking Javanese Ideologies of Gender and Self-Control." In *Bewitching Women, Pious Men: Gender and Body Politics in Southeast Asia*, edited by Aihwa Ong and Michael G. Peletz, 19–50. Berkeley and Los Angeles: University of California Press, 1995.

Bretsky, Nurit. "Yom Huledet Sameah Bhumipol (Happy Birthday Bhumipol)." *Ma'ariv*, December 24, 2001.

Brucker, Guy. "Tayare min yisre'elim be-Tayland" (Israeli male sex tourists in Thailand). MA thesis, University of Haifa, 2007.

Bruins, H. J., Z. Sherzer, H. Ginat, and S. Batarseh. "Degradation of Springs in the Arava Valley: Anthropogenic and Climatic Factors." *Land Degradation & Development* 23, no. 4 (July 2012): 365–83.

Bsoul, Janan. "Hithananti Lalekhet La-Rofe, Aval Ha-Bos Lo Hiskim" (I Begged to Go to the Doctor, but the Boss Didn't Agree). *TheMarker*, September 19, 2016. tinyurl.com/bsoul-thai.

Bunton, Martin. "'Home,' 'Colony,' 'Vilayet': Frames of Reference for the Study of Land in Mandate Palestine." *Journal of Colonialism and Colonial History* 21, no. 1 (2020).

Burawoy, Michael. "The Functions and Reproduction of Migrant Labor: Comparative Material from Southern Africa and the United States." *American Journal of Sociology* 81, no. 5 (March 1976): 1050–87.

———. *Manufacturing Consent: Changes in the Labor Process under Monopoly Capitalism*. Chicago: University of Chicago Press, 1979.

Casanova, Pablo Gonzalez. "Internal Colonialism and National Development." *Studies in Comparative International Development* 1, no. 4 (April 1, 1965): 27–37.

Cassaniti, Julia. *Living Buddhism: Mind, Self, and Emotion in a Thai Community*. Ithaca, NY: Cornell University Press, 2015.

Cazdyn, Eric. "Enlightenment, Revolution, Cure: The Problem of Praxis and the Radical Nothingness of the Future." In *Nothing: Three Inquiries in Buddhism*, by Marcus Boon, Eric Cazdyn, and Timothy B. Morton, 105–84. Chicago: University of Chicago Press, 2015.

Central Arava Regional Council. "Ze Pashut Lo Oved Bli Yadayim Ovdot" (It Just Doesn't Work without Working Hands), August 2006.

Central Bureau of Statistics. *Shnaton Statisti Le-Yisra'el* (Israel Statistical Yearbook). Vol. 41, 1990.

———. *Shnaton Statisti Le-Yisra'el* (Israel Statistical Yearbook). Vol. 62, 2000.

Cerbero, Haim. "Gvul Yisra'el-Yarden Ba-Arava" (The Israel-Jordan Border in the Arabah)." In *Arava En Ketz: Nof, Teva ve-Adam Ba-Arava* (The Arava: Landscape, Nature and People in the Arava Valley), edited by Yair Giladi, Haim Levita, Menahem Marcus, and Amnon Navon, 286–93. Ein Yahav: Arava, 2012.

Chatterjee, Partha. *The Nation and Its Fragments: Colonial and Postcolonial Histories*. Oxford: Oxford University Press, 1994.

Chetrit, Sami Shalom. *Intra-Jewish Conflict in Israel: White Jews, Black Jews*. London: Routledge, 2010.

Chua, Peter, and Dune C. Fujino. "Negotiating New Asian-American Masculinities: Attitudes and Gender Expectations." *Journal of Men's Studies* 7, no. 3 (June 1, 1999): 391–413.

Chyutin, Michael. *Architecture and Utopia: The Israeli Experiment*. London: Routledge, 2016.

CIMI (Center for International Migration and Integration). "Kelim Le-Avoda Ye'ila Bi-Sviva Rav-Tarbutit Im Ovdim Ha-Megi'im Mi-Tayland" (Tools for Effective Work in a Multicultural Environment with Workers Coming from Thailand), 2017. tinyurl.com/CIMI-kelim.

Clarno, Andy. *Neoliberal Apartheid: Palestine/Israel and South Africa after 1994*. Chicago: University of Chicago Press, 2017.

Cohen, Erik. "Ovdim Taylandim ba-Hakla'ut ha-Yisre'elit" (Thai workers in Israeli agriculture). In *Ha-po'alim ha-hadashim: 'Ovdim mi-Medinot Zarot be-Yisra'el* (The new workers: Wage earners from foreign countries in Israel), edited by Roby Nathanson and Lea Achdut, 155–204. Tel Aviv: Hakibbutz Hameuchad, 1999.

Cohen, Miri. "Ma'aneh MASHHAB Li-Fniyat Ha va'ada Ha-Meyuhedet Le-ovdim Zarim Be-Nose Etgarim Be-Ha'asakat Ovdim Zarim Be-anaf Ha-Hakla'ut" (Response of the Health Ministry to the Enquiry of the Special Committee for Foreign Workers on the Challenges of Employing Foreign Workers in the Agricultural Sector). Israel Health Ministry, November 16, 2021.

Cohen, Yeruham. *Tokhnit Allon* (The Allon Plan). Tel Aviv: Hakibbutz Hameuchad, 1972.

Crosby, Alfred W. W. *Ecological Imperialism: The Biological Expansion of Europe, 900–1900*. Cambridge: Cambridge University Press, 2004.

Davis, Mike. *Late Victorian Holocausts: El Niño Famines and the Making of the Third World*. London: Verso, 2001.

De León, Jason. *The Land of Open Graves: Living and Dying on the Migrant Trail*. Berkeley and Los Angeles: University of California Press, 2015.

DeGooyer, Stephanie, Alastair Hunt, Lida Maxwell, Samuel Moyn, and Astra Taylor. *The Right to Have Rights*. London: Verso, 2018.

Deleuze, Gilles, and Félix Guattari. *A Thousand Plateaus: Capitalism and Schizophrenia*. London: Continuum International, 2004.

DeMalach, Daniel. "The Political Economy of Communal Life: Zionist Settlement Policy and Kibbutz Collective Practices, 1920–2010." *Communal Societies* 37, no. 2 (May 2018): 129–52.

Diklo, Shmuel, and Galei Tzahal. "HAK Shlomo Benizri Hursha Be-Kabalat Shohad Meha-Kablan Moshe Sela Uve-Hafarat Emunim" (MK Shlomo Benizri Convicted of Taking Bribes from Contractor Moshe Sela and of Breach of Trust). *Globes*, April 1, 2008. tinyurl.com/globes-benizri.

Dolinka, Benjamin J. "The Rujm Taba Archeological Project (RTAP): Results of the 2001 Survey and Reconnaisance." In *Crossing the Rift: Resources, Routes, Settlement Patterns, and Interaction in the Wadi Arabah*, edited by Piotr Bienkowski and Katharina Galor, 195–214. Oxford: Oxbow Books, 2006.

Dommen, Arthur J. "Laos in 1984: The Year of the Thai Border." *Asian Survey* 25, no. 1 (1985): 114–21.

Doumani, Beshara. *Rediscovering Palestine: Merchants and Peasants in Jabal Nablus, 1700–1900*. Berkeley and Los Angeles: University of California Press, 1995.

Dromi, Uri. "Ben Gurion shel ha-arava: Shai Ben-Eliyahu, ehad mi-meyasde Ein Yahav, 1935–2010" (Ben Gurion of the Arabah: Shai Ben-Eliyahu, one of the founders of Ein Yahav, 1935–2010). *Ha'aretz*, July 23, 2010. tinyurl.com/obit-ben-eliyahu.

Drori, Israel. *Foreign Workers in Israel: Global Perspectives*. Albany: SUNY Press, 2009.

Efrati, Ido. "Tofa'a: Hakla'im megarshim atzma'it ovdim zarim" (Phenomenon: Farmers independently deporting foreign workers). *Ynet*, August 29, 2005. tinyurl.com/indy-deport.

Ehrenreich, Barbara. *Fear of Falling: The Inner Life of the Middle Class*. New York: Twelve, 2020.

Ehrlich, Avishai. "The Crisis in Israel, Danger of Fascism?" *Khamsin*, no. 5 (July 10, 1978). tinyurl.com/ehrlich-fascism.

Eisenman, Tsippy. "Histaglutam shel moshvei ha-arava ha-tikhona li-sviva mishtana" (The adaptation of the moshavim of the Central Arabah to a changing environment). MA thesis, Ben Gurion University, 1994.

El Or, Tamar. "Ha-Horef Shel Ha-Re'ulot: Kisuy ve-Giluy Be-2007/8" (The Winter of the Veiled Women: Covering and Uncovering in 2007/8). *Theory and Criticism* 37 (Fall 2010): 37–68.

———. "The Soul of the Biblical Sandal: On Anthropology and Style." *American Anthropologist* 114, no. 3 (September 1, 2012): 433–45.

El Kurd, Dana. "The Paradox of Peace: The Impact of Normalization with Israel on the Arab World." *Global Studies Quarterly* 3, no. 3 (July 1, 2023): ksad042.

Elmaliach, Tal. *Anshei Ha-Etmol: Ha-Kibbutz Ha-Artzi ve-Mapam, 1956–1977* (Yesterday's People: Ha-Kibbutz Ha-Artzi and Mapam, 1956–1977). Sde Boker: Ben Gurion Institute, 2018.

Elmaliah, Adi. "Avoda Ivrit Zara" (Foreign Hebrew Labor). *Adrikhalut Nof: The Journal of the Israeli Union of Landscape Architects*, no. 64 (September 2017): 44–45.

Enfield, N. J. "How to Define 'Lao,' 'Thai,' and 'Isan' Language? A View from Linguistic Science." *Tai Culture* 7, no. 1 (2002).

Engelberg, Ari. "Fighting Intermarriage in the Holy Land: Lehava and Israeli Ethnonationalism." *Journal of Israeli History* 36, no. 2 (July 3, 2017): 229–47.

Englert, Sai. "Hebrew Labor without Hebrew Workers: The Histadrut, Palestinian Workers, and the Israeli Construction Industry." *Journal of Palestine Studies* 52, no. 3 (July 3, 2023): 23–45.

———. *Settler Colonialism: An Introduction*. London: Pluto Press, 2022.

Ennis, Crystal A., and Nicolas Blarel, eds. *The South Asia to Gulf Migration Governance Complex*. Bristol: Bristol University Press, 2022.

"Face, n." In *Oxford English Dictionary*. Oxford: Oxford University Press, 2009.

Falah, Ghazi. "Dynamics and Patterns of the Shrinking of Arab Lands in Palestine." *Political Geography* 22, no. 2 (February 2003): 179–209.

———. "The Evolution of Semi-Nomadism in Non-Desert Environment: The Case of Galilee in the 19th Century." *GeoJournal* 21, no. 4 (1990): 397–410.

FAO, UNDP, and UNEP. *A Multi-Billion-Dollar Opportunity—Repurposing Agricultural Support to Transform Food Systems*. Rome: FAO, UNDP, and UNEP, 2021. doi.org/10.4060/cb6562en.

Farsakh, Leila. "Palestinian Labor Flows to the Israeli Economy: A Finished Story?" *Journal of Palestine Studies* 32, no. 1 (October 2002): 13–27.

———. *Palestinian Labour Migration to Israel: Labour, Land and Occupation*. Abingdon: Routledge, 2005.

Fields, Gary. *Enclosure: Palestinian Landscapes in a Historical Mirror*. Berkeley and Los Angeles: University of California Press, 2017.

Filc, Danny, and Uri Ram, eds. *Shilton ha-hon: Ha-hevra ha-yisre'elit ba-idan ha-globali* (The rule of capital: Israeli society in the global age). Jerusalem: Van Leer Institute, 2004.

Fischbach, Michael. *Records of Dispossession: Palestinian Refugee Property and the Arab-Israeli Conflict*. New York: Columbia University Press, 2003.

Fisher, Mark. *Capitalist Realism: Is There No Alternative?* Winchester: Zero Books, 2009.

Forman, Geremy, and Alexandre (Sandy) Kedar. "From Arab Land to 'Israel Lands': The Legal Dispossession of the Palestinians Displaced by Israel in the Wake of 1948." *Environment and Planning D: Society and Space* 22, no. 6 (December 2004): 809–30.

Foster, John Bellamy. *Marx's Ecology: Materialism and Nature*. New York: Monthly Review Press, 2000.

Fox, Shlomo. "The Settlement Department Unsettled." In *Rural Cooperatives in Socialist Utopia: Thirty Years of Moshav Development in Israel*, edited by Gideon Kressel, Susan Lees, and Moshe Schwartz, 55–62. Westport, CT: Praeger, 1995.

Frankel, Shlomo, and Shimshon Bichler. *Hameyuhasim: Atzulat Ha-Hon Shel Yisrael* (The Rich Families: Israel's Aristocracy of Finance). Tel Aviv: CADIM, 1984.

Friedmann, Harriet. "The Political Economy of Food: The Rise and Fall of the Postwar International Food Order." *American Journal of Sociology* 88 (January 1982): S248–86.

Gal, Susan. "Language and the 'Arts of Resistance.'" *Cultural Anthropology* 10, no. 3 (August 1, 1995): 407–24.

Galili, Roy. "Hitporerut" (Disintegration). *Aravot*, August 2020.

Gams, Nathanel. "'Me'orer Sh'at Nefesh': Gid'on Sa'ar Metzia Lishlol Pitzuyim Mi-Ovdim Zarim She-Rotzim La'azov ('Revolting': Gideon Sa'ar Suggests Denial of Compensation to Foreign Workers Who Want to Leave)." *TheMarker*, October 22, 2023. tinyurl.com/saar-pitzuyim.

Gardi, Tomer, and Omar Al-Ghabari. *Awdah: Eduyot medumyanot me-atidim efshariyim* (Awdah: Imagined Testimonies from Possible Futures). Tel Aviv: Pardes, 2013.

Gardner, Andrew M. "Engulfed: Indian Guest Workers, Bahraini Citizens and the Structural Violence of the Kafala System." In *The Deportation Regime: Sovereignty, Space, and the Freedom of Movement*, edited by Nicholas De Genova and Nathalie Mae Peutz, 196–223. Durham, NC: Duke University Press, 2010.

Geertz, Clifford. *Agricultural Involution: The Process of Ecological Change in Indonesia*. Berkeley: University of California Press, 1963.

Genovese, Eugene D. *Roll, Jordan, Roll: The World the Slaves Made*. New York: Pantheon Books, 1974.

Gerhards, Jürgen. "Transnational Linguistic Capital: Explaining English Proficiency in 27 European Countries." *International Sociology* 29, no. 1 (January 1, 2014): 56–74.

Ghalayini, Basma, ed. *Palestine +100: Stories from a Century after the Nakba*. Manchester: Comma Press, 2019.

Gillis, Rivi. "Pituah Ha-Zehut: Hakhshara Shel Afrika'im Be-Yisra'el, 1958–1980" (The Development of Identity: Training of Africans in Israel, 1958–1980). PhD diss., Tel Aviv University, 2017.

Gilman, Sander L. "'Stand Up Straight': Notes Toward a History of Posture." *Journal of Medical Humanities* 35, no. 1 (March 1, 2014): 57–83.

Glassman, Jim. "Cracking Hegemony in Thailand: Gramsci, Bourdieu and the Dialectics of Rebellion." *Journal of Contemporary Asia* 41, no. 1 (February 2011): 25–46.

———. "Lineages of the Authoritarian State in Thailand: Military Dictatorship, Lazy Capitalism and the Cold War Past as Post-Cold War Prologue." *Journal of Contemporary Asia* 50, no. 4 (August 7, 2020): 571–92.

———. *Thailand at the Margins: Internationalization of the State and the Transformation of Labour.* Oxford: Oxford University Press, 2004.

Gluckman, Max. "Analysis of a Social Situation in Modern Zululand." *Bantu Studies* 14, no. 1 (January 1940): 1–30.

Goffman, Erving. "On Face-Work." In *Interaction Ritual,* 5–45. New York: Doubleday, 1967.

Goldreich, Yair, and Ora Karni. "Climate and Precipitation Regime in the Arava Valley, Israel." *Israel Journal of Earth Sciences* 50, no. 2 (January 1, 2001): 53–60.

Grabowsky, Volker. "The Isan Up to Its Integration into the Siamese State." In *Regions and National Integration in Thailand, 1892–1992,* edited by Volker Grabowsky, 107–30. Leipzig: Otto Harrassowitz Verlag, 1995.

Grosfoguel, Ramón, and Ana Margarita Cervantes-Rodríguez, eds. *The Modern/ Colonial/Capitalist World-System in the Twentieth Century: Global Processes, Antisystemic Movements, and the Geopolitics of Knowledge.* Westport, CT: Praeger, 2002.

Guha, Ranajit. *Dominance without Hegemony: History and Power in Colonial India.* Cambridge, MA: Harvard University Press, 1997.

Gullette, Gregory S. "Rural–Urban Hierarchies, Status Boundaries, and Labour Mobilities in Thailand." *Journal of Ethnic and Migration Studies* 40, no. 8 (August 3, 2014): 1254–74.

Gutiérrez Rodríguez, Encarnación. "The Coloniality of Migration and the 'Refugee Crisis': On the Asylum-Migration Nexus, the Transatlantic White European Settler Colonialism-Migration and Racial Capitalism." *Refuge* 34, no. 1 (June 18, 2018).

Habermas, Jürgen. *The Structural Transformation of the Public Sphere: An Inquiry into a Category of Bourgeois Society.* Translated by Thomas Burger. Cambridge: Polity Press, 2008.

Hall, Stuart. "Race, Articulation, and Societies Structured in Dominance." In *Black British Cultural Studies: A Reader,* edited by Houston A. Baker, Manthia Diawara, and Ruth H. Lindeborg, 16–60. Chicago: University of Chicago Press, 1996.

HALOT. "עֲרָבָה." In HALOT Online, February 2017.

Halper, Jeff. *Decolonizing Israel, Liberating Palestine: Zionism, Settler Colonialism, and the Case for One Democratic State.* London: Pluto Press, 2021.

———. "The 94 Percent Solution: A Matrix of Control." *Middle East Report,* no. 216 (2000): 14–19.

Handley, Paul M. *The King Never Smiles: A Biography of Thailand's Bhumibol Adulyadej.* New Haven, CT: Yale University Press, 2006.

Hanna, J. M., and D. E. Brown. "Human Heat Tolerance: An Anthropological Perspective." *Annual Review of Anthropology* 12, no. 1 (1983): 259–84.

Harkins, Benjamin. "Thailand Migration Report 2019." Bangkok: United Nations Thematic Working Group on Migration in Thailand, 2019.

Ha-Shkhenim Shelanu—Ha-Bedu'im Shel Ha-Arava (Our Neighbors—the Bedouin of the Arabah), 2018. tinyurl.com/ha-shkhenim.

Hauptmann, Andreas. "Mining Archaeology and Archaeometallurgy in the Wadi Arabah: The Mining Districts of Faynan and Timna." In *Crossing the Rift: Resources, Routes, Settlement Patterns, and Interaction in the Wadi Arabah,* edited by Piotr Bienkowski and Katharina Galor, 125–34. Oxford: Oxbow Books, 2006.

Herzfeld, Michael. "The Absent Presence: Discourses of Crypto-Colonialism." *South Atlantic Quarterly* 101, no. 4 (March 3, 2003): 899–926.

———. *Cultural Intimacy: Social Poetics and the Real Life of States, Societies, and Institutions.* 3rd ed. London and New York: Routledge, 2016.

———. *Siege of the Spirits: Community and Polity in Bangkok.* Chicago: University of Chicago Press, 2016.

Hewes, Gordon W. "World Distribution of Certain Postural Habits." *American Anthropologist* 57, no. 2 (1955): 231–44.

Hirsch, Dafna. "'Hummus Is Best When It Is Fresh and Made by Arabs': The Gourmetization of Hummus in Israel and the Return of the Repressed Arab." *American Ethnologist* 38, no. 4 (November 1, 2011): 617–30.

Hirschfeld, Yizhar. "The Nabatean Presence South of the Dead Sea: New Evidence." In *Crossing the Rift: Resources, Routes, Settlement Patterns, and Interaction in the Wadi Arabah,* edited by Piotr Bienkowski and Katharina Galor, 167–90. Oxford: Oxbow Books, 2006.

Ho, Engseng. "Empire through Diasporic Eyes: A View from the Other Boat." *Comparative Studies in Society and History* 46, no. 2 (April 2004): 210–46.

———. *The Graves of Tarim: Genealogy and Mobility across the Indian Ocean.* Berkeley and Los Angeles: University of California Press, 2006.

Hobsbawm, E. J. *The Age of Extremes: A History of the World, 1914–1991.* New York: Vintage Books, 1996.

Holmes, Seth. *Fresh Fruit, Broken Bodies: Migrant Farmworkers in the United States.* Berkeley and Los Angeles: University of California Press, 2013.

Horden, Peregrine, and Nicholas Purcell. *The Corrupting Sea: A Study of Mediterranean History.* Oxford: Blackwell, 2000.

HRW (Human Rights Watch). "A Raw Deal: Abuses of Thai Workers in Israel's Agricultural Sector," 2015. tinyurl.com/hrw-raw-deal.

Hu, Hsien-chin. "The Chinese Concepts of 'Face.'" *American Anthropologist* 46, no. 1 (1944): 45–64.

Hughes, Geoffrey. "Cutting the Face: Kinship, State and Social Media Conflict in Networked Jordan." *Journal of Legal Anthropology* 2, no. 1 (June 1, 2018): 49–71.

———. "Envious Ethnography and the Ethnography of Envy in Anthropology's 'Orient': Towards a Theory of Envy." *Ethos* 48, no. 2 (2020): 192–211.

Hymes, Dell. "Linguistic Problems in Defining the Concept of Tribe." In *Essays on the Problem of Tribe: Proceedings of the 1967 Annual Spring Meeting of the American Ethnological Society.* Seattle: University of Washington Press, 1968.

Ifergan, Shimon. "Ekstazi La-Aniyim" (The Poor Man's Ecstasy). *Mako,* December 20, 2012. tinyurl.com/ifergan-yaba.

Iijima, A. "The Invention of 'Isan' History." *Journal of the Siam Society,* November 28, 2018.

IIM (Israel Interior Ministry). "Reshimat Haktza'ot Le-Ha'asakat ovdim Zarim Be-anaf Ha-Hakla'ut Li-Shnat 2013" (List of Allocations for the Employment of Foreign Workers in the Agricultural Sector for the Year 2013), 2012. tinyurl.com/alloc-2013.

Ilani, Giora. *Ma'ale Namer: Zikhronot Zo'olog Yisre'eli* (Leopard Steppe: Memoir of an Israeli Zoologist). Bnei Brak: Sifriat Po'alim, 2004.

Ince, Onur Ulaş. *Colonial Capitalism and the Dilemmas of Liberalism.* Oxford: Oxford University Press, 2018.

———. "Deprovincializing Racial Capitalism: John Crawfurd and Settler Colonialism in India." *American Political Science Review* 116, no. 1 (2022): 1–17.

Irvine, Judith T. "When Talk Isn't Cheap: Language and Political Economy." *American Ethnologist* 16, no. 2 (1989): 248–67.

Irvine, Judith, and Susan Gal. "Language Ideology and Linguistic Differentiation." In *Regimes of Language: Ideologies, Polities, and Identities,* 25–84. Santa Fe, NM: School of American Research, 2000.

Ishii, Yoneo. "A Note on Buddhistic Millenarian Revolts in Northeastern Siam." *Journal of Southeast Asian Studies* 6, no. 2, (1975): 121–26.

ISO (International Standards Organization). "ISO 11940–2." International Standards Organization, January 28, 2019. www.iso.org/standard/29544 .html.

Israel Meteorological Service. "Erke Temperatura Rav-Shnatiyim, 1995–2009" (Multi-Annual Temperature Values, 1995–2009). State of Israel, February 2013. tinyurl.com/isratemp1999.

Issara Phromma, Adcharaporn Pagdee, Ananya Popradit, Atsushi Ishida, and Somkid Uttaranakorn. "Protected Area Co-Management and Land Use Conflicts Adjacent to Phu Kao—Phu Phan Kham National Park, Thailand." *Journal of Sustainable Forestry* 38, no. 5 (July 4, 2019): 486–507.

Jackson, Peter A. "The Performative State: Semi-Coloniality and the Tyranny of Images in Modern Thailand." *Sojourn: Journal of Social Issues in Southeast Asia* 19, no. 2 (2004): 219–53.

——. "The Thai Regime of Images." *Sojourn: Journal of Social Issues in Southeast Asia* 19, no. 2 (2004): 181–218.

Jasmin, Michaël. "The Emergence and First Development of the Arabian Trade across the Wadi Arabah." In *Crossing the Rift: Resources, Routes, Settlement Patterns, and Interaction in the Wadi Arabah*, edited by Piotr Bienkowski and Katharina Galor, 143–50. Oxford: Oxbow Books, 2006.

Jobson, Ryan Cecil. "The Case for Letting Anthropology Burn: Sociocultural Anthropology in 2019." *American Anthropologist* 122, no. 2 (2020): 259–71.

Johnson, Andrew Alan. "Deferral and Intimacy: Long-Distance Romance and Thai Migrants Abroad." *Anthropological Quarterly* 91, no. 1 (2018): 307–24.

Johnson, Walter, and Robin D. G. Kelley. *Race Capitalism Justice*. Cambridge, MA: MIT Press, 2018.

Johnston, David B. "Opening a Frontier: The Expansion of Rice Cultivation in Central Thailand in the 1890's." In *Population, Land and Structural Change in Sri Lanka and Thailand*, edited by James Brow, 27–44. Leiden: Brill Academic, 1976.

Jones, Huw, and Tieng Pardthaison. "The Impact of Overseas Labour Migration on Rural Thailand: Regional, Community and Individual Dimensions." *Journal of Rural Studies* 15, no. 1 (January 1, 1999): 35–47.

Joseph, Miranda. *Against the Romance of Community*. Minneapolis: University of Minnesota Press, 2002.

Jung, Moon-Ho. *Coolies and Cane: Race, Labor, and Sugar in the Age of Emancipation*. Baltimore: Johns Hopkins University Press, 2006.

Kalir, Barak. "The Jewish State of Anxiety: Between Moral Obligation and Fearism in the Treatment of African Asylum Seekers in Israel." *Journal of Ethnic and Migration Studies* 41, no. 4 (March 21, 2015): 580–98.

Kamala Tiyavanich. *Forest Recollections: Wandering Monks in Twentieth-Century Thailand*. Honolulu: University of Hawaii Press, 1997.

Kaminer, Matan. "The Abrahamic Ideology: Patrilineal Kinship and the Politics of Peacemaking in the Contemporary Middle East." *Millennium: Journal of International Studies*, online first (November 20, 2023).

——. "The Agricultural Settlement of the Arabah and the Political Ecology of Zionism." *International Journal of Middle East Studies* 54, no. 1 (February 2022): 40–56.

———. "At the Zero Degree/Below the Minimum: Wage as Sign in Israel's Split Labor Market." *Dialectical Anthropology* 43, no. 3 (September 2019): 317–32.

———. "Avoda be-darga efes: Subyektiviyut po'alit be-mahsan ashdodi" (Zero degree labor: Worker subjectivity in an Ashdod warehouse). MA thesis, Tel Aviv University, 2011.

———. "Behind the Well Houses: The Saknat of Abu Kabir." *Maarav*, no. 30 (June 2021). tinyurl.com/behind-well-houses.

———. "By the Sweat of Other Brows: Thai Migrant Labor and the Transformation of Israeli Settler Agriculture." PhD diss., University of Michigan, 2019.

———. "Connections Yet Unmade: The Reception of Balibar and Wallerstein's Race, Nation, Class in Israel." In *"Race, Nation, Class": Rereading a Dialogue for Our Times*, edited by Manuela Bojadzijev and Katrin Klingan, 107–20. Berlin: Argument-Verlag, 2018.

———. "Giving Them the Slip: Israeli Employers' Strategic Falsification of Pay Slips to Disguise the Violation of Thai Farmworkers' Right to the Minimum Wage." *Journal of Legal Anthropology* 3, no. 2 (2019): 124–27.

———. "Ha-zman she-aharei ha-'Post'" (The time after the 'post')." *Hazman Hazeh*, May 11, 2021. hazmanhazeh.org.il/post/.

———. "In Israel, Thai Migrant Workers Are Caught in Other People's War." *Jacobin*, December 4, 2023. tinyurl.com/jacobin-kaminer-thais.

———. "In the Shadow of the Mountains: The Jordan Valley and Israel/Palestine's Marginalized East." *Jadaliyya*, September 9, 2020. tinyurl.com/kaminer-shadow.

———. "Learning About 'Life in Israel' from Thai Migrant Farmworkers." *Discover Rackham* (blog), November 14, 2018. tinyurl.com/kaminer-learning.

———. "A Lonely Songkran in the Arabah." *Middle East Report* 279 (2016): 34–37.

———. "Mabatim musatim ba-arava" (Averted gazes in the Arabah). *Hazman Hazeh*, October 23, 2019. hazmanhazeh.org.il/thaiworkers/.

———. "The Oksana Affair: Ambiguous Resistance in an Israeli Warehouse." *Ethnography* 19, no. 1 (March 2018): 25–43.

———. "The Rebirth of the 'Natural Worker': Racialisation and Class Formation in Zionist Agriculture." *New Socialist*, September 30, 2023. tinyurl.com/kaminer-rebirth.

———. "Saving the Face of the Arabah: Thai Migrant Workers and the Asymmetries of Community in an Israeli Agricultural Settlement." *American Ethnologist* 49, no. 1 (February 2022): 118–31.

Käng, Dredge Byung'chu. "Kathoey 'In Trend': Emergent Genderscapes, National Anxieties and the Re-Signification of Male-Bodied Effeminacy in Thailand." *Asian Studies Review* 36, no. 4 (December 1, 2012): 475–94.

Kasaba, Reşat. *A Moveable Empire: Ottoman Nomads, Migrants, and Refugees.* Seattle: University of Washington Press, 2009.

Katriel, Tamar. "Kiturim: Griping as a Verbal Ritual in Israeli Discourse." In *Communal Webs: Communication and Culture in Contemporary Israel*, 35–50. Albany: SUNY Press, 2012.

———. *Talking Straight: Dugri Speech in Israeli Sabra Culture.* Cambridge: Cambridge University Press, 1986.

Keane, Webb. "Semiotics and the Social Analysis of Material Things." *Language & Communication* 23, no. 3–4 (July 2003): 409–25.

Kedar, Nir. "Ben-Gurion's Mamlakhtiyut: Etymological and Theoretical Roots." *Israel Studies* 7, no. 3 (2002): 117–33.

Kemp, Adriana, and Rebeca Raijman. "Bringing in State Regulations, Private Brokers, and Local Employers: A Meso-Level Analysis of Labor Trafficking in Israel." *International Migration Review* 48, no. 3 (2014): 604–42.

———. *Ovdim u-zarim: Ha-kalkala ha-politit shel hagirat avoda le-Yisra'el* (Migrants and Workers: The Political Economy of Labour Migration in Israel). Tel Aviv: Hakibbutz Hameuchad, 2008.

Keyes, Charles F. *Finding Their Voice: Northeastern Villagers and the Thai State.* Chiang Mai: Silkworm Books, 2014.

———. "Hegemony and Resistance in Northeastern Thailand." In *Regions and National Integration in Thailand, 1892–1992*, edited by Volker Grabowsky, 154–82. Leipzig: Otto Harrassowitz Verlag, 1995.

———. "In Search of Land: Village Formation in the Central Chi River Valley, Northeastern Thailand." In *Population, Land and Structural Change in Sri Lanka and Thailand*, edited by James Brow, 45–63. Leiden: Brill, 1976.

———. "Mother or Mistress but Never a Monk: Buddhist Notions of Female Gender in Rural Thailand." *American Ethnologist* 11, no. 2 (May 1, 1984): 223–41.

Khalidi, Walid. *All That Remains: The Palestinian Villages Occupied and Depopulated by Israel in 1948.* Washington, DC: Institute for Palestine Studies, 2006.

Khan, A., P. Martin, and P. Hardiman. "Expanded Production of Labor-Intensive Crops Increases Agricultural Employment." *California Agriculture* 58, no. 1 (January 1, 2004): 35–39.

Kim, Min Ji. "The Republic of Korea's Employment Permit System (EPS): Background and Rapid Assessment." International Migration Papers. Geneva: International Labour Organization, 2015.

Kimmerling, Baruch. *Ketz shilton ha-ahusalim* (The end of Ashkenazi hegemony). Jerusalem: Keter, 2001.

———. *Zionism and Territory: The Socio-Territorial Dimensions of Zionist Politics.* Berkeley: University of California Press, 1983.

Klima, Alan. *The Funeral Casino: Meditation, Massacre, and Exchange with the Dead in Thailand*. Princeton, NJ: Princeton University Press, 2002.

———. "Spirits of 'Dark Finance' in Thailand: A Local Hazard for the International Moral Fund." *Cultural Dynamics* 18, no. 1 (March 1, 2006): 33–60.

Kozłowska, Magdalena, and Michał Lubina. "The Burmese Road to Israeli-Style Cooperative Settlements: The Namsang Project, 1956–63." *Journal of Southeast Asian Studies* 52, no. 4 (December 2021): 701–25.

Krasner, Stephen D. "Structural Causes and Regime Consequences: Regimes as Intervening Variables." *International Organization* 36, no. 2 (1982): 185–205.

Kressel, Gideon. "'He Who Stays in Agriculture Is Not a "Freier"': The Spirit of Competition among Members of the Moshav Is Eroded When Unskilled Arab Labor Enters the Scene." In *Perspectives on Israeli Anthropology*, edited by Esther Hertzog, Orit Abuhav, and Harvey Goldberg, 191–216. Detroit: Wayne State University Press, 2010.

Kressel, Gideon M., Joseph Ben-David, and Khalil Abu Rabi'a. "Changes in the Land Usage by the Negev Bedouin Since the Mid-19th Century. The Intra-Tribal Perspective." *Nomadic Peoples*, no. 28 (1991): 28–55.

Kurlander, Yahel. "Mis'hur Ha-Hagira: Al Tzmihata, Sigsuga ve-Shinuya Shel Ta'asiyat Ha-Giyus Veha-Tivukh Le-Hagirat Avoda Le-Hakla'ut Mi-Tayland Le-Yisra'el" (The Marketization of Migration: On the Emergence, Flourishment and Change of the Recruitment Industry for Agricultural Migrant Workers from Thailand to Israel). PhD diss., University of Haifa, 2019.

———. "On the Establishment of Agricultural Migration Industry in Israel's Countryside." *Geography Research Forum* 41, no. 1 (July 15, 2022): 19–34.

Kurlander, Yahel, and Avinoam Cohen. "BLAs as Sites for the Meso-Level Dynamics of Institutionalization: A Cross-Sectoral Comparison." *Theoretical Inquiries in Law* 23, no. 2 (July 19, 2022).

Kurlander, Yahel, and Matan Kaminer. "Ovdim Kvu'im Me-Ahorei Ha-Bayit: Ha'asakat Mehagrei Avoda Mi-Tayland Ba-Hakla'ut Ba-Merhav Ha-Kafri" (Permanent Workers in the Backyard: The Employment of Migrant Workers from Thailand in Agriculture in the Countryside). *Horizons in Geography* 98 (2020): 131–48.

Kushnirovich, Nonna, and Rebeca Raijman. "The Impact of Bilateral Agreements on Labor Migration to Israel: A Comparison between Migrant Workers Who Arrived before and after the Implementation of Bilateral Agreements." Jerusalem: CIMI, 2017.

Lakoff, George, and Mark Johnson. *Metaphors We Live By*. Chicago: University of Chicago Press, 2003.

Leach, Edmund Ronald. *Political Systems of Highland Burma: A Study of Kachin Social Structure*. Boston: Beacon Press, 1965.

Lees, Susan. *The Political Ecology of the Water Crisis in Israel*. Lanham, MD: University Press of America, 1997.

Lemon, Alaina. "'Your Eyes Are Green like Dollars': Counterfeit Cash, National Substance, and Currency Apartheid in 1990s Russia." *Cultural Anthropology* 13, no. 1 (February 1, 1998): 22–55.

Levi-Strauss, Claude. *The Savage Mind*. Chicago: University of Chicago Press, 1966.

Levita, Haim. "Hilufe Shtahim Ba-Arava" (Territory Swaps in the Arabah). In *Arava En Ketz: Nof, Teva ve-Adam Ba-Arava* (The Arava: Landscape, Nature and People in the Arava Valley), edited by Yair Giladi, Haim Levita, Menahem Marcus, and Amnon Navon, 294–97. Ein Yahav: Arava, 2012.

Li, Tania Murray. *Land's End: Capitalist Relations on an Indigenous Frontier*. Durham, NC: Duke University Press, 2014.

Liebelt, Claudia. *Caring for the "Holy Land": Filipina Domestic Workers in Israel*. New York: Berghahn, 2011.

Livnat, Yuval, and Hila Shamir. "Gaining Control? Bilateral Labor Agreements and the Shared Interest of Sending and Receiving Countries to Control Migrant Workers and the Illicit Migration Industry." *Theoretical Inquiries in Law* 23, no. 2 (July 26, 2022): 65–94.

Locke, John. *The Second Treatise of Government*. New York: Liberal Arts Press, 1952.

Lockman, Zachary. *Comrades and Enemies: Arab and Jewish Workers in Palestine, 1906–1948*. Berkeley and Los Angeles: University of California Press, 1996.

London, Bruce. "Internal Colonialism in Thailand: Primate City Parasitism Reconsidered." *Urban Affairs Quarterly* 14, no. 4 (June 1, 1979): 485–513.

Loss, Joseph. "Buddha-Dhamma in Israel: Explicit Non-Religious and Implicit Non-Secular Localization of Religion." *Nova Religio* 13, no. 4 (May 2010): 84–105.

Losurdo, Domenico. *Liberalism: A Counter-History*. Translated by Gregory Elliott. London: Verso Books, 2011.

Lowe, Lisa. *The Intimacies of Four Continents*. Durham, NC: Duke University Press, 2015.

Lustick, Ian S. "Israel as a Non-Arab State: The Political Implications of Mass Immigration of Non-Jews." *Middle East Journal* 53, no. 3 (1999): 417–33.

Lysa, Hong. "'Stranger within the Gates': Knowing Semi-Colonial Siam as Extraterritorials." *Modern Asian Studies* 38, no. 2 (2004): 327–54.

Manig, Winfried. "The Taxation of the Agricultural Sector in Thailand: The Effects of the Rice Premium." *Verfassung Und Recht in Übersee/Law and Politics in Africa, Asia and Latin America* 10, no. 2 (1977): 289–317.

Marcus, George E. "Ethnography in/of the World System: The Emergence of Multi-Sited Ethnography." *Annual Review of Anthropology* 24 (1995): 95–117.

le Mare, Ann, Buapun Promphaking, and Jonathan Rigg. "Returning Home: The Middle-Income Trap and Gendered Norms in Thailand." *Journal of International Development* 27, no. 2 (2015): 285–306.

Marghescu, T. "Restoration of Degraded Forest Land in Thailand: The Case of Khao Kho." UN Food and Agriculture Organization, n.d. tinyurl.com/fao-degraded.

Marks, Tom. *Making Revolution: The Insurgency of the Communist Party of Thailand in Structural Perspective*. Chon Buri: White Lotus, 1994.

Marx, Karl. *Capital: A Critique of Political Economy*. Vol. 1. Translated by Ben Fowkes. Middlesex: Penguin, 1990.

Mashash, Inbal. "Hozer Rosh Minhal 123202: Hakla'im Ba'alei Heterim Le-Ha'asakat Oved Zar" (Authority Director's Circular 123202: Farmers with a Permit to Employ a Foreign Worker). Population and Immigration Authority, May 31, 2023. tinyurl.com/mashash-hozer.

Mauss, Marcel. "Techniques of the Body." *Economy and Society* 2, no. 1 (February 1973): 70–88.

Mayblin, Lucy, and Joe B. Turner. *Migration Studies and Colonialism*. Cambridge, UK, and Medford, MA: Polity Press, 2021.

McCargo, Duncan, and Krisadawan Hongladarom. "Contesting Isan-ness: Discourses of Politics and Identity in Northeast Thailand." *Asian Ethnicity* 5, no. 2 (June 2004): 219–34.

McWilliams, Carey. *Factories in the Field: The Story of Migratory Farm Labor in California*. Boston: Little, Brown, 1939.

Meillassoux, Claude. *Maidens, Meal, and Money: Capitalism and the Domestic Community*. Cambridge: Cambridge University Press, 1981.

Mies, Maria. *Patriarchy and Accumulation on a World Scale: Women in the International Division of Labour*. London: Zed Books, 2014.

Mills, E. "Census of Palestine: Population of Villages, Towns and Administrative Areas." Jerusalem: British Mandate for Palestine, 1932.

Mills, Mary Beth. "Attack of the Widow Ghosts: Gender, Death and Modernity in Northeast Thailand." In *Bewitching Women, Pious Men: Gender and Body Politics in Southeast Asia*, edited by Aihwa Ong and Michael G. Peletz, 244–73. Berkeley and Los Angeles: University of California Press, 1995.

———. "Engendering Discourses of Displacement: Contesting Mobility and Marginality in Rural Thailand." *Ethnography* 6, no. 3 (September 1, 2005): 385–419.

———. "Gendered Encounters with Modernity: Labor Migrants and Marriage Choices in Contemporary Thailand." *Identities* 5, no. 3 (November 1, 1998): 301–34.

——. *Good Daughters, Modern Women: Modernity, Identity, and Female Labor Migration in Thailand.* New Brunswick, NJ: Rutgers University Press, 1999.

Mirovsky, Arik. "Israel Tops World in Increase in Housing Prices." *Haaretz,* March 13, 2017. www.haaretz.com/israel-news/1.776849.

Mitchell, James. *Luk Thung: The Culture and Politics of Thailand's Most Popular Music.* Silkworm Books, 2015.

Mitchell, Timothy. *Carbon Democracy: Political Power in the Age of Oil.* London: Verso, 2011.

——. "Everyday Metaphors of Power." *Theory and Society* 19, no. 5 (October 1, 1990): 545–77.

Moore, Jason W. *Capitalism in the Web of Life: Ecology and the Accumulation of Capital.* London: Verso, 2016.

Moore, Jeffrey M. *The Thai Way of Counterinsurgency.* Miami Beach, FL: Muir Analytics, 2014.

Mor, Liron. *Conflicts: The Poetics and Politics of Palestine-Israel.* New York: Fordham University Press, 2023.

Morris, Rosalind C. "Failures of Domestication: Speculations on Globality, Economy, and the Sex of Excess in Thailand." *Differences* 13, no. 1 (May 1, 2002): 45–76.

Nasasra, Mansour. *The Naqab Bedouins: A Century of Politics and Resistance.* New York: Columbia University Press, 2017.

Navon, Amnon. "Hitpathut Ha-Hityashvut Ba-Arava Ha-Tikhona" (The Development of the Settlement of the Central Arabah). In *Arava En Ketz: Nof, Teva ve-Adam Ba-Arava* (The Arava: Landscape, Nature and People in the Arava Valley), edited by Yair Giladi, Haim Levita, Menahem Marcus, and Amnon Navon, 182–99. Ein Yahav: Arava, 2012.

Navon, Avi. "Rishonim Ba-Arava" (First in the Arabah). In *Arava En Ketz: Nof, Teva ve-Adam Ba-Arava* (The Arava: Landscape, Nature and People in the Arava Valley), edited by Yair Giladi, Haim Levita, Menahem Marcus, and Amnon Navon, 156–69. Ein Yahav: Arava, 2012.

Neumann, Boaz. *Land and Desire in Early Zionism.* Translated by Haim Watzman. Waltham, MA: Brandeis University Press, 2011.

Ngai, Mae M. "American Orientalism." *Reviews in American History* 28, no. 3 (September 1, 2000): 408–15.

Nichols, Robert. *Theft Is Property! Dispossession and Critical Theory.* Durham, NC: Duke University Press, 2020.

NII (National Insurance Institute of Israel). "Skhar minimum" (The minimum wage). Accessed March 30, 2018. tinyurl.com/nii-miniwage.

Nitzan, Jonathan, and Shimshon Bichler. *The Global Political Economy of Israel.* London: Pluto Press, 2002.

Nkrumah, Kwame. *Neo-Colonialism: The Last Stage of Imperialism*. New York: International, 1966.

NSOT (National Statistics Office of Thailand). "Per Capita Income of Population, New Series by Region and Province: 1995–2011." Bangkok. Accessed August 22, 2018. tinyurl.com/nso-income.

OECD (Organisation for Economic Co-operation and Development). "OECD Review of Agricultural Policies: Israel 2010." OECD, 2010. tinyurl.com/OECD-israel.

Ohnuma, Reiko. "Gift." In *Critical Terms for the Study of Buddhism*, edited by Donald S. Lopez, 103–23. Chicago: University of Chicago Press, 2005.

Ong, Aihwa. "The Family Romance of Mandarin Capital." In *Flexible Citizenship: The Cultural Logics of Transnationality*, 139–57. Durham, NC: Duke University Press, 1999.

Oppenheimer, Franz. *Merchavia: A Jewish Co-Operative Settlement in Palestine*. New York: Co-operative Society Eretz-Israel, 1914.

Or, Iair G. "Regime Changes and the Impact of Informal Labor: The Case of Thai Workers in Southern Israel." *Linguistic Landscape* 7 (February 19, 2021).

Or, Iair G., and Elana Shohamy. "'Youth Should Be Sent Here to Absorb Zionism': Jewish Farmers and Thai Migrant Workers in Southern Israel." In *Sociolinguistic Perspectives on Migration Control: Language Policy, Identity and Belonging*, edited by Markus Rheindorf and Ruth Wodak, 148–69. Bristol: Multilingual Matters, 2020.

Oren, O., Y. Yechieli, J. K. Böhlke, and A. Dody. "Contamination of Groundwater under Cultivated Fields in an Arid Environment, Central Arava Valley, Israel." *Journal of Hydrology* 290, no. 3 (May 25, 2004): 312–28.

Ovetz, Robert, ed. *Worker's Inquiry and Global Class Struggle: Strategies, Tactics, Objectives*. London: Pluto Press, 2020.

Pachirat, Timothy. *Every Twelve Seconds: Industrialized Slaughter and the Politics of Sight*. New Haven, CT: Yale University Press, 2011.

Panyamee, Tipparin. "A Struggle for Getting Free from Social Exclusion of Tribe-War Volunteers: A Case Study of Ban Khiangfa of Sa Doe Phong Subdistrict in Khao Kho District of Phetchabun Province." PhD diss., National Institute of Development Administration, 2021.

Park, Joseph Sung-Yul, and Lionel Wee. *Markets of English: Linguistic Capital and Language Policy in a Globalizing World*. New York: Routledge, 2012.

Pattana Kitiarsa. *The "Bare Life" of Thai Migrant Workmen in Singapore*. Chiang Mai: Silkworm, 2014.

——. "Beyond Syncretism: Hybridization of Popular Religion in Contemporary Thailand." *Journal of Southeast Asian Studies* 36, no. 3 (October 1, 2005): 461–87.

——. "The Lyrics of Laborious Life: Popular Music and the Reassertion of Migrant Manhood in Northeastern Thailand." *Inter-Asia Cultural Studies* 10, no. 3 (September 1, 2009): 381–98.

——. "Village Transnationalism: Transborder Identities among Thai-Isan Migrant Workers in Singapore." SSRN Scholarly Paper. Rochester, NY, August 1, 2006.

Paz, Alejandro. "The Circulation of Chisme and Rumor: Gossip, Evidentiality, and Authority in the Perspective of Latino Labor Migrants in Israel." *Journal of Linguistic Anthropology* 19, no. 1 (2009): 117–43.

——. *Latinos in Israel: Language and Unexpected Citizenship.* Bloomington: Indiana University Press, 2018.

Pedreño, Pedro. "Sustainability, Resilience and Agency in Intensive Agricultural Enclaves." *Ager. Revista de Estudios Sobre Despoblación y Desarrollo Rural*, no. 18 (April 15, 2015): 139–60.

Peled, Yoav. "Profits or Glory? The Twenty-Eighth Elul of Arik Sharon." *New Left Review* 29 (October 2004).

Peleg, Bar, and Josh Breiner. "They Came to Study in Israel—and Ended Up Victims of Slavery and Trafficking." *Haaretz*, November 28, 2022. tinyurl.com/haaretz-slaves2.

Penslar, Derek J. *Zionism and Technocracy: The Engineering of Jewish Settlement in Palestine, 1870–1918.* Bloomington: Indiana University Press, 1991.

PIBA (Population and Immigration Authority) and CIMI (Center for International Migration and Integration). "Labor Migration to Israel," 2016. tinyurl.com/labmigisr.

Pilapa Esara. "Imagining the Western Husband: Thai Women's Desires for Matrimony, Status and Beauty." *Ethnos* 74, no. 3 (September 1, 2009): 403–26.

——. "Moral Scrutiny, Marriage Inequality: Cohabitation in Bangkok, Thailand." *Asia Pacific Journal of Anthropology* 13, no. 3 (June 1, 2012): 211–27.

Piya Pangsapa. *Textures of Struggle: The Emergence of Resistance among Garment Workers in Thailand.* Ithaca: ILR Press, 2007.

Pomeroy, Anne Fairchild. *Marx and Whitehead: Process, Dialectics, and the Critique of Capitalism.* Albany: SUNY Press, 2004.

Porat, Hanina. "Mediniut Rekhishat Karka'ot Veha-Hityashvut Ba-Negev erev Milhemet Ha-Atzma'ut (Land Purchase and Settlement Policy in the Negev on the Eve of the War of Independence)." *Cathedra* 62 (December 1991): 123–54.

Porphant Ouyyanont. *A Regional Economic History of Thailand.* Singapore: ISEAS-Yusof Ishak Institute, 2017.

——. "Thailand's Northeast 'Problem' in Historical Perspective." Edited by Daljit Singh and Malcolm Cook. *Southeast Asian Affairs* (2017): 367–84.

Puangthong Rungswasdisab (Pawakapan). *The Central Role of Thailand's Internal Security Operations Command in the Post-Counter-insurgency Period.* Singapore: ISEAS—Yusof Ishak Institute, 2017.

———. "Thailand's Response to the Cambodian Genocide." Case Study. Yale University Genocide Studies Program. New Haven, CT: Yale University, 2004. gsp.yale.edu/thailands-response-cambodian-genocide.

Quijano, Aníbal. "Coloniality of Power and Eurocentrism in Latin America." *International Sociology* 15, no. 2 (June 1, 2000): 215–32.

Rabie, Kareem. *Palestine Is Throwing a Party and the Whole World Is Invited: Capital and State Building in the West Bank.* Durham, NC: Duke University Press, 2021.

Ragolsky, Gidon. "Al ha-bedu'im ha-hayim ba-arava" (On the Bedouin who live in the Arabah). Accessed June 15, 2021. tinyurl.com/ragolsky-bedouin.

Raijman, Rebeca, and Adriana Kemp. "The New Immigration to Israel: Becoming a de-Facto Immigration State in the 1990s." In *Immigration Worldwide*, by U. Segal, N. Mayadas, and D. Elliot, 227–43. Oxford: Oxford University Press, 2010.

Raijman, Rebeca, and Nonna Kushnirovich. "Labor Migrant Recruitment Practices in Israel." Jerusalem: JDC, March 2012.

Rainwater, Katie. "Gold Diggers and Their Housewives: The Gendered Political Economy of Thai Labor Export to Saudi Arabia, 1975–1990." *Critical Asian Studies* 51, no. 4 (2019): 515–36.

Rainwater, Katie, and Lindy Brooks Williams. "Thai Guestworker Export in Decline: The Rise and Fall of the Thailand-Taiwan Migration System." *International Migration Review* 53, no. 2 (June 2019): 371–95.

Ram, Uri. *The Globalization of Israel: McWorld in Tel Aviv, Jihad in Jerusalem.* New York: Routledge, 2008.

Regev, David. "Hadash: Mitnadvim Mi-Tayland" (New: Volunteers from Thailand). *Yedioth Ahronoth,* June 9, 1989.

Reid, Anthony. "Female Roles in Pre-Colonial Southeast Asia." *Modern Asian Studies* 22, no. 3 (January 1, 1988): 629–45.

Reuters. "Labor Abuse Fears Rise for Thai Migrant Workers in Israel under New Deal." *Jerusalem Post,* July 21, 2020. tinyurl.com/jpost-iom.

Rigg, Jonathan, and Albert Salamanca. "Connecting Lives, Living, and Location: Mobility and Spatial Signatures in Northeast Thailand, 1982–2009." *Critical Asian Studies* 43, no. 4 (December 1, 2011): 551–75.

Rigg, Jonathan, Albert Salamanca, and Michael Parnwell. "Joining the Dots of Agrarian Change in Asia: A 25 Year View from Thailand." *World Development* 40, no. 7 (July 2012): 1469–81.

Roberts, William Clare. *Marx's Inferno: The Political Theory of Capital.* Princeton, NC: Princeton University Press, 2018.

Robinson, Cedric J. *Black Marxism: The Making of the Black Radical Tradition.* Chapel Hill: University of North Carolina Press, 2000.

Roediger, David R., and Elizabeth D. Esch. *The Production of Difference: Race and the Management of Labor in U.S. History.* New York: Oxford University Press, 2012.

Rogan, Eugene L. *Frontiers of the State in the Late Ottoman Empire: Transjordan, 1850–1921.* Cambridge: Cambridge University Press, 1999.

Rose, Sonya O. "Class Formation and the Quintessential Worker." In *Reworking Class*, edited by John R. Hall, 133–66. Ithaca, NY: Cornell University Press, 2018.

Rosenfeld, Henry. "The Class Situation of the Arab National Minority in Israel." *Comparative Studies in Society and History* 20, no. 3 (1978): 374–407.

Ross, Andrew. *Stone Men: The Palestinians Who Built Israel.* London: Verso, 2019.

Sabar, Galia. *Lo banu lehisha'er: Mehagre avoda me-Afrika le-Yisrael uve-Hazara* (We're Not Here to Stay: African Migrant Workers in Israel and Back in Africa). Tel Aviv: Tel Aviv University Press, 2008.

Sabbagh-Khoury, Areej. *Colonizing Palestine: The Zionist Left and the Making of the Palestinian Nakba.* Stanford, CA: Stanford University Press, 2023.

Saiyud Kerdphol. *The Struggle for Thailand: Counter-Insurgency, 1965–1985.* Bangkok: S. Research Center Co., 1986.

Samooha, Shahar. "Ben Ha-Moshavnikim Ba-Arava La-Ovdim Ha-Zarim She-Hem Ma'asikim Hitpatha Ma'rekhet Yahasim Murkevet. Doktor Matan Kaminer Hakar et Ha-Tofa'a" (A Complex Relationship Has Developed between the Moshavniks of the Arabah and the Foreign Workers They Employ. Dr. Matan Kaminer Has Researched the Phenomenon). *Globes*, March 14, 2020. tinyurl.com/samooha-globes.

Sanya Hitakun. *Mak Saaw Israel* (Israeli Woman), 2011. YouTube. tinyurl.com/sanya-song.

Sanyal, Kalyan. *Rethinking Capitalist Development: Primitive Accumulation, Governmentality & Post-Colonial Capitalism.* London: Routledge, 2014.

Sayegh, Fayez A. *Zionist Colonialism in Palestine.* Beirut: Palestine Liberation Organization Research Center, 1965.

Sayer, Derek. *The Violence of Abstraction: The Analytic Foundations of Historical Materialism.* Oxford: Blackwell, 1987.

Schayegh, Cyrus. *The Middle East and the Making of the Modern World.* Cambridge, MA: Harvard University Press, 2017.

Scholz, Ulrich. "Deforestation in the Asian Tropics—Causes and Consequences." *ASIEN: The German Journal on Contemporary Asia*, no. 21 (1986): 1–29.

Schwartz, Moshe. "The Decooperativization of Israel's Moshavim, 1985–1994." In *Rural Cooperatives in Socialist Utopia: Thirty Years of Moshav Development in Israel*, edited by Gideon Kressel, Susan Lees, and Moshe Schwartz, 223–44. Westport, CT: Praeger, 1995.

Sciortino, Rosalia, and Sureeporn Punpuing. "International Migration in Thailand 2009." Bangkok: International Organization for Migration, Thailand Office, 2009.

Scott, James C. *The Art of Not Being Governed: An Anarchist History of Upland Southeast Asia*. New Haven, CT: Yale University Press, 2009.

———. *Domination and the Arts of Resistance: Hidden Transcripts*. New Haven, CT: Yale University Press, 1990.

———. *The Moral Economy of the Peasant: Rebellion and Subsistence in Southeast Asia*. New Haven, CT: Yale University Press, 1976.

Segev, Yael. "Zarim Intimiyim: Hatzayat Gvulot Etno-Le'umiyim Be-Sipur Ha-Mitnadvim Ha-Skandinaviyim Ba-Kibbutz" (Intimate Strangers: Crossing Ethno-National Boundaries in the Story of Scandinavian Kibbutz Volunteers). PhD diss., Bar-Ilan University, 2022.

Segre, D. V. "The Philosophy and Practice of Israel's International Cooperation." In *Israel in the Third World*, edited by Michael Curtis and Susan Aurelia Gitelson, 7–26. New Brunswick, NJ: Transaction Books, 1976.

Sella, T., I. Goren, V. Shalev, H. Shapira, J. Zandbank, J. Rosenblum, M.G. Kimlin, and G. Chodick. "Incidence Trends of Keratinocytic Skin Cancers and Melanoma in Israel 2006–11." *British Journal of Dermatology* 172, no. 1 (January 1, 2015): 202–7.

Seo, Seonyoung. "Temporalities of Class in Nepalese Labour Migration to South Korea." *Current Sociology*, October 4, 2018.

Shacham, Ami. "Mayim Ba-Arava" (Water in the Arabah). In *Arava En Ketz: Nof, Teva ve-Adam Ba-Arava* (The Arava: Landscape, Nature and People in the Arava Valley), edited by Yair Giladi, Haim Levita, Menahem Marcus, and Amnon Navon, 216–31. Ein Yahav: Arava, 2012.

Shafir, Gershon. "From Overt to Veiled Segregation: Israel's Palestinian Arab Citizens in the Galilee." *International Journal of Middle East Studies* 50, no. 1 (February 2018): 1–22.

———. *Land, Labor, and the Origins of the Israeli-Palestinian Conflict, 1882–1914*. Cambridge: Cambridge University Press, 1989.

Shalev, Michael. *Labour and the Political Economy in Israel*. Oxford: Oxford University Press, 1992.

Shamir, Hila, and Maayan Niezna. "An Alternative Anti-Trafficking Action Plan: A Proposed Model Based on a Labor Approach to Trafficking, TraffLab Research Group Policy Paper, Tel Aviv University." SSRN Scholarly Paper. Rochester, NY, November 1, 2020.

Shani, Liron. "Of Trees and People: The Changing Entanglement in the Israeli Desert." *Ethnos* 83, no. 4 (March 30, 2017): 1–19.

——. *Shitat Ha-Arava: Antropologia Shel Teva Tarbut ve-Hakla'ut* (The Arava Approach: Anthropology of Nature and (Agri)Culture). Ra'anana: Lamda, 2021.

Shapira, Anita. *Ha-ma'avak ha-nikhzav: Avoda ivrit, 1929–1939* (The Futile Struggle: Hebrew Work 1929–1939). Tel Aviv: Hakibbutz Hameuchad, 1977.

Shapira, Jonathan. *Ilit lelo mamshichim: Dorot manhigim ba-hevra ha-yisre'elit* (An Elite without Successors: Generations of Political Leaders in Israel). Tel Aviv: Sifriat Po'alim, 1984.

Shapiro, Maya. "The Development of a 'Privileged Underclass,' Locating Undocumented Migrant Women and Their Children in the Political Economy of Tel Aviv, Israel." *Dialectical Anthropology* 37, no. 3/4 (2013): 423–41.

Sharon, Smadar. *"Kach Kovshim Moledet": Tihknun ve-Yishuv Hevel Lakhish Bi-Shnot Ha-Hamishim* ("And Thus a Homeland Is Conquered": Planning and Settlement in 1950s Lakhish Region). Tel Aviv: Pardes, 2017.

Shauer, Noa, and Matan Kaminer. "Below the Minimum—Violation of Wage Laws in the Employment of Migrant Farmworkers." Tel Aviv: Kav LaOved, 2014. tinyurl.com/below-min1.

Shawcross, William. *The Quality of Mercy: Cambodia, Holocaust, and Modern Conscience*. New York: Simon & Schuster, 1985.

Shek, Yen Ling. "Asian American Masculinity: A Review of the Literature." *Journal of Men's Studies* 14, no. 3 (June 1, 2007): 379–91.

Sheriff, Abdul, and Engseng Ho, eds. *The Indian Ocean: Oceanic Connections and the Creation of New Societies*. London: Hurst, 2014.

Shnider, Avi. *Bimkom Moshavo: Solidariyut Be-Moshav Ha-Ovdim Ha-Mithadesh* (Sense of Place: Solidarity in the Renewed Moshav Ovdim). Ramat Gan: Yad Tabenkin, 2022.

——. "Dunam Po Ve-Dunam Sham Regev Ahar Regev: Tahalikh Hafratat Ha-Aguda Ha-Shitufit Be-Moshav Ovdim Ba-Arava" (A Dunam Here and a Dunam There, One Clod after the Other: The Process of Privatization of the Cooperative Association in a Workers' Moshav in the Arabah). MA thesis, Ben Gurion University, 2008.

——. "Gendered Division of Labor in a Post-Privatization Moshav: A Case Study of Moshav Tzin in Southern Israel." *Journal of Rural Cooperation* 42, no. 2 (2014): 181–97.

Shoham, Hizky. "'Buy Local' or 'Buy Jewish'? Separatist Consumption in Interwar Palestine." *International Journal of Middle East Studies* 45, no. 3 (August 2013): 469–89.

Shoham, Shahar. "The Heroes from Isaan Working in Israel: The Production of Migrants in the Thailand-Israel Migration Regime." PhD diss., Humboldt-Universität, 2024.

——. "Pickers and Packers: Translocal Narratives of Returning Thai Agriculture Labour Migrants from Israel." MA thesis, Humboldt-Universität, 2017.

Shoham, Shahar, and Yahel Kurlander. "Niyar Avoda Be-Nose Alimut Minit Klape Mehagrot Avoda Be-Anaf Ha-Hakla'ut Be-Yisra'el" (Working Paper on Sexual Violence against Women Migrant Workers in the Agricultural Sector in Israel). Tel Aviv: TraffLab, October 2021. tinyurl.com/shoham-kurlander-women.

Shryock, Andrew. "History and Historiography among the Belqa Tribes of Jordan." PhD diss., University of Michigan, 1993.

——. "Other Conscious/Self Aware: First Thoughts on Cultural Intimacy and Mass Mediation." In *Off Stage/On Display: Intimacy and Ethnography in the Age of Public Culture,* edited by Andrew Shryock, 3–28. Stanford, CA: Stanford University Press, 2004.

Shvarzberg, Zohar. "Landscapes in Migration: The Gardens of Thai Agricultural Migrants in Central Israel." MA thesis, Technion, 2023.

Silver, Beverly. "The Contradictions of Semiperipheral Success: The Case of Israel." In *Semiperipheral States in the World-Economy,* edited by William G. Martin, 161–81. New York: Greenwood Press, 1990.

Slavin, Gil, and Ya'ir Giladi. "Tayarut Ba-Arava" (Tourism in the Arabah). In *Arava En Ketz: Nof, Teva ve-Adam Ba-Arava* (The Arava: Landscape, Nature and People in the Arava Valley), edited by Yair Giladi, Haim Levita, Menahem Marcus, and Amnon Navon, 232–43. Ein Yahav: Arava, 2012.

Sopranzetti, Claudio. "Burning Red Desires: Isan Migrants and the Politics of Desire in Contemporary Thailand." *South East Asia Research* 20, no. 3 (2012): 361–79.

——. "Framed by Freedom: Emancipation and Oppression in Post-Fordist Thailand." *Cultural Anthropology* 32, no. 1 (February 27, 2017): 68–92.

——. *Owners of the Map: Motorcycle Taxi Drivers, Mobility, and Politics in Bangkok.* Berkeley: University of California Press, 2017.

——. *Red Journeys: Inside the Thai Red-Shirt Movement.* Chiang Mai: Silkworm Books, 2012.

——. "Thailand's Relapse: The Implications of the May 2014 Coup." *Journal of Asian Studies* 75, no. 2 (2016): 299–316.

Spolter, Simi. "'Mi-Tokh 30 Elef She-Nirshemu Rak 200 Higi'u': Mashber Ha-Ovdim Ma'amik Vele-Misrad Ha-Hakla'ut En Pitronot" ('Out of 30 Thousand Who Signed up Only 200 Have Arrived': The Labor Crisis Is Deepening and the Agriculture Ministry Has No Solutions). *TheMarker,* December 20, 2023. tinyurl.com/mashber-maamik.

Stavi, Ilan, Gidon Ragolsky, Rahamim Shem-Tov, Yanai Shlomi, Oren Ackermann, Henri Rueff, and Judith Lekach. "Ancient through Mid-Twentieth Century Runoff Harvesting Agriculture in the Hyper-Arid Arava Valley of Israel." *CATENA* 162 (March 1, 2018): 80–87.

Stein, Ron. "Ha-Mosdiyim Sakhru et ROAH Barlev Lahkor Nefilata Shel Agrexco" (Institutionals Hire CPA Barlev to Investigate the Fall of Agrexco). *Globes*, August 25, 2011. tinyurl.com/globes-agrexco.

Stoler, Ann. "Colony." *Political Concepts* 1 (2011). tinyurl.com/pc-stoler.

———. *Race and the Education of Desire: Foucault's History of Sexuality and the Colonial Order of Things.* Durham, NC: Duke University Press, 2012.

Stonington, Scott. "Facing Death, Gazing Inward: End-of-Life and the Transformation of Clinical Subjectivity in Thailand." *Culture, Medicine, and Psychiatry* 35, no. 2 (May 15, 2011): 113–33.

———. "Karma Masters: The Ethical Wound, Hauntological Choreography, and Complex Personhood in Thailand." *American Anthropologist* 122, no. 4 (2020): 759–70.

———. *The Spirit Ambulance: Choreographing the End of Life in Thailand.* Oakland: University of California Press, 2020.

Streckfuss, David. "An 'Ethnic' Reading of 'Thai' History in the Twilight of the Century-Old Official 'Thai' National Model." *South East Asia Research* 20, no. 3 (September 1, 2012): 305–27.

Streckman, Rotem. "Pilpelim Atzuvim: Kach Karas Mikhre Ha-Zahav Shel Hakla'e Ha-Arava" (Sad Peppers: This Is How the Arabah Farmers' Goldmine Collapsed). *TheMarker*, May 6, 2014. tinyurl.com/sad-peppers.

Strom, Marjorie. "The Thai Revolution: The Development of Agriculture in the Arava in the 1990s." MA thesis, Hebrew University, 2004.

Suchit Bunbongkan. *The Military in Thai Politics, 1981–86.* Singapore: Institute of Southeast Asian Studies, 1987.

Sudarat Musikawong and Panida Rzonca. "Debt Bondage Scales of Intensity: Thai Overseas Agricultural Workers in the United States." In *On the Move: Critical Migration Themes in ASEAN*, edited by Supang Chantavanich, Carl Middleton, and Michiko Ito. Chiang Mai: Chulalongkorn University Press, 2014.

Supang Chantavanich. "Thailand's Responses to Transnational Migration during Economic Growth and Economic Downturn." *Journal of Social Issues in Southeast Asia* 14, no. 1 (April 1999): 159–77.

Swirski, Shlomo, and Deborah Bernstein. "Mi Avad Be-Ma, Avur Mi, ve-Tmurat Ma? Ha-Pituah Ha-Kalkali Shel Yisra'el ve-Hithavut Halukat Ha-Avoda Ha-Adatit" (Who Worked at What, for Whom and for How Much? Israel's Economic Development and the Emergence of the Ethnic Division of Labor). In *Ha-Hevra Ha-Yisra'elit: Hebetim Bikortiyim* (Israeli Society: Critical Perspectives), edited by Uri Ram, 120–47. Tel Aviv: Breirot, 1993.

Tamari, Salim. "The Dislocation and Re-Constitution of a Peasantry: The Social Economy of Agrarian Palestine in the Central Highlands and the Jordan Valley, 1960–1980." University of Manchester, 1983.

——. *Mountain against the Sea: Essays on Palestinian Society and Culture.* Berkeley and Los Angeles: University of California Press, 2008.

Tambiah, Stanley Jeyaraja. *The Buddhist Saints of the Forest and the Cult of Amulets: A Study in Charisma, Hagiography, Sectarianism, and Millennial Buddhism.* Cambridge: Cambridge University Press, 1984.

Taussig, Michael T. *Shamanism, Colonialism, and the Wild Man: A Study in Terror and Healing.* Chicago: University of Chicago Press, 1991.

Taylor, J. L. "Living on the Rim: Ecology and Forest Monks in Northeast Thailand." *Sojourn: Journal of Social Issues in Southeast Asia* 6, no. 1 (1991): 106–25.

Tegbaru, Amare. "The Racialization of Development Expertise and the Fluidity of Blackness: A Case from 1980s Thailand." *Asian Anthropology* 19, no. 3 (July 2, 2020): 195–212.

Thak Chaloemtiarana. *Thailand: The Politics of Despotic Paternalism.* Ithaca: Cornell University Press, 2007.

Thanapauge Chamaratana, Dusadee Ayuwat, Luuk Knippenberg, and Edwin de Jong. "Connecting the Disconnected: Background, Practices and Motives of Labour Brokers in Isan, Thailand—an Explorative Study." *International Journal of Interdisciplinary Social Sciences* 5, no. 5 (2010): 359–72.

Thomas, Robert J. *Citizenship, Gender, and Work: The Social Organization of Industrial Agriculture.* Berkeley and Los Angeles: University of California Press, 1985.

Thomason, Sarah Grey. *Language Contact.* Washington, DC: Georgetown University Press, 2001.

Thompson, E. P. "The Moral Economy of the English Crowd in the Eighteenth Century." *Past & Present,* no. 50 (1971): 76 136.

Thompson, Gabriel, ed. *Chasing the Harvest: Migrant Workers in California Agriculture.* London: Verso, 2017.

Thongchai Winichakul. *Siam Mapped: A History of the Geo-Body of a Nation.* Honolulu: University of Hawaii Press, 1994.

——. "Siam's Colonial Conditions and the Birth of Thai History." In *Unraveling Myths in Southeast Asian Historiography,* edited by Volker Grabowsky, 23–45. Bangkok: Rivers Books, 2011.

Tipparin Panyamee. "A Struggle for Getting Free from Social Exclusion of Tribe-War Volunteers: A Case Study of Ban Khiangfa of Sa Doe Phong Subdistrict in Khao Kho District of Phetchabun Province." PhD dissertation, National Institute of Development Administration, 2021.

Turner, Victor. "Liminality and Communitas." In *Culture and Society: Contemporary Debates*, edited by Jeffrey C. Alexander and Steven Jay Seidman, 147–54. Cambridge: Cambridge University Press, 1990.

Tzfadia, Erez, and Haim Yacobi. *Rethinking Israeli Space: Periphery and Identity*. 20. Abingdon: Routledge, 2011.

Uhlig, Harald. "The 'Problem-Region' Northeastern Thailand." In *Regions and National Integration in Thailand, 1892–1992*, edited by Volker Grabowsky, 130–44. Leipzig: Otto Harrassowitz Verlag, 1995.

UNSCOP. "United Nations Special Committee on Palestine Report," 1947. tinyurl.com/unscop-report.

Valentine, P. "The Gender Distinction in Communization Theory." *LIES: A Journal of Materialist Feminism* 1 (2012): 191–208.

van Schendel, Willem. "Geographies of Knowing, Geographies of Ignorance: Jumping Scale in Southeast Asia." *Environment and Planning D: Society and Space* 20, no. 6 (December 2002): 647–68.

van der Steen, Eveline J. "Nineteenth-Century Travellers in the Wadi Arabah." In *Crossing the Rift: Resources, Routes, Settlement Patterns, and Interaction in the Wadi Arabah*, edited by Piotr Bienkowski and Katharina Galor, 243–50. Oxford: Oxbow Books, 2006.

Vanwey, Leah K. "Altruistic and Contractual Remittances between Male and Female Migrants and Households in Rural Thailand." *Demography* 41, no. 4 (November 1, 2004): 739–56.

Vitman, Ariel. "Netanyahu: 'Livhon bitul skhar ha-minimum le-ovdim zarim'" (Netanyahu: 'Look into abolishing the minimum wage for foreign workers'). *Israel Hayom*, August 12, 2018. tinyurl.com/abolish-wage.

"Wadi." In *Wikipedia*, July 3, 2018. tinyurl.com/wiki-wadi.

Walker, Andrew. "The Rural Constitution and the Everyday Politics of Elections in Northern Thailand." *Journal of Contemporary Asia* 38, no. 1 (February 1, 2008): 84–105.

Wallerstein, Immanuel. *The Capitalist World-Economy*. Cambridge: Cambridge University Press, 1979.

———. *World-Systems Analysis: An Introduction*. Durham, NC: Duke University Press, 2004.

Weiss, Hadas. "Social Reproduction." In *Cambridge Encyclopedia of Anthropology*. Cambridge: Cambridge University Press, 2021.

Weitz, Yosef. "Emek Ha-Arava Mi-Nekudat Mabat Hakla'it" (The Arabah Valley from an Agricultural Perspective). In *Ha-Ma'avak al Ha-Adama (The Battle over Land)*, 209–306. Tel Aviv: N. Tversky, 1950.

Weizman, Eyal. *Hollow Land: Israel's Architecture of Occupation*. London: Verso, 2007.

Wexler, Fallon. "Female Migrant Agricultural Workers in Israel and Gender-Based Violations of Labor Rights." Tel Aviv: Kav LaOved, December 2013. tinyurl.com/fallon-klo.

Whitcomb, Donald. "Land behind Aqaba: The Wadi Arabah during the Early Islamic Period." In *Crossing the Rift: Resources, Routes, Settlement Patterns, and Interaction in the Wadi Arabah*, edited by Piotr Bienkowski and Katharina Galor, 239–42. Oxford: Oxbow Books, 2006.

Willen, Sarah S. "Toward a Critical Phenomenology of 'Illegality': State Power, Criminalization, and Abjectivity among Undocumented Migrant Workers in Tel Aviv, Israel." *International Migration* 45, no. 3 (2007): 8–38.

———. *Transnational Migration to Israel in Global Comparative Context*. Lanham, MD: Lexington Books, 2007.

Williams, Eric. *Capitalism and Slavery*. Chapel Hill: University of North Carolina Press, 1994.

Willis, Paul E. *Learning to Labor: How Working Class Kids Get Working Class Jobs*. New York: Columbia University Press, 1977.

Wilson, Ara. *The Intimate Economies of Bangkok: Tomboys, Tycoons, and Avon Ladies in the Global City*. Berkeley and Los Angeles: University of California Press, 2004.

Wittgenstein, Ludwig. *Philosophical Investigations*. Oxford: Basil Blackwell, 1968.

Wolf, Eric R. *Europe and the People without History*. Berkeley and Los Angeles: University of California Press, 2010.

Wolpe, Harold. "Capitalism and Cheap Labour-Power in South Africa: From Segregation to Apartheid." *Economy and Society* 1, no. 4 (November 1, 1972): 425–56.

World Bank. "GDP Growth (Annual %)—Thailand, World | Data." Accessed December 22, 2022. tinyurl.com/gdp-thai-world.

Yacobi, Haim, Chen Misgav, and Smadar Sharon. "Technopolitics, Development and the Colonial-Postcolonial Nexus: Revisiting Settlements Development Aid from Israel to Africa." *Middle Eastern Studies* 56, no. 6 (November 1, 2020): 937–52.

Yahav, Telem. "Arba'a Taylandim She-Putru Tov'im 1.5 Milyon Shekel" (Four Thais who were Fired are Suing for 1.5 Million Shekels). *Ynet*, March 11, 2011. tinyurl.com/fired-thais.

Yeoh, Brenda. "Migration and Gender Politics in Southeast Asia." *Migration, Mobility, & Displacement* 2, no. 1 (March 2, 2016).

Yisha'ayahu, Kobi. "Rokhshe Karka'ot Yecholim La'asot Tsu'a Yafa al Ha-Hashka'a" (Land Buyers Can Make a Nice Return on Their Investment). *Globes*, March 18, 2016. tinyurl.com/globes-land.

Yılmaz, Ferruh. "Right-Wing Hegemony and Immigration: How the Populist Far-Right Achieved Hegemony through the Immigration Debate in Europe." *Current Sociology* 60, no. 3 (May 1, 2012): 368–81.

Yonah, Yossi. "Israel's Immigration Policies: The Twofold Face of the 'Demographic Threat.'" *Social Identities* 10, no. 2 (March 1, 2004): 195–218.

Zertal, Idith, and Akiva Eldar. *Lords of the Land: The Settlers and the State of Israel, 1967–2004.* Hevel Modi'in: Kinneret Zmora-Bitan Dvir, 2005.

Zivan, Zeev. *Mi-Nitzana ad Eilat: Sipuro Shel Ha-Negev Ha-Dromi, 1949–1957* (From Nitzana to Eilat: The Story of the Southern Negev, 1949–1957). Sde Boker: Ben Gurion University Press, 2012.

Žižek, Slavoj. *The Sublime Object of Ideology.* London: Verso, 1989.

INDEX

acacia trees, 26, 39, 171
accommodation. *See* acquiescence
acquiescence, 13, 16, 21, 63, 147;
and paternalism, 58, 144, 155,
163; and sexuality, 137–42. *See
also* face
affect. *See* emotions
Africa, 8, 67–68, 78, 96; East, 8, 88,
114, 140; North, 5, 8, 40
Africans, 6, 96, 117, 130, 140
afternoon, 115–21. *See also* day
Agrexco, 90
Agricultural Bank (Thailand), 70–71,
201n74
agriculture: commodity, 4–8, 25,
32–56, 62–63, 66–122, 172–75;
enclaves, 4, 54, 56; flowers, 79, 86;
subsistence, 25–27, 30, 58–61; vegetable, 46–47, 51, 78–79, 105, 110,
211n19. *See also* food: production

ahusalim. See Ashkenazim; LSM
air conditioning, 79, 109, 132
alcohol, 97, 102–3, 121, 134, 138, 158,
161–63
al-Misk family, 39, 191n95
al-Misk, 'Ali, 27
'Amrani family, 39, 191n95
anger, 143, 145–46, 166, 169
anonymization, xix–xx, 178n1–3
anthropology, 16, 20–21, 167–75;
linguistic, 10–12, 181n28. *See also*
ethnography
anxiety, 137, 140–41, 160–65. *See also*
exploitation anxiety
'Aqaba (Ayla), 27–28
aquifers, 10, 25, 41–42, 45–46
Arab countries. *See* Middle East
Arab labor. *See* Palestinians: as
workers in Zionist enterprises
Arab Revolt (1936–39), 28, 33